(

The Yalta
Conference

PROBLEMS IN AMERICAN CIVILIZATION

Under the editorial direction of
Edwin C. Rozwenc
Amherst College

The Yalta Conference

Second Edition

Edited and with an introduction by

Richard F. Fenno, Jr.
The University of Rochester

D. C. HEATH AND COMPANY
LEXINGTON, MASSACHUSETTS   TORONTO   LONDON

CONTENTS

V YALTA, REVISIONISM, AND THE COLD WAR

IV YALTA REVISITED

INTRODUCTION

Livadia Palace is, today, a resort sanatorium on Russia's Crimean coast. In February of 1945, this summer home of the Tsars at Yalta was the scene of the most controversial summit conference of World War II. Winston Churchill, Franklin Roosevelt, and Joseph Stalin, wartime allies, met to plan an end to the war and a beginning of the peace. In the first aim, they succeeded; in the second, they did not. Their failure, symbolized by the ensuing "Cold War," has made the Yalta Conference a subject of debate, recrimination, reassessment and analysis ever since.

In America, the controversy over Yalta has proceeded on many levels and in different frames of reference depending on the vantage point of the viewer and the context of the times. Indeed, the controversy has gone on for so long and in so many contexts that it has created its own history. Once the storm center of a bitter partisan debate—between Republicans and Democrats—it has more recently become grist for an equally sharp controversy among historians—orthodox and revisionist. The subject matter, throughout, has been American foreign policy. What has it been? Could it have been different? What should it have been? What should it be? It is the continuing importance of these questions which accounts for the intensity and the longevity of argument about our foreign policy at, and after, Yalta.

The spring of 1945 was a time of transition. It was also a time of hope. And the Yalta Protocol was greeted in that spirit. *Time* exulted that "all doubts about The Big Three's ability to cooperate in peace as well as in war seem now to have been swept away." And *Pravda* editorialized, "the alliance of the three big Powers possesses not only a historic yesterday and victorious today, but also a great tomorrow." The very height of such hopes magnified the depths of the disillusionment which followed. For Americans, grappling with the consequences of their emergence as a great power, Yalta focussed hope, disillusionment and, above all, uncertainty. It might be helpful for the student to begin his examination of Yalta with that same sense of uncertainty. Suspending the advantages of hindsight, he might put himself in the shoes of the various participants and commentators—adopting their perspectives, their knowledge and their environments—before coming to any final judgment of his own.

Surely the uncertainties of the period have reflected themselves in the succeeding waves of controversy. The student must address himself to the following range of questions: Should the United States have considered Russia as an ally or as an antagonist, as trustworthy or untrustworthy at Yalta? Were the terms of the Yalta agreements favorable or unfavorable for the United States? Were there any practical alternatives to the substance of those agreements? Was Roosevelt's conception of "American national interest" the correct one? Was the United States in a strong or a weak bargaining position at Yalta? Should we judge the Yalta agreements according to standards of "realistic" power politics, or on the basis of "idealistic" moral principles, or as a give-and-take bargaining process? Did the agreements themselves, Russian violation of those agreements, or, perhaps, American violation of them help to trigger the Cold War? Or was the onset of the Cold War totally unrelated to the Yalta Conference? Was the Cold War, in the final analysis, inevitable?

Some of these questions were generated in the period of partisan debate. Others were generated in the succeeding period of historiographic debate. In both cases, outside circumstances—Soviet hegemony in Eastern Europe and the Chinese Communist victory in the first case, the Vietnam War in the second—have helped to structure the terms of debate over Yalta. It may be helpful in threading one's way through the readings to keep in mind that the way people look at American foreign policy generally is affected by the particular circumstances in which they write. And, in turn, the way they look at American foreign policy generally affects the way they look at any given exercise in diplomacy such as Yalta.

Several of the readings help describe the setting of the conference, placing the events at Yalta in the context of the times and explicating the attitudes of the participants. William McNeill's introductory essay is particularly helpful in describing some of the difficulties confronting the negotiators. He sets forth the conflicting goals and priorities together with the unexamined assumptions which the various participants brought with them to the bargaining table.

The actual give and take among the conferees on a number of key questions is detailed in two firsthand accounts, by Winston Churchill and James Byrnes. The subjects covered include Poland (of special concern to Britain and Russia), France (of special concern to Britain), Germany (of special concern to Russia) and the United Nations (of special concern to the United States). Since the Far Eastern agreement was not the subject of formal Big Three negotiations, detailed descriptions of the bargaining on that subject will have to be gleaned from subsequent readings—by Chamberlin, Wilmot, Harriman and Bohlen, for example. In the Churchill and Byrnes descriptions, especially the former, we see the outlines of a standard Western justification for the Yalta agreements—that they were "the best we could get" in view of the hard realities of the situation. The excerpt from the biography of Harry Hopkins evokes the mood of "the three of us" and the early climate in which their results were received.

The early intellectual critics of Yalta, as typified by William Henry Chamberlin and Chester Wilmot, argued that the agreements were a bad bargain. They argue from different perspectives. Wilmot blames American naiveté and idealism for the Yalta results. He argues that our nonpolitical approach to war caused us to disregard the power factors in international relations and that this blind spot cost us insight, if not success, in planning for a stable postwar world at Yalta. Chamberlin, in a totally different view, sees the agreements as cynical and immoral. He attacks Roosevelt for "selling out" Poland and China, for sacrificing their independence without their consent and for acting in contradiction of our historic foreign policy declarations. Both authors agree, however, that American negotiators underestimated Soviet ambitions and that President Roosevelt placed excessive faith in his personal ability to handle Marshal Stalin.

The Yalta Conference became an issue in American domestic politics; and Athan Theoharis examines it in this light. In the Cold War context of the late forties and early fifties, Republicans blamed the Democrats for our foreign policy failures and breathed life into a series of assertions (or "myths") about Yalta as contributory to those failures. As Theoharis points out, the Democratic defense of Yalta was also partisan. Democrats defended the American negotiators by arguing that they made the best possible bargain, and that subsequent Russian violations of the bargain had triggered the Cold War.

Two Yalta participants who articulated that very defense were Averell Harriman and Charles Bohlen, in a pair of important congressional hearings of the early fifties. The questions of Senate Foreign Relations Committee members and Bohlen's answers summarize many of the issues that divided Americans at the height of the domestic Yalta controversy.

A staple of Yalta's defenders has been to ask what alternatives, resources and bargains were available to the Western negotiators. And a staple answer of early critics—intellectual and domestic—has been that some alternative use of Western military resources would either have vitiated the need for the Yalta bargains (or produced a different set of bargains) or produced compliance with the bargains that were agreed to. A later group of critics has argued that there were nonmilitary resources available to American negotiators—of an economic nature. Their view of Yalta is set within a much larger revisionist critique of American foreign policy.

William Appleman Williams views Yalta as an episode in America's foreign policy tradition of economic "open door" expansionism. He argues that Roosevelt could have negotiated a very different kind of bargain with Stalin and that this primarily economic bargain might have led to a very different set of postwar relations between the two countries. It was, in Williams' view, not Russian aggressiveness but American expansionism that prevented the alternative bargain from being struck, and this, therefore, helped precipitate the Cold War.

The revisionist perspective on American and Russian aims and strategies differs from that of either the other critics or the defenders of Yalta. One of its characteristics is a greater effort to delineate the vantage point of the Russians. Another is its effort to apportion greater American blame for the Cold War. Arthur Schlesinger, Jr. updates and defends the more traditional view of "The Origins of the Cold War" and, by implication, of the Yalta Conference. Schlesinger

Wide World Photos

contrasts the American and Soviet views of international politics, and he finds it reasonable that the Russians should have mistrusted the Americans. But he returns to the orthodox theme of Soviet ambition and aggressiveness as the root cause of the Cold War.

Christopher Lasch's commentary on the historiographical controversy makes it clear that one can no longer assess the Yalta Conference without some attention to the larger debate over American foreign policy in the period immediately succeeding Yalta. If a standard defense of Yalta is to be that Russia broke the agreements, it becomes necessary to entertain the revisionist claim that America may have forced the Soviet hand in this regard.

In the final selection, Diane Clemens returns to focus directly on the Yalta Conference—much in the same vein as the McNeill excerpt with which this collection begins. She analyzes Yalta as a diplomatic bargaining process to find out who wanted what and who got what. In those terms, she finds it to be a normal exercise in diplomatic compromise, and assigns considerable blame to the Americans for breaking the compromise. Her concluding question is one with which students might profitably begin their independent assessments.

Foreign policy controversies provide an opportunity for self-examination as well as debate. This case study invites the reader to engage in both. He should come to some judgments on the clash of issues concerning Yalta. But he should also think broadly, critically and constructively about America's position in the world. Decades after Yalta, that remains the nub of the controversy.

The Clash of Issues

Was the conference an American success?

> The second conference of the Big Three held at Yalta in February 1945 represented the high point of Soviet diplomatic success and the low point of American appeasement.
>
> WILLIAM HENRY CHAMBERLIN

> The record of the conference shows clearly that the Soviet Union made greater concessions at Yalta to the United States and Great Britain than were made to the Soviets. The agreements reached among President Roosevelt, Prime Minister Churchill and Marshal Stalin were, on the whole, a diplomatic triumph for the United States and Great Britain.
>
> EDWARD R. STETTINIUS, JR.

By what criteria should we judge the Yalta agreements?

> Aside from such things as the restoration of Russian sovereignty in Sakhalin or the Kuriles, the Western allies conceded nothing that Russia did not already have or could not have taken.
>
> HENRY STEELE COMMAGER

> The real issue for the world and for the future is not what Stalin would or could have taken, but what he was given the right to take.
>
> CHESTER WILMOT

Did Soviet violation of the Yalta agreements promote the Cold War?

> The United States and Great Britain have at least the moral right and technically, the legal right to use Soviet violations as the basis for repudiation of Allied concessions at Yalta, for it was the Soviet breach of contract that started the "Cold War."
>
> FORREST C. POGUE

> Within a few months after the Conference, the United States attempted to undo those agreements at Yalta which reflected Soviet interests. . . . The Soviets, for their part, generally complied with the Yalta decisions sponsored by and beneficial to the West.
>
> DIANE S. CLEMENS

Might an alternative American policy at Yalta have averted the Cold War?

> America was in a position at Yalta to speak the only language the Communists understand, the language of power. The President of the

United States at Yalta was in command of the greatest land, navy and air force ever assembled on earth. One quiet sentence to Marshal Stalin in that language could have indicated that America could have required him to keep his solemn agreements.

PATRICK J. HURLEY

He [Roosevelt] never got his priorities straight. Short of war, economic aid was the one effective tool he had in negotiating with the Soviets. But he never used it.

WILLIAM APPLEMAN WILLIAMS

The most rational American policies could hardly have averted the Cold War.

ARTHUR SCHLESINGER, JR.

Note: The statement above by Edward R. Stettinius, Jr. is quoted from *Roosevelt and the Russians* (Garden City, 1949), p. 295; that by Henry Steele Commager from "Was Yalta a Calamity? A Debate," *New York Times Magazine,* August 3, 1952, p. 49; that by Forrest C. Pogue from John L. Snell (editor) *The Meaning of Yalta* (Baton Rouge, 1956), p. 207; that by Diane S. Clemens from *Yalta* (New York, 1970), pp. 268 and 269. The statement by Patrick J. Hurley is quoted from *Hearings on the Military Situation in the Far East* before the Committees on Armed Services and Foreign Relations, U.S. Senate, 82nd Congress, 1st Session, 1951, p. 2839; that by William Appleman Williams is quoted in the *New York Times,* September 24, 1967, p. 33.

I YALTA IN CONTEXT

William H. McNeill

THE YALTA CONFERENCE, 4–11 FEBRUARY 1945

One of the earliest histories of World War II was one by American historian William Hardy McNeill. Written in England under the auspices of the Royal Institute of International Affairs, it conveys an Anglo-American perspective. McNeill's brief introduction to his own account of the Yalta Conference sets the stage for our readings. He describes some of the problems confronting the Big Three leaders and the attitudes which each of those leaders brought with him to their meeting.

The Yalta Conference, 4–11 February 1945, was probably the most important war-time meeting of the Big Three. It came at the time of transition from war planning to peace planning, at a critical moment when the mold of post-war relations between the great Allies was still malleable by words. At Teheran, military strategy had dominated the discussion; by the time of the Potsdam Conference, on the other hand, the relations between the Russians and the West had so hardened that there was little to be done but ratify the existing fact by agreeing to disagree. At Yalta, on the other hand, the Big Three seemed (though the seeming may have been illusory) to have a wider margin of choice. They met at a time when each country's post-war role was yet to be clearly formulated; at a time when it seemed possible to turn their respective policies either towards agreement or towards conflict with one another. For the first time, Roosevelt, Churchill, and Stalin met with a full retinue of political and military advisers; and the atmosphere as well as the organization of the conference was that of a full-dress international gathering. By comparison, Teheran had been an informal, personal encounter between the three chiefs of government, supplemented by military staff conversations.

The United States, Britain, and Russia each approached the Yalta

From William H. McNeill: *America, Britain and Russia, Their Cooperation and Conflict, 1941–1946* in *Survey of International Affairs* (Wartime Series) edited by A. J. Toynbee and published by Oxford University Press under the auspices of the Royal Institute of International Affairs. Used with permission.

Conference with definite goals in view. For the Americans, two aims took precedence over all others. First, Roosevelt and his advisers wished to smooth out the obstacles to agreement with the Russians which had arisen at Dumbarton Oaks in order to assure the speedy establishment of a United Nations organization. Secondly, the Americans hoped to settle future strategy in both Europe and the Far East. The strategic problem in Europe hinged upon the dispute between British and American Chiefs of Staff as to how best to invade Germany; in the Far East it centered upon Russia's part in the war against Japan.

In comparison, local European political problems took second rank. The Americans still looked forward to a rapid withdrawal of their troops from Europe as soon as Germany had been beaten. Roosevelt told Stalin and Churchill at Yalta that it would be impossible for the American Government to keep any troops in Europe for more than two years after Hitler's overthrow; and, long before that, plans called for the transfer of combat units to the Pacific as fast as ships could be found to carry them. Moreover, many of Roosevelt's most trusted advisers did not expect that public opinion would support an active American policy in Europe after the end of the war. Roosevelt certainly had no desire to repeat President Wilson's fiasco of 1918–1920. The spectacle of a new American arbiter of Europe repudiated by his own country could only lead to confusion and misunderstanding. It would be much better if Europeans settled their own affairs to suit themselves, so long as they did so within the general world framework envisaged by the proposals of Dumbarton Oaks, and paid more or less respectful attention to the principles of the United Nations Declaration and the Atlantic Charter.

According to this line of reasoning, the first thing Americans should try to achieve was to secure an agreement with the Russians about the United Nations organization. That done, European disputes could be left to the Europeans, with a little helpful advice and perhaps some prodding from the United States. It is true that the experts of the State Department came to Yalta with some definite ideas as to how the outstanding disputes in Europe should be solved, but Roosevelt was not inclined to take their advice very seriously. In the debates at the Conference, the President in general preferred not to act as champion of any particular formula. Instead he assumed the role of mediator between Churchill and Stalin whenever he could, leaving the positive initiative for settlement of the tangled affairs of Europe largely to the British and Russians.

On the military side, the British were as anxious as the Americans to settle the dispute over European strategy which had arisen between the two countries; and as usual they were prepared to leave to the Americans the problems of war in the Pacific. But the facts of geography, if nothing else, reversed in British eyes the priority among the political issues to be solved. The problem of Allied policy towards Germany and Poland; the role of France in the post-war balance of power on the Continent; the future of British influence in the Balkans and Persia—these were pressing and important matters, and only after they had been amicably settled by the Great Powers did it seem sensible to go ahead with the formation of a world-wide United Nations organization. High principles and professions of friendship would, after all, mean next to nothing if they could not be translated into detailed agreements about the future fate of particular countries and regions.

Stalin approached the Yalta Conference in a somewhat similar spirit. It seems reasonable to impute to him three general aims. He wanted what help he could get for the economic reconstruction of the Soviet Union. This meant reparations from Germany and, if possible, loans from the United States. Secondly, in return for his intervention against Japan in Manchuria, Stalin wished to acquire the territories and special rights which the Tsarist Government had lost in the Far East after the Russo-Japanese war of 1904–1905. Thirdly, and this was by all odds the most important of his aims, Stalin wished to lay the basis for the future security of his country against Germany. This, he probably believed, required the continuation of the general understanding which the war had brought about among the Big Three. To maintain that understanding he was prepared to make concessions, and he did make several that must have seemed to him very great indeed.

But Stalin also believed that the future security of the Soviet Union required the establishment of governments friendly to Russia in the East European countries that lay between Russia and Germany. It is possible, even probable, that Stalin had not yet come fully to realize the dilemma which this very natural wish created for him. As later

events were to show, a government which satisfied the Soviet definition of friendliness could hardly at the same time satisfy the Western
Powers' definition of a democracy. But the forcible imposition of
"friendly" governments in countries like Poland or Rumania was
likely to offend, even antagonize, Britain and America. Thus the two
basic requirements for Soviet security as Stalin saw them in February
1945 were to prove mutually incompatible in the long run. . . .

It thus appears probable that at the time of the Yalta Conference
Stalin felt that if he refrained from interfering in British and American
zones of influence he could expect the Western nations to do the
same in the Russian zone in Eastern Europe. The problem was merely
to fix amicably the limits of the Russian zone; and the recent agreement reached by the European Advisory Commission which defined
the Russian zone of occupation in Germany, combined with the
agreements which he had made with Churchill at Moscow in October
1944 with respect to the Balkans and Danubian Europe, seemed already to have solved a large part of that problem. There remained
the Far East and, most difficult of all, Poland.

In each area Stalin had what must have seemed to him good bargaining counters. In the Far East he could offer the help of the Red
Army against Japan and an agreement to recognize the Government
of Chiang Kai-shek at the expense of the Chinese Communists. As
for Poland, there were hints that he considered France a sort of
equivalent. The bargain he hoped to make was simple. In return for
his recognition of and support for de Gaulle's Provisional Government (sealed by the Treaty concluded in December 1944) he felt
he could demand British and American recognition of and support
for the new Provisional Government of Poland.

But neither Britain nor America saw things in such a light. Churchill was anxious to rescue Poland from Russian domination; and
what seemed to Stalin a friendly Polish Government seemed to Churchill to promise a mere puppet show. Roosevelt, for his part, hoped
that the whole problem of spheres of influence could be transcended
by basic agreement upon the principles of international relations—
an agreement which would obviate the need for unilateral intervention by any one of the Great Powers in any part of Europe. For
practical purposes, his view coincided with Churchill's: Poland, he
felt, should be genuinely free to run her own affairs and the Polish

people should be permitted to elect whatever sort of government they preferred.

Neither Roosevelt nor Churchill seems frankly to have faced the fact that, in Poland at least, genuinely free democratic elections would return governments unfriendly to Russia—certainly by Stalin's definition, and, indeed, by any definition of international friendliness. Stalin's dilemma—his wish at once to maintain harmony with the Western Powers and to create a belt of friendly governments between himself and Germany—was matched by a similar dilemma in the policy of the West. The democratic process upon which so many eulogies were expended could not produce governments in Eastern Europe (or in many other parts of the world) that would further the harmony of the Great Powers and prove acceptable to all of them. Men were not so uniform, so rational, nor possessed of such good will, as the democratic theory presupposed; and in talking of East European governments which would be both democratic and friendly to Russia the Western Powers were in large part deluding themselves.

In February 1945, however, these truths had yet to be demonstrated by the progress of events. Stalin, as much as Roosevelt, and Churchill, as much as Stalin, talked of the importance of free democratic elections to determine as soon as possible the future form of government in the various countries of Europe which had been liberated from the Nazis; and the identity of their phrases disguised the divergence of their hopes and intentions. It was because the Big Three failed to cut through the smoke-screen of words and face frankly the differences that existed among them that the agreements reached at Yalta in so many cases were no more than verbal and did not long endure the test of practice. In the course of the long discussions over the formation of a Polish government—the topic which took more time than anything else at Yalta—the real differences between Russia and the West were often very near the surface, but neither side dared to grasp the nettle.

Reading the record in retrospect one is tempted to scorn the pious phrases which were used so freely on all sides; but it is perhaps overhasty to do so. War-time propaganda and military cooperation had obscured the great differences between Russian and Western ideas of democracy; and it seemed imperative to many good, honest, and intelligent men to retain the common slogans in the hope that the reality of agreement might gradually grow up under the shelter of an identity of verbal formulae. Deliberately to uncover the disagreements which a common profession of faith in democracy hid might have made things worse, might even have fractured the Grand Alliance before Germany and Japan had been defeated. With a war yet to win, such an alternative was rejected out of hand by all the participants in the Yalta Conference. . . .

II YALTA NEGOTIATED

Winston Churchill

RUSSIA AND POLAND:
THE SOVIET PROMISE

Winston Churchill, Prime Minister of Great Britain (1940–1945 and 1951–1955), is the only one of the major participants to have written about the Yalta Conference. In this excerpt from his memoirs, he describes the negotiations over "the Polish question." More time was spent on the issues of Poland's postwar boundaries and government than on any other topic during the eight days. As Churchill's account makes clear, finding a satisfactory solution to these problems was a matter of the highest priority for the British government.

Poland was discussed at no fewer than seven out of the eight plenary meetings of the Yalta Conference, and the British record contains an interchange on this topic of nearly eighteen thousand words between Stalin, Roosevelt, and myself. Aided by our Foreign Ministers and their subordinates, who also held tense and detailed debate at separate meetings among themselves, we finally produced a declaration which represented both a promise to the world and agreement between ourselves on our future actions. The painful tale is still unfinished and the true facts are as yet imperfectly known, but what is here set down may perhaps contribute to a just appreciation of our efforts at the last but one of the war-time Conferences. The difficulties and the problems were ancient, multitudinous, and imperative. The Soviet-sponsored Lublin Government of Poland, or the "Warsaw" Government as the Russians of all names preferred to call it, viewed the London Polish Government with bitter animosity. Feeling between them had got worse, not better, since our October meeting in Moscow. Soviet troops were flooding across Poland, and the Polish Underground Army was freely charged with the murder of Russian soldiers and with sabotage and attacks on their rear areas and their lines of communication. Both access and information were denied to the Western Powers. In Italy and on the Western Front over 150,000 Poles were fighting valiantly for the final destruction of the Nazi

The selections from Winston Churchill, *Triumph and Tragedy,* are reprinted by permission of and arrangement with Houghton Mifflin Company, the authorized publishers.

armies. They and many others elsewhere in Europe were eagerly looking forward to the liberation of their country and a return to their homeland from voluntary and honorable exile. The large community of Poles in the United States anxiously awaited a settlement between the three Great Powers.

The questions which we discussed may be summarized as follows:

> How to form a single Provisional Government for Poland.
> How and when to hold free elections.
> How to settle the Polish frontiers, both in the east and west.
> How to safeguard the rear areas and lines of communication of the advancing Soviet Armies.

The reader should bear in mind the important correspondence between the President and Stalin, and my share in it, about Poland, which is set forth in an earlier chapter. Poland had indeed been the most urgent reason for the Yalta Conference, and was to prove the first of the great causes which led to the breakdown of the Grand Alliance.

When we met on February 6 President Roosevelt opened the discussion by saying that, coming from America, he had a distant view on the Polish question. There were five or six million Poles in the United States, mostly of the second generation, and most of them were generally in favor of the Curzon Line. They knew they would have to give up East Poland. They would like East Prussia and part of Germany, or at any rate something with which to be compensated. As he had said at Teheran, it would make it easier for him if the Soviet Government would make some concession such as Lvov, and some of the oil-bearing lands, to counterbalance the loss of Konigsberg. But the most important point was a permanent Government for Poland. General opinion in the United States was against recognizing the Lublin Government, because it represented only a small section of Poland and of the Polish nation. There was a demand for a Government of national unity, drawn perhaps from the five main political parties.

He knew none of the members of either the London or Lublin Governments. He had been greatly impressed by Mikolajczyk when he had come to Washington, and felt he was an honest man. He therefore hoped to see the creation of a Government of Poland which would be representative, and which the great majority of Poles would support even if it was only an interim one. There were many ways in which it might be formed, such as creating a small Presidential Council to take temporary control and set up a more permanent institution.

I then said it was my duty to state the position of His Majesty's Government. I had repeatedly declared in Parliament and in public my resolution to support the claim of the U.S.S.R. to the Curzon Line as interpreted by the Soviet Government. That meant including Lvov in the U.S.S.R. I had been considerably criticized in Parliament (as had the Foreign Secretary) and by the Conservative Party for this. But I had always thought that, after the agonies Russia had suffered in defending herself against the Germans, and her great deeds in driving them back and liberating Poland, her claim was founded not on force but on right. If however she made a gesture of magnanimity to a much weaker Power, and some territorial concession, such as the President had suggested, we should both admire and acclaim the Soviet action.

But a strong, free, and independent Poland was much more important than particular territorial boundaries. I wanted the Poles to be able to live freely and live their own lives in their own way. That was the object which I had always heard Marshal Stalin proclaim with the utmost firmness, and it was because I trusted his declarations about the sovereignty, independence, and freedom of Poland that I rated the frontier question as less important. This was dear to the hearts of the British nation and the Commonwealth. It was for this that we had gone to war against Germany—that Poland should be free and sovereign. Everyone knew what a terrible risk we had taken when we had gone to war in 1939 although so ill-armed. It had nearly cost us our life, not only as an Empire but as a nation. Great Britain had no material interest of any kind in Poland. Honor was the sole reason why we had drawn the sword to help Poland against Hitler's brutal onslaught, and we could never accept any settlement which did not leave her free, independent, and sovereign. Poland must be mistress in her own house and captain of her own soul. Such freedom must not cover any hostile design by Poland or by any Polish group, possibly in intrigue with Germany, against Russia; but the World Organization that was being set up would surely never tolerate such action or leave Soviet Russia to deal with it alone.

At present there were two Governments of Poland, about which we differed. I had not seen any of the present London Government of Poland. We recognized them, but had not sought their company. On the other hand, Mikolajczyk, Romer, and Grabski were men of good sense and honesty, and with them we had remained in informal but friendly and close relations. The three Great Powers would be criticized if they allowed these rival Governments to cause an apparent division between them, when there were such great tasks in hand and they had such hopes in common. Could we not create a Government or governmental instrument for Poland, pending full and free elections, which could be recognized by all? Such a Government could prepare for a free vote of the Polish people on their future constitution and administration. If this could be done we should have taken one great step forward towards the future peace and prosperity of Central Europe. I said I was sure that the communications of the Russian Army, now driving forward in victorious pursuit of the Germans, could be protected and guaranteed.

After a brief adjournment Stalin spoke. He said that he understood the British Government's feeling that Poland was a question of honor, but for Russia it was a question both of honor and security; of honor because the Russians had had many conflicts with the Poles and the Soviet Government wished to eliminate the causes of such conflicts; of security, not only because Poland was on the frontiers of Russia, but because throughout history Poland had been a corridor through which Russia's enemies had passed to attack her. During the last thirty years the Germans had twice passed through Poland. They passed through because Poland had been weak. Russia wanted to see a strong and powerful Poland, so that she would be able to shut this corridor of her own strength. Russia could not keep it shut from the outside. It could only be shut from the inside by Poland herself, and it was for this reason that Poland must be free, independent, and powerful. This was a matter of life and death for the Soviet State. Their policy differed greatly from that of the Czarist Government. The Czars had wanted to suppress and assimilate Poland. Soviet Russia had started a policy of friendship, and friendship moreover with an independent Poland. That was the whole basis of the Soviet attitude, namely, that they wanted to see Poland independent, free, and strong.

He then dealt with some of the points which Mr. Roosevelt and I had put forward. The President, he said, had suggested there should be some modification of the Curzon Line and that Lvov and perhaps certain other districts should be given to Poland, and I had said that this would be a gesture of magnanimity. But the Curzon Line had not been invented by the Russians. It had been drawn up by Curzon and Clemenceau and representatives of the United States at the conference in 1919, to which Russia had not been invited. The Curzon Line had been accepted against the will of Russia on the basis of ethnographical data. Lenin had not agreed with it. He had not wished to see the town and province of Bialystok given to Poland. The Russians had already retired from Lenin's position, and now some people wanted Russia to take less than Curzon and Clemenceau had conceded. That would be shameful. When the Ukrainians came to Moscow they would say that Stalin and Molotov were less trustworthy defenders of Russia than Curzon or Clemenceau. It was better that the war should continue a little longer, although it would cost Russia much blood, so that Poland could be compensated at Germany's expense. When Mikolajczyk had been in Russia during October he had asked what frontier for Poland Russia would recognize in the West, and he had been delighted to hear that Russia thought that the western frontier of Poland should be extended to the Neisse. There were two rivers of that name, said Stalin, one near Breslau, and another farther west. It was the Western Neisse he had in mind, and he asked the Conference to support his proposal. . . .

That evening the President wrote a letter to Stalin, after consultation with and amendment by us, urging that two members of the Lublin Government and two from London or from within Poland should come to the Conference and try to agree in our presence about forming a Provisional Government which we could all recognize to hold free elections as soon as possible. I favored this course, and supported the President when we met again on February 7. Mr. Roosevelt once more emphasized his concern. Frontiers, he said, were important, but it was quite within our province to help the Poles to set up a united temporary Government, or even to set one up ourselves until they could produce one of their own founded on free elections. "We ought to do something," he said, "that will come like a breath of fresh air in the murk that exists at the moment on the Polish question." He then asked Stalin if he would like to add anything to what he had said the day before.

Stalin replied that he had received the President's letter only about an hour and a half before, and had immediately given instructions for Bierut and Morawski to be found so that he could talk to them on the telephone. He had just learned that they were in Cracow and Lodz respectively, and he promised to ask them how representatives from the opposition camp could be traced, as he did not know their addresses. In case there might not be time to get them to the Conference, Molotov had elaborated some proposals which to some extent met the President's suggestions. . . . As for the river Neisse, mentioned in the second of Molotov's proposals, I reminded my hearers that in previous talks I had always qualified the moving of the Polish frontier westward by saying that the Poles should be free to take territory in the West, but not more than they wished or could properly manage. It would be a great pity to stuff the Polish goose so full of German food that it died of indigestion. I was conscious of a large body of opinion in Great Britain which was frankly shocked at the idea of moving millions of people by force. A great success had been achieved in disentangling the Greek and Turkish populations after the last war, and the two countries had enjoyed good relations ever since; but in that case under a couple of millions of people had been moved. If Poland took East Prussia and Silesia as far as the Oder, that alone would mean moving six million Germans back to Germany. It might be managed, subject to the moral question, which I would have to settle with my own people.

Stalin observed that there were no Germans in these areas, as they had all run away.

I replied that the question was whether there was room for them in what was left of Germany. Six or seven million Germans had been killed and another million (Stalin suggested two millions) would probably be killed before the end of the war. There should therefore be room for these migrant people up to a certain point. They would be needed to fill the vacancies. I was not afraid of the problem of transferring populations, so long as it was proportionate to what the Poles could manage and to what could be put into Germany. But it was a matter which required study, not as a question of principle, but of the numbers which would have to be handled.

In these general discussions maps were not used, and the distinction between the Eastern and Western Neisse did not emerge as clearly as it should have done. This was however soon to be made clear. . . .

When we met again on February 8 Mr. Roosevelt read out his revised proposals based on Molotov's draft. "No objection," he stated, "is perceived to the Soviet proposal that the eastern boundary of Poland should be the Curzon Line, with modifications in favor of Poland in some areas of from five to eight kilometres." Here at least was one matter on which we could all agree, and although I had invited the Russians to make some minor concessions it seemed better not to multiply our difficulties, which were already serious enough. But the President was firm and precise about the frontier in the West. He agreed that Poland should receive compensation at the expense of Germany, "including that portion of East Prussia south of the Konigsberg line, Upper Silesia, and up to the line of the Oder; but," he continued, *"there would appear to be little justification for extending it up to the Western Neisse."* This had always been my view, and I was to press it very hard when we met again at Potsdam five months later.

There remained the question of forming a Polish Government which we could all recognize and which the Polish nation would accept. Mr. Roosevelt suggested a Presidential Committee of three Polish leaders who would go to Moscow, form a provisional Government from representatives in Warsaw, London, and inside Poland itself, and hold free elections as soon as possible.

After a short adjournment Molotov voiced his disagreement. The Lublin Government, he said, was now at the head of the Polish people. It had been enthusiastically acclaimed by most of them and enjoyed great authority and prestige. The same could not be said of the men from London. If we tried to create a new Government the Poles themselves might never agree so it was better to try to enlarge the existing one. It would only be a temporary institution, because all our proposals had but one object, namely, to hold free elections in Poland as soon as possible. How to enlarge it could best be discussed in

Moscow between the American and British Ambassadors and himself. He said he greatly desired an agreement, and he accepted the President's proposals to invite two out of the five people mentioned in his letter of February 6. There was always the possibility, he said, that the Lublin Government would refuse to talk with some of them, like Mikolajczyk, but if they sent three representatives and two came from those suggested by Mr. Roosevelt conversations could start at once.

"What about the Presidential Committee?" asked Mr. Roosevelt.

"Better avoid it," he answered. "It will mean having two bodies to deal with instead of one."

"This," I said, "is the crucial point of the Conference. The whole world is waiting for a settlement, and if we separate still recognizing different Polish Governments the whole world will see that fundamental differences between us still exist. The consequences will be most lamentable, and will stamp our meeting with the seal of failure. On the other hand of course we take different views about the basic facts in Poland, or at any rate some of them. According to British information, the Lublin Government does not commend itself to the great majority of the Polish people, and we cannot feel that it would be accepted abroad as representing them. If the Conference is to brush aside the existing London Government and lend all its weight to the Lublin Government there will be a world outcry. As far as can be foreseen, the Poles outside of Poland will make a virtually united protest. There is under our command a Polish army of 150,000 men, who have been gathered from all who have been able to come together from outside Poland. This army has fought, and is still fighting, very bravely. I do not believe it will be at all reconciled to the Lublin Government, and if Great Britain transfers recognition from the Government which it has recognized since the beginning of the war they will look on it as a betrayal.

"As Marshal Stalin and M. Molotov well know," I proceeded, "I myself do not agree with the London Government's action, which has been foolish at every stage. But the formal act of transferring recognition from those whom we have hitherto recognized to this new Government would cause the gravest criticism. It would be said that His Majesty's Government have given way completely on the eastern frontier (as in fact we have) and have accepted and championed the

Soviet view. It would also be said that we have broken altogether with the lawful Government of Poland, which we have recognized for these five years of war, and that we have no knowledge of what is actually going on in Poland. We cannot enter the country. We cannot see and hear what opinion is. It would be said we can only accept what the Lublin Government proclaims about the opinion of the Polish people, and His Majesty's Government would be charged in Parliament with having altogether forsaken the cause of Poland. The debates which would follow would be most painful and embarrassing to the unity of the Allies, even supposing that we were able to agree to the proposals of my friend M. Molotov.

"I do not think," I continued, "that these proposals go nearly far enough. If we give up the Polish Government in London a new start should be made from both sides on more or less equal terms. Before His Majesty's Government ceased to recognize the London Government and transferred their recognition to another Government they would have to be satisfied that the new Government was truly representative of the Polish nation. I agree that this is only one point of view, as we do not fully know the facts, and all our differences will of course be removed if a free and unfettered General Election is held in Poland by ballot and with universal suffrage and free candidatures. Once this is done His Majesty's Government will salute the Government that emerges without regard to the Polish Government in London. It is the interval before the election that is causing us so much anxiety."

Molotov said that perhaps the talks in Moscow would have some useful result. It was very difficult to deal with this question without the participation of the Poles themselves, who would have to have their say. I agreed, but said that it was so important that the Conference should separate on a note of agreement that we must all struggle patiently to achieve it. The President supported me. He said that it was the great objective of the Americans that there should be an early General Election in Poland. The only problem was how the country was to be governed in the meantime, and he hoped it would be possible to hold elections before the end of the year. The problem was therefore limited in time.

Stalin now took up my complaint that I had no information and no way of getting it.

"I have a certain amount," I replied.

"It doesn't agree with mine," he answered, and proceeded to make a speech, in which he assured us that the Lublin Government was really very popular, particularly Bierut, Osobka-Morawski, and General Zymierski. They had not left the country during the German occupation, but had lived all the time in Warsaw and came from the underground movement. That made a deep impression on the Poles, and the peculiar mentality of people who had lived under the German occupation should be borne in mind. They sympathized with all those who had not left the country in difficult times, and they considered the three persons he had named to be people of that kind. He said he did not believe that they were geniuses. The London Government might well contain cleverer people, but they were not liked in Poland because they had not been seen there when the population was suffering under the Hitlerite occupation. It was perhaps a primitive feeling, but it certainly existed.

It was, he said, a great event in Poland that the country had been liberated by Soviet troops, and this had changed everything. It was well known that the Poles had not liked the Russians, because they had three times helped to partition Poland. But the advance of the Soviet troops and the liberation of Poland had completely changed their mood. The old resentment had disappeared, and had given way to goodwill and even enthusiasm for the Russians. That was perfectly natural. The population had been delighted to see the Germans flee and to feel that they were liberated. Stalin said it was his impression that the Polish population considered the driving out of the Germans a great patriotic holiday in Polish life, and they were astonished that the London Government did not take any part in this festival of the Polish nation. They saw on the streets the members of the Provisional Government, but asked where were the London Poles. This undermined the prestige of the London Government, and was the reason why the Provisional Government, though not great men, enjoyed great popularity.

Stalin thought that these facts could not be ignored if we wanted to understand the feelings of the Polish people. I had said that I feared the Conference separating before agreement was reached. What then was to be done? The various Governments had different information, and drew different conclusions from it. Perhaps the first thing was to call together the Poles from the different camps and hear what they had to say.

There was dissatisfaction, he continued, because the Polish Government was not elected. It would naturally be better to have a Government based on free elections, but the war had so far prevented that. But the day was near when elections could be held. Until then we must deal with the Provisional Government, as we had dealt, for instance, with General de Gaulle's Government in France, which also was not elected. He did not know whether Bierut or General de Gaulle enjoyed greater authority, but it had been possible to make a treaty with General de Gaulle, so why could we not do the same with an enlarged Polish Government, which would be no less democratic? It was not reasonable to demand more from Poland than from France. So far the French Government had carried out no reform which created enthusiasm in France, whereas the Polish Government had enacted a land reform which had aroused great enthusiasm. If we approached the matter without prejudice we should be able to find common ground. The situation was not as tragic as I thought, and the question could be settled if too much importance was not attached to secondary matters and if we concentrated on essentials.

"How soon," asked the President, "will it be possible to hold elections?"

"Within a month," Stalin replied, "unless there is some catastrophe on the front, which is improbable."

I said that this would of course set our minds at rest, and we could wholeheartedly support a freely elected Government which would supersede everything else, but we must not ask for anything which would in any way hamper the military operations. These were the supreme ends. If however the will of the Polish people could be ascertained in so short a time, or even within two months, the situation would be entirely different and no one could oppose it.

We thereupon agreed to let our Foreign Secretaries talk the matter over.

The three Ministers accordingly met at noon on February 9. They were unable to agree. When however the Conference assembled in plenary session at four o'clock in the afternoon Molotov produced some fresh proposals which were much nearer to the American draft. The Lublin Government was to be "reorganized on a wider democratic basis, with the inclusion of democratic leaders from Poland itself, and also from those living abroad." He and the British and American Ambassadors should consult together in Moscow about how this would be done. Once reorganized the Lublin Government would be pledged to hold free elections as soon as possible, and we should then recognize whatever Government emerged. Mr. Stettinius had desired a written pledge that the three Ambassadors in Warsaw should observe and report that the elections were really free and unfettered, but Molotov opposed this, because, he alleged, it would offend the Poles. Subject to this and to a few minor amendments, he accepted the United States plan.

This was a considerable advance, and I said so, but I felt it my duty to sound a general warning. This would be the last but one of our meetings. There was an atmosphere of agreement, but there was also a desire to put foot in the stirrup and be off. We could not, I declared, afford to allow the settlement of these important matters to be hurried and the fruits of the Conference lost for lack of another twenty-four hours. A great prize was in view and decisions must be unhurried. These might well be among the most important days in our lives.

Mr. Roosevelt declared that the differences between us and the Russians were now largely a matter of words, but both he and I were anxious that the elections should really be fair and free. I told Stalin that we were at a great disadvantage, because we knew so little of what was going on inside Poland and yet had to take decisions of great responsibility. I knew, for instance, that there was bitter feeling among the Poles and that M. Osubka-Morawski had used very fierce language, and I had been told that the Lublin Government had openly said it would try as traitors all members of the Polish Home Army and underground movement. This, I said, caused me anxiety and distress. Of course I put the security of the Red Army first, but I begged Stalin to consider our difficulty. The British Government did not know what was going on inside Poland, except through dropping brave men by parachute and bringing members of the underground movement out. We had no other means of knowing, and did not like getting our information in this way. How could this be remedied without in any way hampering the movements of the Soviet troops? Could any facilities be granted to the British (and no doubt to the United States) for seeing how these Polish quarrels were being settled? Tito had said that when elections took place in Yugoslavia he would not object to Russian, British, and American observers being present to report impartially to the world that they had been carried out fairly. So far as Greece was concerned, His Majesty's Government would greatly welcome American, Russian, and British observers to make sure the elections were conducted as the people wished. The same question would arise in Italy. When Northern Italy was delivered there would be a vast change in the Italian political situation, and there would have to be an election before it was possible to form a Constituent Assembly or Parliament. The British formula there was the same—Russian, American, and British observers should be present to assure the world that everything had been done in a fair way. It was impossible, I said, to exaggerate the importance of carrying out elections fairly. For instance, would Mikolajczyk be able to go back to Poland and organize his party for the elections?

"That will have to be considered by the Ambassadors and M. Molotov when they meet the Poles," said Stalin.

I replied, "I must be able to tell the House of Commons that the elections will be free and that there will be effective guarantees that they are freely and fairly carried out."

Stalin pointed out that Mikolajczyk belonged to the Peasant Party, which, as it was not a Fascist party, could take part in the elections and put up its candidates. I said that this would be still more certain if the Peasant Party were already represented in the Polish Government, and Stalin agreed that the Government should include one of their representatives.

I said that we should have to leave it at that, and added that I hoped that nothing I had said had given offense, since nothing had been further from my heart.

"We shall have to hear," he answered, "what the Poles have to say."

I explained that I wanted to be able to carry the eastern frontier question through Parliament, and I thought this might be done if Parliament was satisfied that the Poles had been able to decide for themselves what they wanted.

"There are some very good people among them," he replied. "They are good fighters, and they have had some good scientists and musicians, but they are very quarrelsome."

"All I want," I answered, "is for all sides to get a fair hearing."

"The elections," said the President, "must be above criticism, like Caesar's wife. I want some kind of assurance to give to the world, and I don't want anybody to be able to question their purity. It is a matter of good politics rather than principle."

"I am afraid," said Molotov, "that if we insert the American draft the Poles will feel they are not trusted. We had better discuss it with them."

I was not content with this, and resolved to raise it with Stalin later on. The opportunity presented itself next day.

Just before our last effective meeting, on February 10, Mr. Eden and I had a private conversation with Stalin and Molotov at the Yusupov Villa, at which I once more explained how difficult it was for us to have no representatives in Poland who could report what was going on. The alternatives were either an Ambassador with an embassy staff or newspaper correspondents. The latter was less desirable, but I pointed out that I should be asked in Parliament about the Lublin Government and the elections and I must be able to say that I knew what was happening.

"After the new Polish Government is recognized it would be open to you to send an Ambassador to Warsaw," Stalin answered.

"Would he be free to move about the country?"

"As far as the Red Army is concerned, there will be no interference with his movements, and I promise to give the necessary instructions, but you will have to make your own arrangements with the Polish Government."

Stalin also pointed out that de Gaulle had a representative in Poland.

We then agreed to add the following to our declaration:

> As a consequence of the above, recognition should entail an exchange of Ambassadors, by whose reports the respective Governments would be informed about the situation in Poland.

This was the best I could get. . . .

At noon on February 27 I asked the House of Commons to approve the results of the Crimea Conference. I said:

I am anxious that all parties should be united in this new instrument, so that these supreme affairs shall be, in Mr. Gladstone's words, "high and dry above the ebb and flow of party politics." . . . The Crimea Conference leaves the Allies more closely united than before, both in the military and in the political sphere. Let Germany ever recognize that it is futile to hope for division among the Allies and that nothing can avert her utter defeat. Further resistance will only be the cause of needless suffering. The Allies are resolved that Germany shall be totally disarmed, that Nazism and militarism in Germany shall be destroyed, that war criminals shall be justly and swiftly punished, that all German industry capable of military production shall be eliminated or controlled, and that Germany shall make compensation in kind to the utmost of her ability for damage done to Allied nations. On the other hand, it is not the purpose of the Allies to destroy the people of Germany, or leave them without the necessary means of subsistence. Our policy is not revenge; it is to take such measures as may be necessary to secure the future peace and safety of the world. There will be a place one day for Germans in the comity of nations, but only when all traces of Nazism and militarism have been effectively and finally extirpated.

Poland was the issue which disturbed the House.

The three Powers are agreed that acceptance by the Poles of the provisions on the eastern frontiers, and, so far as can now be ascertained, on the western frontiers, is an essential condition of the establishment and future welfare and security of a strong, independent, homogeneous Polish State. . . . But even more important than the frontiers of Poland, within the limits now disclosed, is the freedom of Poland. The home of the Poles is settled. Are they to be masters in their own house? Are they to be free, as we in Britain and the United States or France are free? Are their sovereignty and their independence to be untrammelled, or are they to become a mere projection of the Soviet State, forced against their will by an armed minority to adopt a Communist or totalitarian system? I am putting the case in all its bluntness. It is a touchstone far more sensitive and vital than the drawing of frontier lines. Where does Poland stand? Where do we all stand on this?

Most solemn declarations have been made by Marshal Stalin and the Soviet Union that the sovereign independence of Poland is to be maintained, and this decision is now joined in both by Great Britain and the United States. Here also the World Organization will in due course assume a measure of responsibility. The Poles will have their future in their own hands, with the single limitation that they must honestly follow, in harmony with their Allies, a policy friendly to Russia. That is surely reasonable. . . .

The agreement provides for consultations, with a view to the establishment in Poland of a new Polish Provisional Government of National Unity, with which the three major Powers can all enter into diplomatic relations, instead of some recognizing one Polish Government and the rest another. . . . His Majesty's Government intend to do all in their power to ensure that . . . representative Poles of all democratic parties are given full freedom to come and make their views known.

I felt bound to proclaim my confidence in Soviet good faith in the hope of procuring it. In this I was encouraged by Stalin's behavior about Greece.

The impression I brought back from the Crimea, and from all my other contacts, is that Marshal Stalin and the Soviet leaders wish to live in honorable friendship and equality with the Western democracies. I feel also that their word is their bond. I know of no Government which stands to its obligations, even in its own despite, more solidly than the Russian Soviet Government. I decline absolutely to embark here on a discussion about Russian good faith. It is quite evident that these matters touch the whole future of the world. Somber indeed would be the fortunes of mankind if some awful schism arose between the Western democracies and the Russian Soviet Union.

I continued:

We are now entering a world of imponderables, and at every stage occasions for self-questioning arise. It is a mistake to look too far ahead. Only one link in the chain of destiny can be handled at a time.

I trust the House will feel that hope has been powerfully strengthened by our meeting in the Crimea. The ties that bind the three Great Powers together and their mutual comprehension of each other have grown. The United States has entered deeply and constructively into the life and salvation of Europe. We have all three set our hands to far-reaching engagements at once practical and solemn. . . .

The general reaction of the House was unqualified support for the attitude we had taken at the Crimea Conference. There was however intense moral feeling about our obligations to the Poles, who had suffered so much at German hands and on whose behalf as a last resort we had gone to war. A group of about thirty Members felt so strongly on this matter that some of them spoke in opposition to the motion which I had moved. There was a sense of anguish lest we should have to face the enslavement of a heroic nation. Mr. Eden supported me. In the division on the second day we had an overwhelming majority, but twenty-five Members, most of them Conservatives, voted against the Government, and in addition eleven members of the Government abstained. Mr. H. G. Strauss, who was

Parliamentary Secretary to the Ministry of Town and Country Planning, resigned.

It is not permitted to those charged with dealing with events in times of war or crisis to confine themselves purely to the statement of broad general principles on which good people agree. They have to take definite decisions from day to day. They have to adopt postures which must be solidly maintained, otherwise how can any combinations for action be maintained? It is easy, after the Germans are beaten, to condemn those who did their best to hearten the Russian military effort and to keep in harmonious contact with our great Ally, who had suffered so frightfully. What would have happened if we had quarrelled with Russia while the Germans still had two or three hundred divisions on the fighting front? Our hopeful assumptions were soon to be falsified. Still, they were the only ones possible at the time.

James F. Byrnes

YALTA: HIGH TIDE OF BIG THREE UNITY

James F. Byrnes, adviser to President Roosevelt, was Director of the Office of War Mobilization and Reconversion at the time of Yalta. It was a position which earned him the unofficial title of "Assistant President" in Washington. He had been a Justice of the U. S. Supreme Court and was later to become Secretary of State under President Truman. His shorthand notes provide us with a firsthand account of formal negotiations over issues other than Poland.

The Yalta Conference opened on Sunday, February 4, 1945, on a rising tide of Allied victories. The German counteroffensive in the west had been stopped in the bloody snow of the Ardennes Forest, and we were preparing to launch our drive across the Rhine. The Russians had begun the drive on Germany's eastern frontier that was to end in Berlin three months later. The situation was such that

From *Speaking Frankly* by James F. Byrnes. Copyright, 1947, by James F. Byrnes. Reprinted by permission of Harper & Brothers.

at one time President Roosevelt and Marshal Stalin engaged in light banter as to whether they should wager that the Red Army would get to Berlin before the American Army recaptured Manila.

Our chief objective for the conference was to secure agreement on the Dumbarton Oaks proposal for the creation of an international peace organization. But the rapid advance of our armies required also that urgent consideration be given to European political and military problems. It was natural, then, that the President, with the agreement of the other members, opened the conference with the suggestion to discuss "what we shall do with Germany."

Stalin immediately made it clear that he wanted to discuss the terms of the German surrender, the future form of the German state or states, reparations, and the allocation of a zone of occupation to France.

In the fall of 1944 the Soviet Union and the Provisional Government of France had entered into a treaty of friendship. It was immediately obvious at Yalta, however, that the treaty and the friendly words exchanged over it by the diplomats had not changed in any degree Marshal Stalin's opinion on the contribution of France to the war. He thought France should play little part in the control of Germany, and stated that Yugoslavia and Poland were more entitled to consideration than France.

When Roosevelt and Churchill proposed that France be allotted a zone of occupation, Stalin agreed. But it was clear he agreed only because the French zone was to be taken out of the territory allotted to the United States and the United Kingdom. And he especially opposed giving France a representative on the Allied Control Council for Germany. He undoubtedly concurred in the opinion expressed to the President by Mr. Molotov that this should be done "only as a kindness to France and not because she is entitled to it."

"I am in favor of France being given a zone," Stalin declared, "but I cannot forget that in this war France opened the gates to the enemy." He maintained it would create difficulties to give France a zone of occupation and a representative on the Allied Control Council and refuse the same treatment to others who had fought more than France. He said France would soon demand that de Gaulle attend the Big Three's conferences.

Churchill argued strongly in favor of France's being represented on the Council. He said the British public would not understand if questions affecting France and the French zone were settled without her participation in the discussion. It did not follow, as Stalin had suggested, that France would demand de Gaulle's participation in the conferences of the Big Three, he added. And, in his best humor, Mr. Churchill said the conference was "a very exclusive club, the entrance fee being at least five million soldiers or the equivalent."

Stalin, however, feared there would be such a demand. He said General de Gaulle was "very unrealistic," and reiterated that even though "France had not done much fighting in the war, yet de Gaulle has demanded equal rights with the Soviets, the British and the Americans, who have done the fighting."

President Roosevelt did not take issue with Stalin on de Gaulle. The President had great admiration for France and its people but he did not admire de Gaulle. On several occasions he referred to a conversation at Casablanca in which de Gaulle compared himself with Joan of Arc as the spiritual leader of France, and with Clemenceau as the political leader.

President Roosevelt's first opinion was not to insist upon giving France representation on the Allied Council if she were allotted a zone. As the argument proceeded, however, the President said he wished to consider further that phase of the question and asked that action be delayed. The following day Mr. Hopkins, Averell Harriman, our Ambassador to the Soviet Union, and I urged upon the President the view that France should be represented on the Council, that they could not accept a zone without such representation, and that any other action would greatly humiliate them. The President finally reached the same conclusion, and he later succeeded in inducing Stalin to agree with him.

The major problem in connection with the surrender of Germany arose from an informal suggestion, broached at Teheran, that the future security of Europe required Germany to be cut up into a number of individual states.

The discussion was brief but there seemed to be general agreement among all three that Germany should be divided into an unspecified number of states. Marshal Stalin was of the opinion that the Germans in surrendering should be told about this plan. Mr.

Churchill suggested that the questions involved were so complex that further study should be made. The President then suggested that the Foreign Ministers study the matter and submit recommendations within the next thirty days.

At the later meeting in London, in which Ambassador John G. Winant represented the United States, no agreement was reached. When Mr. Hopkins saw Marshal Stalin late in May it was apparent that the Soviet leader had changed his views and had reached the conclusion that we and the British were opposed to dismemberment. He said it was evident there was no agreement at Yalta; and that at the London meeting the British had interpreted the Crimean discussions to represent not a positive plan but something to hold over Germany's head in case of bad behavior. He suggested that the matter be discussed at the forthcoming meeting of the Big Three at Potsdam. By the time that meeting occurred, however, the thinking of all three governments had veered away from dismemberment and the issue did not arise.

During all the consideration of the German question at Yalta, reparations were the chief interest of the Soviet delegation.

At the conference table Marshal Stalin sat between Mr. Molotov and I. M. Maisky, Deputy Commissar for Foreign Affairs. Maisky had served as the Russian Ambassador in London for eleven years, and at Yalta often acted as interpreter as well as adviser to Stalin. It was he who presented the Soviet proposal on German reparations.

"Our plan foresees that reparations in kind should be demanded from Germany in two ways," Mr. Maisky explained. "First, withdrawals from the national wealth of Germany. That means factories, land, machinery, machine tools, rolling stock of railways, investments in foreign enterprises, and so on. Second, yearly payments in kind after the war in the course of ten years."

He proposed that 80 percent of all German industry should be withdrawn, specifying the iron and steel, engineering, metal and chemical industries. He added that aviation plants, facilities for the production of synthetic oil and all other military enterprises and factories should be withdrawn entirely.

"By withdrawal I mean to confiscate and carry away physically and use as reparations payments," he emphasized.

Retention of 20 percent of Germany's heavy industry would be adequate to sustain the country's economic life, he said. All reparations should be terminated within ten years and the removal of factories and other wealth should be completed in two years. German enterprises important as war potentials should be internationalized with representatives of the three powers sitting on the boards of these enterprises for as many years as the three countries should desire.

Reparations funds should be paid only to those countries that had sustained direct material losses such as damage to factories, land and homes and the losses of personal property by citizens, Mr. Maisky maintained. Because such losses were so huge he proposed that a system of priorities be established among the countries to receive reparations based on their contribution to the winning of the war and the value of their direct material losses.

He then stated that reparations should be fixed at twenty billions of dollars and that the share of the Soviet Union in the reparations fund should not be less than ten billion dollars.

Mr. Churchill responded first to Mr. Maisky's statement. He recalled the experience of the United Kingdom after World War I.

"The process was a very disappointing one," he said. "With great difficulty about 1,000 million pounds was extracted from Germany, and that would never have been extracted if the United States, at the same time, had not loaned Germany a larger sum."

"Removal of plants and factories to a certain extent is a proper step," he declared, "but I am quite sure you will never be able to get out of ruined Germany for Russia alone anything like 215 million pounds a year." He pictured Britain's losses and heavy debts and referred to the severe losses of other countries which must be considered in allotting reparations.

"Secondly," Mr. Churchill continued, "there arises in my mind the specter of an absolutely starving Germany."

"If our treatment of Germany's internal economy is such as to leave eighty million people virtually starving, are we to sit still and say, 'It serves you right,' or will we be required to keep them alive? If so, who is going to pay for that? . . . If you have a horse and you want him to pull the wagon you have to provide him with a certain amount of corn—or at least hay."

"But the horse must not kick you," Mr. Maisky objected.

Mr. Churchill switched to a nonkicking illustration by saying:

"If you have a motorcar you must give it a certain amount of petrol to make it go. I am in favor of having a reparations inquiry committee set up to explore this subject with the object of getting the most we can in a sensible way."

In presenting the position of the United States, President Roosevelt pointed out that after the last war we loaned to Germany billions of dollars, and emphasized "We cannot let that happen again."

"We are in the position of not wanting any of Germany's manpower," the President said. "We do not want any of her machinery, tools, or her factories. There will be some German assets in the United States that might be credited against what Germany owes the United States, but it will amount to very little." After the meeting I advised the President that the best estimate placed the value of German assets in this country at 150 million dollars and that the value certainly would not exceed 200 million. He later used these figures to point out what an exceedingly small amount we would receive in contrast to other nations.

The American people want the Germans to live, the President told the conference, but do not want them to have a higher standard of living than other states, such as the Soviet Republic. He stressed that the United States would emerge from the war in poor financial condition and that we would have no money to send into Germany for food, clothing or housing.

"All I can say is that we will do the best we can in an extremely bad situation," the President said, and concluded by adding we would support the creation of a reparations commission as proposed by the Soviet Union.

Marshal Stalin then entered the discussion. "The root of the trouble the last time," he asserted, "was that reparations were demanded in money. Then, the question arose of transferring the German mark into foreign currencies. That was the rock upon which reparations broke down."

Marshal Stalin urged that the three powers that carried the burden of the war should have priority in reparations. He said it must be admitted that "France did not have any sacrifice to compare to the three powers I have in mind." And then to clinch the argument, he said, "France at this time has in the war eight divisions while the

Lublin government has ten divisions." There is no doubt that his opinion as to the claims of a government was influenced by the number of its divisions. He is credited with having said at Yalta, when reference was made to the views of the Pope, "How many divisions does he have?" The Marshal did not make that statement at Yalta. But it was the yardstick he frequently used.

Stalin concluded his statement with a proposal that a decision be made as to whether reparations should be based upon the contributions made in the prosecution of the war or upon the losses sustained, or whether both should be considered. During the discussion, the President made a statement which still remains a source of misunderstanding between ourselves and the Russians. He said the Reparations Commission "should take, in its initial studies as a basis for discussion, the suggestion of the Soviet government, that the total sum of reparations should be twenty billions and that 50 percent of it should go to the Soviet Union."

This language was later incorporated in the Conference Protocol, the document prepared by a committee appointed to set forth in writing the agreements reached during a conference. The protocol, which on the last day of the conference was submitted to the heads of government for final approval, also contained the statement that the Reparations Commission could consider "the use of labor" as a possible source of reparations. There was no discussion of this proposal at the conference table except a passing reference by the President in which he said the United States "cannot take manpower as the Soviet Republics can." Later I learned the language was added by Mr. Maisky, the Soviet representative, and subsequently agreed to by the other delegations. At any rate, I did not know of it at the time I left Yalta. Had I known it, I would have urged the President to oppose the inclusion in the protocol of any provision for the use of large groups of human beings as enforced or slave laborers. The program later drafted by the Reparations Commission contained no provision for "the use of labor." But I regret to say that Germans and Japanese still are being held in Allied hands for use as laborers.

In the days that followed Yalta, as our armies fought their way into Germany from the east and the west, and as our combined air power and artillery pounded the cities of Germany into rubble, it became fully apparent there was no adequate answer to Prime

Minister Churchill's contention that Germany would be unable to reimburse the Allies for all the losses inflicted on the people in the various Allied countries. . . .

In October 1943, Secretary of State Cordell Hull had taken with him to Moscow the first proposal that finally developed into the Dumbarton Oaks plan for a United Nations organization. He and the President believed it would be far easier to obtain agreement on a plan for a peace organization while the war was still in progress. How right they were!

At the conclusion of the Dumbarton Oaks Conference, in the autumn of 1944, the only major point remaining at issue was the formula for voting in the Security Council. The Soviet delegation had insisted that all decisions in the Security Council must be by a unanimous vote on the part of the major powers. We agreed that no decision committing our military forces to action should be taken without our consent but did not believe the right of veto should extend to all matters.

We finally had devised a compromise formula which we hoped the Soviets could be persuaded to accept, and the President sent it direct to Marshal Stalin on December 5. At the same time, the State Department prepared and delivered to the Soviet and British embassies in Washington lengthy statements in explanation and support of the President's proposal.

We sought to meet the Soviet insistence that the votes of the five permanent members of the Security Council must be unanimous on all questions by suggesting that Paragraph 3 in the section of the plan dealing with voting procedure in the Security Council should state that unanimity would be required for all categories of decisions except one: in those decisions involving promotion of peaceful settlement of disputes, a permanent member of the council would not cast a vote if it were party to the dispute in question. Such cases, we believed, would be quasi-judicial in character and no nation should be placed above the law in an organization based on the principle of equality under the law. Where the decisions might require the use of force, we felt justified in placing the permanent members in a special position, since they would have to bear the principal responsibility for such action.

It was on the second day of the conference that Secretary Stettinius formally presented our proposal, and the President then asked for its immediate consideration. In supporting the plan, the President referred to the agreement reached at Teheran in which the three heads of government declared: "We recognize fully that supreme responsibility resting upon us and all the United Nations to make a peace that will command the good will of the overwhelming mass of the peoples of the world and banish the scourge and terror of war for many generations."

Conflicting reports of the exchange that followed were presented in the Security Council of the United Nations in the spring of 1947 by the Soviet and the British representatives during a discussion of the veto power and its relationship to the control of atomic energy. Because of this, and because the veto power has remained one of the most controversial issues of the United Nations structure, it may be of interest to present here the major portion of my shorthand record of the views expressed on the veto issue at Yalta.

Since the United States, as the author of the proposal, had clearly stated its position, the exchange was almost entirely between Prime Minister Churchill and Marshal Stalin. It follows:

> Prime Minister. *The peace of the world depends upon the lasting friendship of the three great powers, but His Majesty's Government feel we should be putting ourselves in a false position if we put ourselves in the position of trying to rule the world when our desire is to serve the world and preserve it from a renewal of the frightful horrors which have fallen upon the mass of its inhabitants. We should make a broad submission to the opinion of the world within the limits stated. We should have the right to state our case against any case stated by the Chinese, for instance, in the case of Hongkong. There is no question that we could not be required to give back Hongkong to the Chinese if we did not feel that was the right thing to do. On the other hand, I feel it would be wrong if China did not have an opportunity to state its case fully. In the same way, if Egypt raises a question against the British affecting the Suez Canal, as has been suggested, I would submit to all the procedure outlined in this statement. I would do this without fear because British rights would be preserved under paragraph 3 when our veto would kill action if we chose to use it.*
>
> *I presume, Mr. President, if Argentina raises a question against the United States, that the United States will submit to all the procedure of the last five paragraphs and would not vote on the issue. However, the United States could raise its fundamental objections in respect to all the measures to be taken under paragraph 3. . . .*

His Majesty's Government see no danger from their point of view in associating themselves with the proposals of the United States. We see great advantages in the three great powers not assuming the position of rulers of all of the rest of the world without even allowing them to state their case. It would not be right for us with the great power we possess to take that position, denying them the right to state their case, and to have measures taken to adjust difficulties short of the powers set out in paragraph 3, on which powers we rely if we are not convinced by our friends and colleagues on the Security Council.

The Marshal. *I would like to have this document to study because it is difficult on hearing it read to come to any conclusion. I think that the Dumbarton Oaks decisions have, as an objective, not only to secure to every nation the right to express its opinion, but if any nation should raise a question about some important matter, it raises the question in order to get a decision in the matter. I am sure none of those present would dispute the right of every member of the Assembly to express his opinion.*

Mr. Churchill thinks that China, if it raised the question of Hongkong, would be content only with expressing opinion here. He may be mistaken. China will demand a decision in the matter and so would Egypt. Egypt will not have much pleasure in expressing an opinion that the Suez Canal should be returned to Egypt, but would demand a decision on the matter. Therefore, the matter is much more serious than merely expressing an opinion. Also, I would like to ask Mr. Churchill to name the power which may intend to dominate the world. I am sure Great Britain does not want to dominate the world. So one is removed from suspicion. I am sure the United States does not wish to do so, so another is excluded from the powers having intentions to dominate the world.

Mr. Churchill. *May I answer?*

The Marshal. *In a minute. When will the great powers accept the provisions that would absolve them from the charge that they intend to dominate the world? I will study the document. At this time it is not very clear to me. I think it is a more serious question than the right of a power to express its intentions or the desire of some power to dominate the world.*

Prime Minister. *I know that under the leaders of the three powers as represented here we may feel safe. But these leaders may not live forever. In ten years' time we may disappear. A new generation will come which did not experience the horrors of war and may probably forget what we have gone through. We would like to secure the peace for at least fifty years. We have now to build up such a status, such a plan, that we can put as many obstacles as possible to the coming generation quarreling among themselves.*

The Marshal. *I think that the task is to secure our unity in the future, and, for this purpose, we must agree upon such a covenant as would best serve that purpose. The danger in the future is the possibility of con-*

flicts among ourselves. If there be unity, then the danger from Germany will not be great. Now we have to think how we can create a situation where the three powers here represented, and China—

Prime Minister. *—and France.*

The Marshal. *Yes, and we will keep a united front. I must apologize to the conference. I have been very busy with other matters and had no chance to study this question in detail. As far as I understand what was said in the American proposal, all conflicts are being divided into two categories—conflicts which demand sanctions of a military nature; the other category includes conflicts which could be regulated by peaceful means without military sanctions. Then I understand that, in the consideration of conflicts of both kinds, it is contemplated there should be first a free discussion of the conflict. I understand, also, that in considering the disputes of the first category, which demand military sanctions, that a permanent member being a party to the dispute has a right to vote. But in conflicts of the second category, which could be regulated by peaceful means, and do not require sanctions, the party in dispute is not allowed to vote.*

We are accused of attaching too great importance to the procedure "how to vote." We are guilty. We attach great importance to the question of voting. All questions are decided by votes and we are interested in the decisions and not in the discussions. Suppose China is a permanent member and demands Hongkong be returned to her. I can assure Mr. Churchill that China will not be alone. They will have some friends in the Assembly. That would be true of Egypt in the case mentioned.

Prime Minister. *I could say "no." I would have a right to say that the powers of the World Security Organization could not be used against us if we remained unconvinced.*

The Marshal. *There is another danger. My colleagues in Moscow cannot forget the case which occurred in 1939 during the Russian-Finnish War, when Britain and France used the League of Nations against us and eventually expelled us and isolated us.*

The President. *It is entirely satisfactory for the Marshal to have sufficient time to study the proposal.*

I was deeply disturbed by the clear evidence that Stalin had not considered or even read our proposal on voting in the Security Council even though it had been sent to him by diplomatic air pouch on December 5. This was February 6, and it occurred to me that if in those sixty-three days he had not familiarized himself with the subject, he could not be greatly interested in the United Nations organization. It was all the more impressive since this certainly was the only proposal on the agenda with which he was not entirely familiar. My concern remained even though at the next day's meeting Mr. Molotov announced the Soviet Union's acceptance of our proposal, which was later adopted in substantially the same form at San Francisco. . . .

Immediately after announcing the Soviet Union's acceptance of the President's proposal on voting procedure in the Security Council, Mr. Molotov expressed the hope that Byelorussia, the Ukraine and Lithuania would be admitted to the United Nations. In any event, he said, he hoped the first two would be admitted. Marshal Stalin made a forceful plea in support of the suggestion.

Prime Minister Churchill supported the Soviet request, stating: "My heart goes out to White Russia, bleeding from her wounds while beating down the tyrants."

Not wishing to agree and yet not wanting to oppose Churchill and Stalin directly while the issue of the international organization was in the balance, the President made this statement: "The British Empire has great populations in its dominions, like Australia, Canada and South Africa. The Soviet Government has great masses of population like the three dominions mentioned. The United States has no colonies but has a large population. Brazil is smaller than the Soviet Union but larger in area than the United States. There are many countries with small population, like Honduras and Liberia. We must study the question of whether any country should be given more than one vote. I do not want to break down the principle of one vote to each nation. Therefore, we can decide on the general plan of a meeting to organize the association and then before the meeting, through the Foreign Secretaries, or at that meeting, we can decide these questions and I will be glad to take them up."

There was no dissent. Because I was strongly opposed to granting the Soviet request, I thought the President had done a good job and that we might hear no more of the proposal. But at the conference table the next afternoon the President began reading a report of the meeting of the Foreign Ministers which had just been handed him and said:

"Paragraph 2 is that it will be for the conference to determine the list of the original members of the organization. At that stage the delegates of the United Kingdom and the United States will support the proposal to admit to original membership two Soviet Socialist republics."

The report was agreed to.

I learned later that at the Foreign Ministers' meeting, Mr. Eden, who wanted to be certain of the admission of all members of the British Commonwealth including India, which was not an independent state, agreed with Mr. Molotov on the votes for Byelorussia and the Ukraine. Mr. Stettinius then also agreed to the arrangement. As the meeting opened, the Secretary advised the President of the action which the President later announced, and the heads of government approved.

I was surprised at the agreement which, in my opinion was very unwise. After the meeting I urged my view upon the President. I reminded him that before we left Washington he told a group of Senators that if Stalin proposed granting membership to Byelorussia and the Ukraine, he would insist upon membership for each of our forty-eight states. The truth is, the Soviet republics are no more independent than the states of our Union.

I recalled to him how effectively the opponents of the League of Nations had argued that the British, because of their dominions, would have five votes in the Assembly while we would have but one. Our people had come to realize that the dominions were independent states and frequently held views different from the United Kingdom, but that was not true of the Soviet republics. I feared the opponents of the United Nations might use the allotment of three votes to the Soviet Union as effectively as the foes of the League had used the argument against the British votes twenty-six years earlier. I urged the President at least to ask that the United States be granted a number of votes equal to those of the Soviet Union. The President feared it was too late but said he would consider it.

I convinced Hopkins that, at the very least, we should secure an agreement from Stalin and Churchill whether or not we afterward exercised the right. He then joined me in urging the President to withdraw his agreement regarding the two Soviet republics unless Russia agreed the United States also should have three votes. The President finally told us he would present it to Marshal Stalin. On the last day I spent at Yalta, February 10, the President wrote him a letter which stated:

> *I am somewhat concerned lest it be pointed out that the United States will have only one vote in the Assembly. It may be necessary for me,*

therefore, if I am to insure wholehearted acceptance by the Congress and people of the United States of our participation in the World Organization, to ask for additional votes in the Assembly in order to give parity to the United States.

I would like to know, before I face this problem, that you perceive no objection and would support a proposal along this line if it is necessary for me to make it at the forthcoming conference.

The following day Marshal Stalin advised the President that he entirely agreed with him that "since the number of votes for the Soviet Union is increased to three in connection with the inclusion of the Soviet Ukraine and Soviet White Russia among the members of the Assembly, the number of votes for the USA should also be increased.

"The number of votes for the USA might be increased to three as in the case of the Soviet Union and its two basic republics," he said. "If it is necessary I am prepared officially to support this proposal."

President Roosevelt also asked Churchill for his views, and Churchill stated he would support the President in any proposal he made to achieve American equality with other nations.

When I arrived in Washington there was waiting for me in the White House Map Room the following cable:

For Justice Byrnes from Mr. Hopkins
THE PRESIDENT HAS RECEIVED COMPLETELY SATISFACTORY REPLIES FROM THE PRIME MINISTER AND MARSHAL STALIN ON ADDITIONAL VOTES TO ACHIEVE PARITY FOR THE UNITED STATES, IF NECESSARY. IN VIEW OF THE FACT THAT NOTHING ON THIS WHOLE SUBJECT APPEARS IN THE COMMUNIQUÉ, THE PRESIDENT IS EXTREMELY ANX-IOUS NO ASPECT OF THIS QUESTION BE DISCUSSED EVEN PRIVATELY.

I assumed he had some very good reason for not wishing this matter to be discussed, and I complied with the request.

The President and his advisers concluded not to ask at San Francisco for compliance with the agreement that we have as many votes as were given to Russia. He did not again discuss the subject with me, and I did not know he had changed his mind. I admit that the public opposition to Russia's three votes as against our one was not so great as I had expected. But nevertheless I think we should have insisted at San Francisco on the agreement made at Yalta. I felt then and feel now that the smaller states would have opposed the request of the Soviets and the United States. This course would have been just and it would have resulted in both governments having only one vote. That would have been the best solution.

In granting three votes to the Soviet Union, we established a precedent. The Soviets do not overlook precedents favorable to themselves. At the Peace Conference in Paris, for example, Byelorussia and the Ukraine were members. They will demand membership in every other conference. This means the Soviet Union has three arguments as well as three votes. They never fail to make the three arguments or cast the three votes.

The Paris Peace Conference agreed upon two kinds of recommendations, one requiring only a majority vote, the other requiring a two-thirds vote. The Soviet representatives announced that in the Council of Foreign Ministers they would not consider any recommendation adopted by less than a two-thirds vote.

There were twenty-one members of the peace conference. Therefore, eight votes in opposition to a recommendation would prevent its receiving the two-thirds endorsement. When the Soviets opposed a proposal, it was much easier for them to secure these eight votes because they had three votes to start with. Had the Soviets possessed only one vote, or had the United States been given three votes, as was agreed at Yalta, many of the recommendations which received thirteen votes, one short of two-thirds, would have been adopted.

Another agreement was made at Yalta which was to confront me later. This was the "Top Secret" Protocol in which it was agreed that in return for Soviet participation in the war against Japan, the Kurile Islands would be "handed over" to the Soviet Union. It also provided that "the former rights of Russia violated by the treacherous attack of Japan in 1904 shall be restored," and listed these as the return of the southern half of Sakhalin Island, internationalization of the Port of Dairen, the lease of Port Arthur as a Russian naval base, and joint Russo-Chinese operation of the Chinese Eastern and South Manchurian railroads. The United States was to use its influence to have China agree to that part affecting China's territory.

I did not know of this agreement, but the reason is understandable. At that time I was not Secretary of State. Mr. Stettinius was Secretary.

Because of problems that had arisen in Washington, the President wanted me to return with Admiral King, who was leaving at noon on February 10. We expected the conference would end that evening and that the President would leave the following day. But that afternoon Stalin requested the President to remain one more day. He said they could not conclude their work and he wished to discuss some matter he deemed important. The President complied. The agreement as to the Kurile Islands was reached in private conversations among the Big Three instead of at the conference table, and the protocols, including this one, were signed on February 11. Had I been in Yalta that day it is probable I would have learned of it.

When the President returned, he did not mention it to me and the protocol was kept locked in his safe at the White House. In the early summer I learned that President Roosevelt had undertaken to induce China to make the concessions affecting Port Arthur, Dairen, and the railroad, but it was not until some time after I became Secretary of State that a news story from Moscow caused me to inquire and learn of the full agreement. I presented the matter to President Truman and he requested Admiral Leahy to transfer to the State Department those documents at the White House containing agreements with foreign governments. I wanted to know how many IOUs were outstanding.

In considering the wisdom of these Pacific agreements entered into by President Roosevelt, one should be fair enough to consider the circumstances under which the promises were made. It was six weeks after the serious German counterattack on the western front. Although progress was being made in both the east and the west, neither the President nor anyone else at that time knew how long the Germans could hold out and how many casualties we would suffer before they surrendered. The President had with him at Yalta the Joint Chiefs of Staff. They knew the situation.

The evidence is clear that the agreement was, in great part, a military decision. The military leaders already had their plans for the invasion of Japan under way. They undoubtedly gave the President their estimate of what such an invasion would cost us in human lives with Russia in the war and what the cost would be if Russia were out of the war. They naturally wanted Russia in the war to engage the Japanese armies in the north. But once Stalin knew our plans for invasion were under way, he knew also that we would want his armies and he could demand more for them. Mr. Stalin is not bashful about making demands.

Nor should President Roosevelt be criticized for keeping the agreement secret. The Soviet Union was party to a treaty with Japan and we could not announce Russia's intention to go to war with her. Furthermore, Russia's military strength was then concentrated on the German campaign. Any hint of the agreement would have been an invitation to the Japanese troops on Russia's borders to launch an invasion. It was in the interest of all of us to allow the Soviets ninety days after Germany's surrender to transfer troops from the European front. It is, therefore, quite understandable that both Marshal Stalin and President Roosevelt wished to maintain strict secrecy.

Robert E. Sherwood

THE MOOD OF YALTA

As anyone who recalls President Nixon's trip to China knows, after-dinner toasts are among the inevitable accoutrements of summit diplomacy. Some Yalta toasts, from Robert Sherwood's biography of Harry Hopkins, help convey the mood of the wartime Allies as of February 1945. Hopkins was perhaps President Roosevelt's closest confidant, and his own assessment of the conference is of special interest in that light.

A large dinner was given by Stalin on the evening of February 8 and a smaller one (with only the principals attending) by Churchill on the last evening, February 10. The record of the principal toasts at the former dinner was as follows:

From *Roosevelt and Hopkins* by Robert E. Sherwood. Copyright, 1948, by Robert E. Sherwood. Reprinted by permission of Harper & Brothers.

Marshal Stalin proposed a toast to the health of the Prime Minister, whom he characterized as the bravest governmental figure in the world. He said that due in large measure to Mr. Churchill's courage and staunchness, England, when she stood alone, had divided the might of Hitlerite Germany at a time when the rest of Europe was falling flat on its face before Hitler. He said that Great Britain, under Mr. Churchill's leadership, had carried on the fight alone irrespective of existing or potential allies. The Marshal concluded that he knew of few examples in history where the courage of one man had been so important to the future history of the world. He drank a toast to Mr. Churchill, his fighting friend and a brave man.

The Prime Minister, in his reply, toasted Marshal Stalin as the mighty leader of a mighty country, which had taken the full shock of the German war machine, had broken its back and had driven the tyrants from her soil. He said he knew that in peace no less than in war Marshal Stalin would continue to lead his people from success to success.

Marshal Stalin then proposed the health of the President of the United States. He said that he and Mr. Churchill in their respective countries had had relatively simple decisions. They had been fighting for their very existence against Hitlerite Germany but there was a third man whose country had not been seriously threatened with invasion, but who had had perhaps a broader conception of national interest and even though his country was not directly imperilled had been the chief forger of instruments which had led to the mobilization of the world against Hitler. He mentioned in this connection Lend-Lease as one of the President's most remarkable and vital achievements in the formation of the Anti-Hitler combination and in keeping the allies in the field against Hitler.

The President, in reply to this toast, said he felt the atmosphere at this dinner was as that of a family, and it was in those words that he liked to characterize the relations that existed between our three countries. He said that great changes had occurred in the world during the last three years, and even greater changes were to come. He said that each of the leaders represented here were working in their own way for the interests of their people. He said that fifty years ago there were vast areas of the world where people had little opportunity and no hope, but much had been accomplished, although there were still great areas where people had little opportunity and little hope, and their objectives here were to give to every man, woman and child on this earth the possibility of security and well being.

In a subsequent toast to the alliance between the three great powers, *Marshal Stalin* remarked that it was not so difficult to keep unity in time of war since there was a joint aim to defeat the common enemy which was clear to everyone. He said the difficult task came after the war when diverse interests tended to divide the Allies. He said he was confident that the present alliance would meet this test also and that it was our duty to see that it would, and that our relations in peacetime should be as strong as they had been in war.

The Prime Minister then said he felt we were all standing on the crest of a hill with the glories of future possibilities stretching before us. He said that in the modern world the function of leadership was to lead the people out from the forests into the broad sunlit plains of peace and happiness. He felt this prize was nearer our grasp than anytime before in history and it would be a tragedy for which history would never forgive us if we let this prize slip from our grasp through inertia or carelessness.

The mood of the American delegates, including Roosevelt and Hopkins, could be described as one of supreme exultation as they left Yalta. They were confident that their British colleagues agreed with them that this had been the most encouraging conference of all, and the immediate response of the principal spokesmen for British and American public opinion added immeasurably to their sense of satisfaction with the job that had been done. As soon as Roosevelt came on board the *Quincy* on Great Bitter Lake (so ominously and perhaps so appropriately named) he received floods of messages telling of the enthusiastic response to the publication of the Yalta communiqués in the United States. One of the cables quoted Herbert Hoover as saying. "It will offer a great hope to the world." William L. Shirer called it "a landmark in human history." Raymond Gram Swing said, "No more appropriate news could be conceived to celebrate the birthday of Abraham Lincoln." Senator Barkley cabled, "Accept my sincere felicitations upon the historic Joint Statement released today. I had it read to the Senate immediately upon release and it made a profound impression. Senator White, Minority Leader, joined me in the expressions of commendation and satisfaction on the floor of the Senate. I regard it as one of the most important steps ever taken to promote peace and happiness in the world."

Joseph C. Harsch wrote, in the *Christian Science Monitor*, "The Crimea Conference stands out from previous such conferences because of its mood of decision. The meetings which produced the Atlantic Charter, Casablanca, Teheran, Quebec—all these were dominated, politically, by declarative moods. They were declarations of policy, of aspirations, of intents. But they were not meetings of decision. The meeting at Yalta was plainly dominated by a desire, willingness and determination to reach solid decisions."

Hopkins later said to me, "We really believed in our hearts that this was the dawn of the new day we had all been praying for and talking about for so many years. We were absolutely certain that we had won the first great victory of the peace—and, by 'we,' I mean *all* of us, the whole civilized human race. The Russians had proved that they could be reasonable and farseeing and there wasn't any doubt in the minds of the President or any of us that we could live with them and get along with them peacefully for as far into the future as any of us could imagine. But I have to make one amendment to that—I think we all had in our minds the reservation that we could not foretell what the results would be if anything should happen to Stalin. We felt sure that we could count on him to be reasonable and sensible and understanding—but we never could be sure who or what might be in back of him there in the Kremlin."

THE CRIMEA (YALTA) CONFERENCE: DOCUMENTS

PROTOCOL OF PROCEEDINGS, FEBRUARY 11, 1945

The complete texts of the Yalta Protocol and the Far Eastern Agreement are reprinted for reference purposes. Most of the Protocol items were included in the communiqué issued at the conclusion of the conference. The Far

From *Official Documents: Texts of Selected Documents on U.S. Foreign Policy, 1918–1952* (New York: Woodrow Wilson Foundation, 1952), pp. 10–19.

Eastern Agreement was not discussed at any of the formal meetings of the Big Three. It was negotiated privately by Marshal Stalin and President Roosevelt; and, for obvious security reasons, was not made public until later—on February 11, 1946.

The Crimea Conference of the Heads of the Governments of the United States of America, the United Kingdom, and the Union of Soviet Socialist Republics which took place from February 4th to 11th came to the following conclusions:

I. World Organization

It was decided:

(1) that a United Nations Conference on the proposed world organization should be summoned for Wednesday, 25th April, 1945, and should be held in the United States of America.

(2) the Nations to be invited to this Conference should be:

(a) the United Nations as they existed on the 8th February, 1945; and

(b) such of the Associated Nations as have declared war on the common enemy by 1st March, 1945. (For this purpose by the term "Associated Nations" was meant the eight Associated Nations and Turkey). When the Conference on World Organization is held, the delegates of the United Kingdom and United States of America will support a proposal to admit to original membership two Soviet Socialist Republics, i.e. the Ukraine and White Russia.

(3) that the United States Government on behalf of the Three Powers should consult the Government of China and the French Provisional Government in regard to decisions taken at the present Conference concerning the proposed World Organization.

(4) that the text of the invitation to be issued to all the nations which would take part in the United Nations Conference should be as follows:

Invitation

The Government of the United States of America, on behalf of itself and of the Governments of the United Kingdom, the Union of Soviet Socialist Republics, and the Republic of China and the Provisional Government of the French Republic, invite the Government of ———— to send representatives to a Conference of the United Nations to be held on 25th April, 1945, or soon thereafter, at San Francisco in the United States of America to prepare a Charter for a General International Organization for the maintenance of international peace and security.

The above named governments suggest that the Conference consider as affording a basis for such a Charter the Proposals for the Establishment of a General International Organization, which were made public last October as a result of the Dumbarton Oaks Conference, and which have now been supplemented by the following provisions for Section C of Chapter VI:

"C. Voting

"1. Each member of the Security Council should have one vote.

"2. Decisions of the Security Council on procedural matters should be made by an affirmative vote of seven members.

"3. Decisions of the Security Council on all other matters should be made by an affirmative vote of seven members including the concurring votes of the permanent members; provided that, in decisions under Chapter VIII, Section A and under the second sentence of paragraph 1 of Chapter VIII, Section C, a party to a dispute should abstain from voting."

Further information as to arrangements will be transmitted subsequently.

In the event that the Government of —————— desires in advance of the Conference to present views or comments concerning the proposals, the Government of the United States of America will be pleased to transmit such views and comments to the other participating Governments.

Territorial Trusteeship. It was agreed that the five Nations which will have permanent seats on the Security Council should consult each other prior to the United Nations Conference on the question of territorial trusteeship.

The acceptance of this recommendation is subject to its being made clear that territorial trusteeship will only apply to (a) existing mandates of the League of Nations; (b) territories detached from the enemy as a result of the present war; (c) any other territory which might voluntarily be placed under trusteeship; and (d) no discussion of actual territories is contemplated at the forthcoming United Nations Conference or in the preliminary consultations, and it will be a matter for subsequent agreement which territories within the above categories will be placed under trusteeship.

II. Declaration on Liberated Europe

The following declaration has been approved:

The Premier of the Union of Soviet Socialist Republics, the Prime Minister of the United Kingdom and the President of the United States of America have consulted with each other in the common interests of the peoples of their countries and those of liberated Europe. They jointly declare their mutual agreement to concert during the temporary period of instability in liberated Europe the policies of their three governments in assisting the peoples of the former Axis satellite states of Europe to solve by democratic means their pressing political and economic problems.

The establishment of order in Europe and the rebuilding of national economic life must be achieved by processes which will enable the liberated peoples to destroy the last vestiges of Nazism and Fascism and to create democratic institutions of their own choice. This is a priniciple of the Atlantic Charter—the right of all peoples to choose the form of government under which they will live—the restoration of sovereign rights and self-government to those peoples who have been forcibly deprived of them by the aggressor nations.

To foster the conditions in which the liberated peoples may exercise these rights, the three governments will jointly assist the people in any European liberated state or former Axis satellite state in Europe where in their judgment conditions require (a) to establish conditions of internal peace; (b) to carry out emergency measures for the relief of distressed peoples; (c) to form interim governmental authorities broadly representative of all democratic elements in the population and pledged to the earliest possible establishment through free elections of governments responsive to the will of the people; and (d) to facilitate where necessary the holding of such elections.

The three governments will consult the other United Nations and provisional authorities or other governments in Europe when matters of direct interest to them are under consideration.

When, in the opinion of the three governments, conditions in any European liberated state or any former Axis satellite state in Europe make such action necessary, they will immediately consult together on the measures necessary to discharge the joint responsibilities set forth in this declaration.

By this declaration we reaffirm our faith in the principles of the Atlantic Charter, our pledges in the Declaration by the United Nations, and our determination to build in cooperation with other peace-loving nations world order under law, dedicated to peace, security, freedom and general well-being of all mankind.

In issuing this declaration, the Three Powers express the hope that the Provisional Government of the French Republic may be associated with them in the procedure suggested.

III. Dismemberment of Germany

It was agreed that Article 12 (a) of the Surrender Terms for Germany should be amended to read as follows:

The United Kingdom, the United States of America and the Union of

Soviet Socialist Republics shall possess supreme authority with respect to Germany. In the exercise of such authority they will take such steps, including the complete disarmament, demilitarization and dismemberment of Germany as they deem requisite for future peace and security.

The study of the procedure for the dismemberment of Germany was referred to a Committee, consisting of Mr. Eden (Chairman), Mr. Winant and Mr. Gousev. This body would consider the desirability of associating with it a French representative.

IV. Zone of Occupation for the French and Control Council for Germany

It was agreed that a zone in Germany, to be occupied by the French Forces, should be allocated to France. This zone would be formed out of the British and American zones and its extent would be settled by the British and Americans in consultation with the French Provisional Government.

It was also agreed that the French Provisional Government should be invited to become a member of the Allied Control Council of Germany.

V. Reparation

The heads of the three governments agreed as follows:

1. Germany must pay in kind for the losses caused by her to the Allied nations in the course of the war. Reparations are to be received in the first instance by those countries which have borne the main burden of the war, have suffered the heaviest losses and have organized victory over the enemy.

2. Reparation in kind to be exacted from Germany in three following forms:

(a) Removals within 2 years from the surrender of Germany or the cessation of organized resistance from the national wealth of Germany located on the territory of Germany herself as well as outside her territory (equipment, machine-tools, ships, rolling stock, German investments abroad, shares of industrial, transport and other enterprises in Germany etc.), these removals to be carried out chiefly for purpose of destroying the war potential of Germany.

(b) Annual deliveries of goods from current production for a period to be fixed.

(c) Use of German labor.

3. For the working out on the above principles of a detailed plan for exaction of reparation from Germany an Allied Reparation Commission will be set up in Moscow. It will consist of three representatives—one from the Union of Soviet Socialist Republics, one from the United Kingdom and one from the United States of America.

4. With regard to the fixing of the total sum of the reparation as well as the distribution of it among the countries which suffered from the German aggression the Soviet and American delegations agreed as follows:

> The Moscow Reparation Commission should take in its initial studies as a basis for discussion the suggestion of the Soviet Government that the total sum of the reparation in accordance with the points (a) and (b) of the paragraph 2 should be 20 billion dollars and that 50% of it should go to the Union of Soviet Socialist Republics.

The British delegation was of the opinion that pending consideration of the reparation question by the Moscow Reparation Commission no figures of reparation should be mentioned.

The above Soviet-American proposal has been passed to the Moscow Reparation Commission as one of the proposals to be considered by the Commission.

VI. Major War Criminals

The Conference agreed that the question of the major war criminals should be the subject of enquiry by the three Foreign Secretaries for report in due course after the close of the Conference.

VII. Poland

The following Declaration on Poland was agreed by the Conference:

> A new situation has been created in Poland as a result of her complete liberation by the Red Army. This calls for the establishment of a Polish Provisional Government which can be more broadly based than was possible before the recent liberation of Western part of Poland. The Provisional Government which is now functioning in Poland should therefore be recognized on a broader democratic basis with the inclusion of demo-

cratic leaders from Poland itself and from Poles abroad. This new Government should then be called the Polish Provisional Government of National Unity.

M. Molotov, Mr. Harriman and Sir. A. Clark Kerr are authorized as a commission to consult in the first instance in Moscow with members of the present Provisional Government and with other Polish democratic leaders from within Poland and from abroad, with a view to the reorganization of the present Government along the above lines. This Polish Provisional Government of National Unity shall be pledged to the holding of free and unfettered elections as soon as possible on the basis of universal suffrage and secret ballot. In these elections all democratic and anti-Nazi parties shall have the right to take part and to put forward candidates.

When a Polish Provisional Government of National Unity has been properly formed in conformity with the above, the Government of the U.S.S.R., which now maintains diplomatic relations with the present Provisional Government of Poland, and the Government of the United Kingdom and the Government of the United States of America will establish diplomatic relations with the new Polish Provisional Government of National Unity, and will exchange Ambassadors by whose reports the respective Governments will be kept informed about the situation in Poland.

The three Heads of Government consider that the Eastern frontier of Poland should follow the Curzon Line with digressions from it in some regions of five to eight kilometers in favor of Poland. They recognize that Poland must receive substantial accession of territory in the North and West. They feel that the opinion of the new Polish Provisional Government of National Unity should be sought in due course on the extent of these accessions and that the final delimitation of the Western frontier of Poland should therefore await the Peace Conference.

VIII. Yugoslavia

It was agreed to recommend to Marshal Tito and to Dr. Subasic:

(a) that the Tito-Subasic Agreement should immediately be put into effect and a new Government formed on the basis of the Agreement

(b) that as soon as the new Government has been formed it should declare:

(i) that the Anti-Fascist Assembly of National Liberation (Aunoj) will be extended to include members of the last Yugoslav Skupstina who have not compromised themselves by collaboration with the enemy, thus forming a body to be known as a temporary Parliament and

(ii) that legislative acts passed by the Anti-Fascist Assembly of

National Liberation (Aunoj) will be subject to subsequent ratification by a Constituent Assembly; and that this statement should be published in the Communiqués of the Conference.

IX. Italo-Yugoslav Frontier [and] Italo-Austria Frontier

Notes on these subjects were put in by the British delegation and the American and Soviet delegations agreed to consider them and give their views later.

X. Yugoslav-Bulgarian Relations

There was an exchange of views between the Foreign Secretaries on the question of the desirability of a Yugoslav-Bulgarian pact of alliance. The question at issue was whether a state still under an armistice regime could be allowed to enter into a treaty with another state. Mr. Eden suggested that the Bulgarian and Yugoslav Governments should be informed that this could not be approved. Mr. Stettinius suggested that the British and American Ambassadors should discuss the matter further with M. Molotov in Moscow. M. Molotov agreed with the proposal of Mr. Stettinius.

XI. Southeastern Europe

The British Delegation put in notes for the consideration of their colleagues on the following subjects:

(a) The Control Commission in Bulgaria;
(b) Greek claims upon Bulgaria, more particularly with reference to reparations;
(c) Oil equipment in Rumania.

XII. Iran

Mr. Eden, Mr. Stettinius and M. Molotov exchanged views on the situation in Iran. It was agreed that this matter should be pursued through the diplomatic channel.

XIII. Meetings of the Three Foreign Secretaries

The Conference agreed that permanent machinery should be set up for consultation between the three Foreign Secretaries; they should meet as often as necessary, probably about every three or four months.

These meetings will be held in rotation in the three capitals, the first meeting being held in London.

XIV. The Montreux Convention and the Straits

It was agreed that at the next meeting of the three Foreign Secretaries to be held in London, they should consider proposals which it was understood the Soviet Government would put forward in relation to the Montreux Convention and report to their Governments. The Turkish Goverment should be informed at the appropriate moment.

The foregoing Protocol was approved and signed by the three Foreign Secretaries at the Crimean Conference, February 11, 1945.

E. R. Stettinius, Jr.
M. Molotov
Anthony Eden

AGREEMENT REGARDING JAPAN, FEBRUARY 11, 1945

The leaders of the three Great Powers—the Soviet Union, the United States of America and Great Britain—have agreed that in two or three months after Germany has surrendered and the war in Europe has terminated the Soviet Union shall enter into the war against Japan on the side of the Allies on condition that:

1. The status quo in Outer-Mongolia (The Mongolian People's Republic) shall be preserved;
2. The former rights of Russia violated by the treacherous attack of Japan in 1904 shall be restored, viz:
   a. the southern part of Sakhalin as well as all the islands adjacent to it shall be returned to the Soviet Union,
   b. the commercial port of Dairen shall be internationalized, the preeminent interests of the Soviet Union in this port being safeguarded and the lease of Port Arthur as a naval base of the U.S.S.R. restored,
   c. the Chinese-Eastern Railroad and the South-Manchurian Railroad which provides an outlet to Dairen shall be jointly

operated by the establishment of a joint Soviet-Chinese Company, it being understood that the preeminent interests of the Soviet Union shall be safeguarded and that China shall retain full sovereignty in Manchuria;

3. The Kurile islands shall be handed over to the Soviet Union. It is understood, that the agreement concerning Outer-Mongolia and the ports and railroads referred to above will require concurrence of Generalissimo Chiang Kai-Shek. The President will take measures in order to obtain this concurrence on advice from Marshal Stalin.

The Heads of the three Great Powers have agreed that these claims of the Soviet Union shall be unquestionably fulfilled after Japan has been defeated.

For its part the Soviet Union expresses its readiness to conclude with the National Government of China a pact of friendship and alliance between the U.S.S.R. and China in order to render assistance to China with its armed forces for the purpose of liberating China from the Japanese yoke.

> *Joseph V. Stalin*
> *Franklin D. Roosevelt*
> *Winston S. Churchill*

February 11, 1945

III YALTA CRITICIZED

Chester Wilmot

STALIN'S GREATEST VICTORY

Historian Chester Wilmot provides us with a British perspective on the American performance at Yalta. In his judgment, our failure to understand some of the practical realities of international political life severely damaged our efforts. For one thing, our anticolonialism drove a wedge between us and our natural allies, the British. For another thing, our drive for unconditional surrender blinded us to the more limited political goals to be achieved by war. Throughout, Wilmot emphasizes the impact of the military situation on the negotiations, and invites us to do the same.

It was not altogether fortuitous that the Yalta Conference coincided with the Red Army's spectacular victory in Poland, for the timing was determined by Stalin. The original initiative had come from Roosevelt, who had been eager to arrange a meeting of the Big Three at the first opportunity after his re-election as President. On his behalf, therefore, Hopkins had broached the subject with the Soviet Ambassador in Washington, Andrei Gromyko, early in November. When Gromyko had replied that Stalin could not leave the Soviet Union, since he was personally directing the military campaign, Hopkins had suggested that the conference might be held in the Crimea. Gromyko had passed this suggestion on, but no positive response had been forthcoming from Moscow. . . .

There is no reason to believe that Stalin had anticipated Hitler's offensive in the West and had therefore delayed his reply to Roosevelt until the moment of greatest Allied embarrassment. On the other hand, the history of wartime and post-war diplomacy has made it clear that the Russians regard international conferences as opportunities for the recognition of situations which have already been created by the exercise of power, not as occasions for the negotiation of reasonable settlements mutually acceptable. Since he was more concerned with Power than Justice, Stalin was not interested in having another conference with the Western leaders until he had secured for himself the strongest military position his armies seemed capable of gaining. . . .

From *The Struggle for Europe* by Chester Wilmot. Copyright, 1952, by Chester Wilmot. Reprinted by permission of Harper & Brothers.

. . . The commitment of Hitler's entire strategic reserve in the West ensured the success of the Red Army's January offensive in Poland. Accordingly, when he cabled Roosevelt just before Christmas, Stalin had good reason to believe that by the start of the Yalta Conference he would be in possession of Warsaw and at least the greater part of Western Poland. Nevertheless, he proceeded to strengthen his position by a political maneuver designed to present his Allies with a *fait accompli*. On December 30th Roosevelt and Churchill confirmed their willingness to come to Yalta early in February. On the following day, at the instigation of the Kremlin, the Lublin Committee proclaimed itself the "Provisional Government of Liberated Democratic Poland" and in the first week of the new year the Soviet Union extended to this puppet administration the diplomatic recognition it had refused to accord the legitimate Polish Government in London.

Even Stalin, however, can hardly have expected that the turn of events would swing the balance of power so quickly or so far in his favor. In the last fortnight of January, while the Russians were sweeping through Poland and into the Reich, driving before them a rabble of armies, the Americans in the Ardennes were meeting resistance as stubborn and as skillful as any they had encountered since D-day. On January 16th the converging attacks of the First and Third U. S. Armies had met at Houffalize, but no substantial body of German troops had been cut off in the Western Ardennes, and the Wehrmacht had continued to fight a steady rearguard action back to the Siegfried defenses. It was February before the Americans regained the line they had been holding six weeks earlier.

On February 4th the Americans captured the first of the Roer dams towards which they had been attacking when the Germans began their counter-offensive. The forces of the Western Powers were now ready to launch their long-delayed assault on the Rhineland, but they were no nearer Berlin than they had been in September 1944, or for that matter in September 1939. Except in the Roer River sector, the Siegfried Line was still intact; the Rhine had yet to be forced; and, since Eisenhower's engineers then believed that no large-scale crossing of the Lower Rhine could be carried out before May, there seemed little chance of Berlin being taken by attack from the West.

On the Eastern Front by this time Malinovsky, having thwarted the German attempts to relieve Budapest, was 80 miles from Vienna; Konev, having surrounded Breslau and secured several bridgeheads west of the Oder, was 120 miles from Prague; and Zhukov, having reached the Oder at Kuestrin north of Frankfurt, was 45 miles from Berlin. Thus the Soviet armies stood, with all the capitals of Eastern Europe already in their hands and the three great capitals of Central Europe within their grasp.

At Yalta Stalin was to be in a doubly advantageous position, for the conference took place not only on the morrow of a severe Allied reverse and at the moment of the Red Army's greatest victory, but also at a time of Anglo-American suspicion and discord.

En route to the Crimea, Roosevelt and Churchill held a brief preliminary conference at Malta, where they discussed the Yalta agenda and those issues which had introduced a certain acrimony into their relationship since their last meeting at Quebec in September. From these discussions Churchill hoped that there would emerge a common policy which he and the President could then present to Stalin and by their unity offset the advantage of his strength. It was apparent, however, that Roosevelt was as anxious as ever to avoid making commitments or giving the Russians any reason to think that they were dealing with an Anglo-American alliance. He saw himself as "the Good Neighbor of the World," the independent arbiter whose task it was to preserve harmony between Churchill and Stalin and to prevent Anglo-Soviet rivalry from causing a breach in "Big Three Unity." In the course of the Malta meeting the British delegation were dismayed to find that their American colleagues were less suspicious of Russia's post-war intentions than they were of Britain's. The appreciation of this fact—astonishing though it may seem at this distance—is essential to the understanding of what happened at Yalta.

The roots of this suspicion lay deep in history. Ever since 1776 Americans have nurtured a profound prejudice against "colonialism," and have tended to presume that the independence which brought them such benefiits must likewise transform the lives of peoples less fortunate than themselves. With little regard for the merits, or the difficulties, of particular cases, they have consistently favored the early grant of self-government to all dependent peoples, and particularly to those still under the dominion of the British Crown, for to Americans—by virtue of their past—Britain has remained the symbol of all Imperialism. Although ready to concede that British colonial policies were more progressive and more humane than those of any other country, they persisted in the belief that Imperial rule contained such inherent evils that even good empires must be bad. . . .

Roosevelt's "assault" upon the colonial concept began with the Atlantic Charter. The first draft of this declaration was drawn up by Churchill, who endeavored to set forth the principles which should guide the democratic nations in their struggle against German aggression and in the re-establishment of European peace. Reporting to the House of Commons on September 9th, 1941, the Prime Minister said: "At the Atlantic meeting we had in mind the restoration of the sovereignty . . . of the states . . . now under the Nazi yoke." This, he insisted, was "quite a separate problem from the progressive evolution of self-governing institutions in the regions and peoples that owe allegiance to the British Crown."

The President, on the other hand, had no such limited view. During the Atlantic Charter Conference he told Churchill: "I can't believe that we can fight a war against fascist slavery, and at the same time not work to free people all over the world from a backward colonial policy. . . . The peace cannot include any continued despotism. Equality of peoples involves the utmost freedom of competitive trade." Thus, when he added to Churchill's draft the statement that he and the Prime Minister wished to "see sovereign rights and self-government restored to those who have been forcibly deprived of them," Roosevelt was thinking not only of the occupied countries of Europe but also of colonial peoples throughout the world. Furthermore, when he inserted an article declaring that they would endeavor "without discrimination to further the enjoyment by all states, great or small, victor or vanquished, of access, on equal terms, to the trade and to the raw materials of the world," the President was avowedly aiming at the Ottawa Agreements, the foundation of Imperial Preference. Appreciating this, Churchill demanded that the words "without discrimination" should be replaced by the phrase "with due respect to their existing obligations," but this gained him only a brief respite from American pressure.

Five months later, when the master Lend-Lease Agreement was signed, Roosevelt insisted that, in return for American aid, Britain must agree to "the elimination of all forms of discriminatory treatment in international commerce and the reduction of tariffs and trade barriers" after the war. Cordell Hull, the prime advocate of this clause, reports that "a few Tory members of the British Cabinet . . . regarded the Lend-Lease Agreement . . . as an attempt to infringe on British Imperial sovereignty"—which, of course, it was.

In his Memoirs Hull is quite frank about the President's purpose. "We had," he writes, "definite ideas with respect to the future of the British Colonial Empire, on which we differed with the British. It might be said that the future of that Empire was no business of ours; but we felt that unless dependent peoples were assisted toward ultimate self-government and were given it . . . they would provide kernels of conflict." Neither Hull nor Roosevelt were content with the official British explanation that "self-government should be achieved within the British Commonwealth." On one occasion the President told his son, Elliott, "I've tried to make it clear to Winston —and the others—that, while we're their allies and in it to victory by their side, they must never get the idea that we're in it just to help them hang on to the archaic, medieval Empire ideas . . . Great Britain signed the Atlantic Charter. I hope they realize the United States government means to make them live up to it." . . .

Roosevelt's vision of the peace included not only the ending of the colonial system, but the abandonment of what he regarded as its essential concomitants, spheres of influence and regional balances of power. He expected, as Hull told Congress, that when the United Nations organization was established there would "no longer be any need for spheres of influence, for alliances, for balance of power, or any other of the special arrangements through which, in the unhappy past, nations strove to safeguard their security or promote their interests."

This idealistic vision was not shared by Churchill who knew from long experience of European history that nations are less likely to succumb to the temptation of aggrandizement if their ambitions are restrained by a reasonable balance of power, and that such a balance could be preserved only by alliances and other "special arrangements." Churchill was by no means anti-Russian, but as early

as October 1942 he had set down the view that "it would be a mea-
sureless disaster if Russian barbarism were to overlay the culture
and independence of the ancient states of Europe." After Teheran,
while continuing to work for Hitler's defeat and Stalin's friendship,
he had become alive to the danger that the war would leave the
Soviet Union in a position of overwhelming power which could be
counter-balanced only by a strong British Empire, a firm Anglo-
American alliance and a United States of Europe.

The prospect of a Russian advance deep into Central and Southeastern Europe dismayed Churchill, and was one of the main reasons for his unflagging advocacy of those Balkan operations which
Roosevelt and the American Chiefs of Staff so persistently vetoed.

Thwarted in his desire to forestall Russia militarily, Churchill endeavored to restrain her by striking a political bargain direct with
the Kremlin. In the early summer of 1944, before the Red Army had
made any serious inroad on the Balkans, the Prime Minister proposed to Stalin (without the President's knowledge) that the "controlling interest" in Rumania and Bulgaria should be exercised by
the Soviet Union, and in Greece and Yugoslavia by Britain. When
news of this proposal reached Washington, the secretive British
approach to Moscow was resented, and the plan was condemned
by Hull on the ground that it amounted to "the division of the Balkans
into spheres of influence." In reply Churchill argued that he was not
proposing to carve up the Balkans, but that in the reestablishment
of civil government "someone must play the hand" and that this
should be done by the power responsible for military operations in
each country. Roosevelt was not altogether satisfied, but he agreed
to give the arrangement a three months' trial on the understanding
that it would apply only to immediate problems and would not prejudice the post-war settlement. Nevertheless, the plan remained suspect in Washington, particularly as the President gave his consent
to it without consulting, or even advising his Secretary of State!

American suspicions were sharpened when Churchill, during his
visit to Moscow in October 1944, "extended the arrangement still
further, even reducing to percentages the relative degree of influence
which Britain and Russia individually should have in specified Balkan
countries." Each of the major powers placed its own interpretation
on this agreement. The Russians regarded it as a formal acknowledg-

ment of their predominant role and interest in the Danube Basin. The British saw it as the recognition of the *fait accompli* in that region and were thankful to have preserved even a small voice in the affairs of the Danubian states and to have kept Russia out of Greece. In Churchill's opinion it was not a matter of dividing the Balkans between Britain and Russia, but of preventing the Soviet Union extending its sphere of influence over the whole peninsula. The Americans, on the other hand, considered the agreement a betrayal of the Atlantic Charter, a sinister scheme to further Britain's Imperial ambitions. In the State Department it was denounced as "Churchiavellian." . . .

It was most tragic that such suspicion and discord should have developed on the eve of Yalta, for it seems to have led Roosevelt and some of his intimates to presume that the future threat to world peace and the independence of small nations would come not from Russia or international Communism, but from the old colonial powers, and particularly Britain. This peculiar aberration can be explained only if it is remembered that at this time Roosevelt did not believe that Stalin cherished any imperialistic aspirations.

Three days before he set out for Malta and the Crimea, Roosevelt took the oath for the fourth time as President of the United States, and, in the course of his inaugural address, declared, "We have learned to be citizens of the world, members of the human community. We have learned the simple truth, as Emerson said, 'the only way to have a friend is to be one.' "

This was the creed that Roosevelt carried to Yalta. There was, in his view, no fundamental conflict of national interest between the Soviet Union and the United States; the Russian and American peoples had so much in common that they would readily cooperate in the cause of peace and freedom if only there could be a real meeting of minds between their leaders. His trust in Stalin and his faith in his own ability to win the Soviet Union's lasting cooperation were still high, although the unhappy course of Russo-Polish relations during the past year might well have given him reason to doubt both his own personal influence and Russia's post-war intentions.

Three times since Teheran, Roosevelt had made a direct approach to Stalin in the hope of inducing him to reach a reasonable agreement with the Polish Government in London; each time he had been rebuffed and Stalin had shown no inclination whatever to allow the principles of the Atlantic Charter to apply to Poland. Nevertheless, Mikolajczyk reports—and there is no reason to disbelieve him—that, when he was in Washington in June 1944, Roosevelt told him, "Stalin is a realist, and we mustn't forget, when we judge Russian actions, that the Soviet regime has had only two years of experience in international relations. But of one thing I am certain, Stalin is not an Imperialist." Roosevelt explained to Mikolajczyk that he had not been able to take a public stand on the Polish question because it was election year, but "eventually," he said: "I will act as moderator in this problem and effect a settlement." Believing, as he had said after Teheran, that Stalin was "getatable," Roosevelt felt sure that when they met again across the conference table there would be no problem they could not solve on a "man-to-man" basis.

Roosevelt was not alone in thinking that Diplomacy by Friendship would bring a sympathetic response from Stalin. The most influential of his advisers—military and political alike—were agreed, as Hull says, that they "must and could get along with the Soviet Government," and that this would be possible if they were "patient and forbearing." The idea that they could "get along with" the Russians came more easily to the American leaders than to the British, for the United States is the great melting pot and the American people have shown an unparalleled capacity for absorbing into their own society a multitude of nationalities.

Perhaps the best exposition of Roosevelt's idea is to be found in a memorandum which Hopkins wrote six months after Yalta. "We know or believe," he said, "that Russia's interests, so far as we can anticipate them, do not afford an opportunity for a major difference with us in foreign affairs. We believe we are mutually dependent upon each other for economic reasons. We find the Russians as individuals easy to deal with. The Russians undoubtedly like the American people. They like the United States. They trust the United States more than they trust any other power in the world . . . above all, they want to maintain friendly relations with us. . . . They are a tenacious, determined people who think and act just like you and I do."

Eisenhower endorsed this view of the Russian people when he wrote, "In his generous instincts, in his love of laughter, in his devotion to a comrade, and in his healthy, direct outlook on the affairs of workaday life, the ordinary Russian seems to me to bear a marked similarity to what we call an 'average American.' " Eisenhower believed too that there was a special bond between the United States and the Soviet Union, a bond that was inevitably lacking in the Anglo-American association. He felt, he says, that "in the past relations of America and Russia there was no cause to regard the future with pessimism." On the one hand, "the two peoples had maintained an unbroken friendship that dated back to the birth of the United States as an independent republic"; on the other, "both were free from the stigma of colonial empire building by force."

This remarkable statement stems straight from the Founding Fathers. It was the American way of saying that politically both peoples were free from original sin. That this was not true of either was irrelevant; it was believed, not merely by Eisenhower but also by many Americans who should have been better acquainted with their own history. This belief was implicit in Roosevelt's approach to the problems which were to be discussed at Yalta. In his eyes, Britain was an Imperial Power, bearing the "colonial stigma"; Russia was not. That assessment of his allies was a decisive factor in Roosevelt's readiness to make concessions to the Soviet Union both in Europe and Asia in order to ensure Stalin's entry into the Pacific War.

Roosevelt's intimates give two reasons for his determination to enlist the aid of Russia against Japan. His personal Chief of Staff, Admiral Leahy, says that the President was actuated by the belief that "Soviet participation in the Far East operation would insure Russia's sincere cooperation in his dream of a united, peaceful world." On the other hand, his Secretary of State, Stettinius, reports that "immense pressure was put on the President by our military leaders to bring Russia into the Far Eastern War. At this time the atomic bomb was still an unknown quantity and our setback in the Battle of the Bulge was fresh in the minds of all. We had not as yet crossed the Rhine. No one knew how long the European War would last nor how great the casualties would be." Stettinius adds that the American Chiefs of Staff had warned Roosevelt that "without Russia it might cost the United States a million casualties to conquer Japan" and that the Pacific War might not end until 1947.

The chief advocate of this view was Marshall, but Roosevelt's military advisers were by no means unanimous in the belief that it would be necessary to invade the Japanese home islands. Leahy says that at Pearl Harbor, in July 1944, both MacArthur and Nimitz (the two commanders directly concerned) had told the President that "Japan could be forced to accept our terms of surrender by the use of sea and air powers without the invasion of the Japanese homeland." Since then, at the Battle for Leyte Gulf in October, the Japanese Navy had suffered such a crushing defeat that well before Yalta Leahy considered that the war against Japan "had progressed to the point where her defeat was only a matter of time and attrition." This was also the opinion of Arnold, the Chief of the Air Staff, whose Super-Fortresses were already bombing Japan from island airfields. There was no longer any great need for air bases in the Maritime Provinces of the Soviet Union, and, after the unhappy experiment of "shuttle-bombing" in Europe, Arnold did not set much store by any facilities he might be granted in Asia. Nevertheless, the advice of Marshall and King prevailed. . . .

Roosevelt's eagerness to buy Stalin's aid in the war against Japan was principally due to his desire to save lives, but in the light of all the evidence it seems fair to say that he was also actuated by the hope that Russia's intervention would enable the United States to strike the decisive blow at Japan, and compel her surrender, before the British, French or Dutch could regain possession of their colonies. The United States would thus be able to demand that the colonies which had been liberated from the Japanese should now be liberated from the dominion of their original owners. . . .

The plenary sessions of the Yalta Conference were held at Livadia Palace overlooking the Black Sea. The ownership of this palace had changed since it was built by the Romanoffs, but the aims and ambitions of the new owners differed little from those of its former masters. The only significant difference was that the men who now sought to fulfill Russia's imperial destiny were more ruthless and more powerful.

At the opening session on Sunday, February 4th, Stalin made a gesture which was both tactful and tactical. He proposed, as he had at Tehran, that Roosevelt should take the chair, and thus once again he brought the President half-way to his side. Yet Stalin showed no early inclination to follow the chairman's lead, least of all with regard to the President's cherished plan for creating a world peace organization based on the recognition of the sovereign rights of all nations. The first time the subject was raised, "Stalin made it quite plain," says Stettinius, "that the three Great Powers which had borne the brunt of the war should be the ones to preserve the peace." He declared, moreover, that he would "never agree to having any action of any of the Great Powers submitted to the judgment of the small powers." In reply to this argument Churchill spoke for all the Western World in saying, "The eagle should permit the small birds to sing and care not wherefore they sang." That evening, when Stettinius and Eden discussed the outlook, they agreed that "the trend . . . seemed to be more towards a three-power alliance than anything else."

Evidently sensing that the time was not opportune to pursue the question of the world peace organization, Roosevelt, at the start of the second plenary meeting, turned the discussion to the future of Germany. . . . .

As the discussion developed—both in the plenary sessions and at meetings of the Foreign Ministers—Roosevelt and Stettinius endeavored to take an intermediate stand on these issues. The result was that three distinct viewpoints emerged. With regard to partition, Stalin wanted a definite commitment both now and in the surrender terms; Churchill wished to make no commitments either way; and Roosevelt suggested that they should mention dismemberment in the terms without binding themselves to this policy. On the matter of reparations, Stalin demanded explicit acceptance in the Protocol of the overall figure of twenty billion dollars; Churchill opposed any mention of any figure even in a secret document; and Roosevelt inclined to the view that the Russian figure might be taken as "a basis for discussion." As for the occupation of Germany, Churchill insisted that France should have a seat on the Control Commission as well as a zone; Stalin argued against both suggestions; and Roosevelt proposed that France should have a zone but no seat.

On each of these questions the President was in fundamental agreement with the Prime Minister's stand (though not with all his reasons) but in public discussion Roosevelt played the mediator. He was not interested in upholding the balance of power concept, nor was he deeply concerned with the intrinsic merits of the German problem. To him Germany was not an issue in itself, but a bargaining point in the wider issue that was uppermost in his mind—the winning of Stalin's cooperation in the international peace organization, and in the war against Japan.

To some extent the role of arbiter was thrust upon Roosevelt when he became chairman but there is no doubt that he preferred it since he was thus able to preserve greater freedom of action and to avoid committing himself until he had heard the rival views. The results of the President's determination to act as mediator were twofold. On the one hand, the assertion of what were in reality Anglo-American views and principles was frequently left to the British alone—much to Churchill's annoyance; and on the other, as one of Roosevelt's closest advisers [Byrnes] says, "the Soviet leaders did over-estimate the ultimate extent of the President's generosity and his willingness to compromise on principles."

The problem of Germany's future was still undecided when—at the third plenary session on February 6th—Roosevelt returned to the question of post-war peace and asked Stettinius to review the questions which had been in dispute at the Dumbarton Oaks Conference. There the Americans, British, Chinese and Russians had agreed on the principles and purposes of what was to become the United Nations, and had decided there should be a General Assembly, a Security Council and various other instrumentalities. The area of agreement had ended, however, when the Soviet Delegate, Gromyko, had proposed that all sixteen republics of the Soviet Union should have seats in the Assembly (a proposal which "left Stettinius and Cadogan breathless"), and had demanded that in the Security Council the Great Powers should have the right to veto any proposals, except those which related to points of procedure.

It has been alleged by some of Roosevelt's critics that the establishment of the veto power in the Security Council was a concession made by him at Yalta to induce Stalin to join the United Nations. This is not so. The basic principle of the veto was never in dispute. None of the Great Powers was prepared to submit itself and its interests unreservedly to the jurisdiction of an international security organization. All were agreed that there must be "unqualified unanimity of the permanent members of the Council in all major decisions relating to the preservation of peace, including all economic and military enforcement measures." This was inevitable. The President, haunted by the ghost of Wilson, insisted on the veto power because he knew that the United States Senate would not surrender to an international body the right to commit American forces to military action. Churchill was equally insistent on this point because, as he said at Yalta, he would "never consent to the fumbling fingers of forty or fifty nations prying into the life's existence of the British Empire."

Although both Britain and America felt obliged to retain the right to veto any international "police action," they had no desire to curtail discussion or to prevent any small power bringing a cause of grievance to the notice of the Security Council. At Dumbarton Oaks, however, Gromyko had refused to accept this view and had told Stettinius, "The Russian position on voting in the Council will never be departed from!" Nevertheless, on December 5th, 1944, Roosevelt had sent to Stalin and Churchill a compromise formula which, while recognizing the need for unanimity on matters involving the application of sanctions, provided that on questions relating to the peaceful settlement of any dispute no member of the Council would cast its vote, or exercise its veto, if it were a party to that dispute. . . .

When the Big Three met again next afternoon . . . Molotov proceeded to say that the Soviet Union was "happy to accept the entire American proposal" about voting in the Security Council, and would not press for all sixteen Soviet Republics to be members of the United Nations. It would be satisfactory if seats were granted to the Ukraine and White Russia. As it had already been agreed that Britain, the four Dominions and India should have individual representation in the General Assembly, Churchill could not oppose this request, and, although Roosevelt did not give his consent immediately, he told Stettinius that he "did not believe there was anything preposterous about the Russian proposal." Indeed, he regarded it as a small price to pay for Soviet cooperation.

The President and the Prime Minister were delighted at this manifestation of Stalin's willingness to join the United Nations and they felt he had made substantial concessions on two vital issues about which he had previously been intractable. They had feared that Stalin was interested only in securing a Three-Power Alliance, but now Roosevelt, at any rate, believed he had persuaded Stalin not only to recognize the sovereign rights of small nations, but also to act in friendly concert with the other Great Powers in maintaining peace and extending the frontiers of freedom.

This belief was confirmed when Stalin agreed that the Soviet Union would take part in the United Nations Conference to be held in San Francisco in April, and would support there the right of the United States to have three votes in the General Assembly, if the President desired to make such a claim. It seemed to Roosevelt that these concessions were an earnest of Stalin's good faith, for it could not be foreseen then that the Soviet Union would abuse the veto power, as it was to do in the years after the war, employing it to prevent discussion as well as decision and endeavoring to exercise it even on questions of procedure. That afternoon at Yalta it appeared that Anglo-American diplomacy had gained a considerable victory, and the President felt that the long and arduous journey had not been in vain.

During the brief adjournment which followed this discussion about the United Nations the prevailing opinion among the Western delegates was that the concessions Stalin had made represented a decided change of heart. Considered in relation to what followed, however, these concessions appear as a tactical maneuver designed to make the Western delegations more receptive to the Soviet plan for Poland which Molotov put forward while the meeting still glowed with goodwill. This plan did little more than set out in formal terms the attitude Stalin had so forcibly proclaimed the day before. The only hint of any readiness to meet the Western view was contained in the statement that the present Provisional Government (i.e. the Lublin Committee) might be enlarged to include some democratic leaders from Polish *emigre* circles." Since the Russians refused to regard even Mikolajczyk, the leader of the Peasant Party, as a "democrat," that concession meant nothing. The moral of this day's proceedings was that, while Russia was willing to join the United Nations, she was not prepared to rely on it entirely. She intended to safeguard her own security in any event by ensuring that she had subservient neighbors in Europe and a commanding position in Asia.

Stalin's Asiatic ambitions were revealed on the following afternoon during a private discussion with Roosevelt about the Soviet

Union's entry into the Japanese War. This discussion was conducted on a strictly Russo-American basis and in conditions of great secrecy. The only other persons present, apart from the two interpreters, were Molotov and Averell Harriman, the American Ambassador to the Soviet Union.

At the President's request, Churchill was not there and, when the negotiations were continued on the technical level by the Chiefs of Staff, the British did not take part. Even within his own entourage Roosevelt was most uncommunicative. Stettinius, though Secretary of State, was merely notified that talks were in progress. When he asked if the State Department should not be represented, Roosevelt replied that the problem was "primarily a military matter . . . and had best remain on a purely military level." This was a specious answer, for Stalin had long since committed himself on the basic military issue; the main point to be decided at Yalta was the political price of his participation.

It was in October 1943 that Stalin had first promised to join in the war against Japan after the defeat of Germany. He had made this offer to Cordell Hull, who says that it was "entirely unsolicited . . . and had no strings attached to it." At Teheran a month later, Stalin had repeated this promise virtually as a *quid pro quo* for the Second Front and for Lend-Lease. Nevertheless, Roosevelt had then volunteered to restore Russia's rights in the Manchurian port of Dairen and to ensure her free access to warm waters. Finding that the President was a "soft touch," Stalin proceeded to make this gesture his price with the paradoxical result that Soviet demands grew as the American need for Russian assistance in the Eastern War declined. During Churchill's visit to Moscow in October 1944, the Marshal said that "the Soviet Union would take the offensive against Japan three months after Germany's defeat, provided the United States would assist in building up the necessary reserve supplies and *provided the political aspects of Russia's participation had been clarified.*" During this Moscow meeting, as on five other separate occasions in 1944, Stalin gave an assurance that Russian air and naval bases in the Maritime Provinces would be made available to American forces. In December, however, this assurance was withdrawn, presumably with a view to strengthening the bargaining position of the Soviet Union at Yalta. . . .

The President's Chief of Staff (Admiral Leahy) says that, when the Russian terms were mentioned at a subsequent plenary session, there was "little discussion and no argument." It appears that Stalin blandly explained, "I only want to have returned to Russia what the Japanese have taken from my country"; and that Roosevelt replied, "That seems like a very reasonable suggestion from our ally. They only want to get back that which has been taken from them." Churchill must have listened a little incredulously to this exchange for he cannot have forgotten that Roosevelt had once said to him: "Winston . . . you have four hundred years of acquisitive instinct in your blood and you just don't understand how a country might not want to acquire land somewhere if they can get it. A new period has opened in the world's history and you will have to adjust yourself to it."

The British should have known, if the Americans did not, that Stalin's justification could not by any means cover all the Soviet claims. The Kuriles had never formally belonged to Russia. The reclaimed "rights" in Manchuria were those which in the nineteenth century had enabled Russia to exercise in this province a degree of dominion which seriously impinged upon Chinese sovereignty. These "rights" rested on no more substantial foundations than those extraterritorial privileges which the United States, Britain and other countries had given up in 1943 at Roosevelt's own instigation and in fulfillment of his pledge to restore and respect the independence of China. To accept the "status quo" in Outer Mongolia, which Moscow had been sedulously luring away from its allegiance to Chungking, was to acknowledge that the Soviet Union, not China, should enjoy political supremacy in that country. In short, by this agreement Russia was to become, with Anglo-American consent, the political heir of Japan in Manchuria, and thereby in North China.

No arrangement was made at Yalta with regard to the occupation of Korea and the post-war fate of that unhappy country appears to have been mentioned only incidentally. Stalin inquired whether it was to be occupied by any foreign troops. When Roosevelt replied that this was not intended, Stalin, no doubt thinking far into the future, "expressed his approval."

Upon learning the full extent of the Soviet terms, some of Churchill's advisers were deeply concerned, for they discovered that, although Stalin had made no further commitments whatever and although the most important of his claims had to be met by their ally, China, not by Japan, the President and the Prime Minister were required to declare that "these claims of the Soviet Union shall be unquestionably fulfilled after Japan has been defeated." Moreover, Stalin was insisting that for security reasons the Chinese Government should not even be informed until the Soviet Union was ready to attack. Roosevelt had undertaken to secure Chiang Kai-shek's compliance in due course but, as Sherwood says, "If China had refused to agree to any of the Soviet claims, presumably the U.S. and Britain would have been compelled to join in enforcing them." To some of the British delegation it seemed rather incongruous that, while urging Churchill to hand Hong Kong over to China as "a gesture of goodwill," Roosevelt was prepared to promise Stalin substantial concessions in Manchuria, and to do this without so much as consulting the Chinese. This point was appreciated by at least one of his staff, for Leahy reports that he warned Roosevelt, "Mr. President, you are going to lose out on Hong Kong if you agree to give the Russians half of Dairen"; and that Roosevelt replied, "Well, Bill, I can't help it."

Eden did all he could to dissuade the Prime Minister from setting his signature to the terms agreed upon by Roosevelt and Stalin. Churchill replied that he must sign, because he felt that "the whole position of the British Empire in the Far East might be at stake." The Prime Minister had good reason to fear that, since he had been excluded from the negotiations about the Japanese War, Britain might well be excluded from future discussions about the Far East if she did not stand by the United States now. Like Leahy, he may also have foreseen that, if these territorial concessions were made to Russia, Roosevelt would not be in a strong moral position to enforce his oft-repeated "threat" to reform the British Empire.

Of all the agreements reached at Yalta, this is the most controversial and would seem to be the least defensible. Yet it does not appear that the concessions, which Stalin obtained, were wrung from a reluctant Roosevelt. Sherwood records that the President had been "prepared even before the Teheran Conference . . . to agree to the legitimacy of most if not all of the Soviet claims in the Far East," although he expresses the opinion that "Roosevelt would not have agreed to the final firm commitment," if he had not been "tired and anxious to avoid further argument." Stettinius disagrees with this opinion and explains that "the Far Eastern agreement was carefully worked out and was not a snap decision made at Yalta." He endeavors to defend the concessions by asking: "What, with the possible exception of the Kuriles, did the Soviet Union receive at Yalta which she might not have taken without any agreement?"

That question does not pose the real issue which surely was: What did the Soviet Union receive at Yalta which she could not have taken without flagrantly violating the fundamental principles of the Atlantic Charter and the United Nations to which she had subscribed? The real issue for the world and for the future was not what Stalin would or could have taken but what he was given the right to take. This agreement provided Stalin with a moral cloak for his aggressive designs in Asia, and, more important, with almost a legal title enforceable at the Peace Conference to the territories and privileges which he demanded.

The President's surrender on this question is the more remarkable because it involved the sacrifice of those very principles which he had striven to uphold throughout his dealings with Churchill and Stalin. He had always insisted that he would not make any post-war commitments which would prejudice the peace treaties; he would recognize no spheres of influence, no territorial changes except those arrived at by mutual agreement, and no transfers of colonial territory except under conditions of international trusteeship. By making this agreement about the Japanese War, however, Roosevelt weakened both his mediating influence and his bargaining position in relation to problems arising out of the German War. He was not well placed to defend the sovereignty of Poland, once he had agreed to the infringement of China's sovereignty without her consent and in breach of the promise he had given to Chiang Kai-shek at Cairo in 1943. He could not make any effective protest against the Russians' creating a sphere of influence in the Balkans, when he had acknowledged their sphere of influence in Mongolia and Manchuria. Having departed from his principles in Asia, he could not expect to be allowed to apply them in Europe; not against a realist like Stalin. Consequently, the President was now in a less favorable position than he had been at the start of the conference. Stalin's appetite had been whetted, not satisfied.

The records kept by those who were present at Yalta give the impression that the negotiations about Russia's part in the Pacific War on the Thursday afternoon marked the turning point in the week's discussions. If this was not realized by the Western delegations at the time, it seems to have been fully appreciated by Stalin. Thereafter, having gained the concessions which were to enable him to dominate China, he proceeded to consolidate politically the strategic advantages his armies had already secured in Europe. Stalin was better able to press his demands now, for he could play upon the sense of gratitude and cooperation he had built up in the Americans, and to a lesser extent in the British, by his agreement to help in the defeat of Japan and the creation of the international security organization. The remaining negotiations were to prove the truth of the warning which had been sent to Washington two months earlier by the Head of the American Military Mission in Moscow (General Deane), an astute and not unsympathetic observer of the Soviet scene. In a letter to Marshall in December Deane had written, "We never make a request or proposal to the Soviets that is not viewed with suspicion. They simply cannot understand giving without taking, and as a result even our giving is viewed with suspicion. Gratitude cannot be banked in the Soviet Union. Each transaction is complete in itself without regard to past favors.

When the discussions about Poland were continued, as they were at each session on the last four days, the Russians gained their way on almost every point. Nothing more was heard of the President's suggestion that Poland should keep the Lwow region. The Curzon Line was accepted and this fact was duly recorded in the Protocol. With regard to Poland's western frontier, however, Stalin did not press for the formal recognition of a specific line, since he realized that neither Roosevelt nor Churchill was prepared to go beyond the Oder. He readily consented to the suggestion that "the final delimitation of the western frontier should await the Peace Conference," for in the meantime that left him free to make his own arrangements about the German territory between the Oder and the Neisse.

The Russians consented to the holding of free elections and

Molotov told Roosevelt that these could be held "within a month." On the other hand, he bluntly rejected the supervision proposal, arguing that this would be "an affront to the pride and sovereignty of the independent people"! Eden endeavored to insist on this safeguard, for he feared that any unsupervised elections would be a mockery, but at the final meeting of the Foreign Ministers Stettinius announced that "the President was anxious to reach agreement and that to expedite matters he was willing to make this concession." With regard to the setting up of a new administration, the three Ministers eventually decided upon a compromise formula which read: "The Provisional Government which is now functioning in Poland should be reorganized on a broader democratic basis with the inclusion of democratic leaders from Poland itself and from Poles abroad." To this end various Polish leaders from all non-Fascist parties were to be brought together in Moscow for consultations with Molotov and the British and American Ambassadors.

When this formula was adopted at the plenary session on February 10th the Western delegates, with few exceptions, believed that they had reached, as Sherwood says, "an honorable and equitable solution." They were acting in good faith and they presumed that Stalin was equally sincere, for he also set his hand to a "Declaration on Liberated Europe" which reaffirmed the principles of the Atlantic Charter. By this Declaration the three Powers bound themselves "to build . . . a world order under law, dedicated to peace, security and freedom and the general well-being of all mankind," and agreed to act in concert "in assisting the peoples liberated from the dominion of Nazi Germany and the peoples of the former Axis satellite states of Europe . . . to create democratic institutions of their own choice."

These fine phrases were to prove less important than the terms of the Polish formula, which was so loosely worded that it left the Russians ample room to maneuver. Roosevelt certainly entertained some doubts on this score, for he concurred when Leahy said to him, "Mr. President, this is so elastic that the Russians can stretch it all the way from Yalta to Washington without ever technically breaking it." The essential fact was that, while the British and Americans started by refusing to accord any recognition whatever to the Lublin Committee, they ended by allowing it to be described in the communiqué as "the present Provisional Government of Poland." Moreover, although they had originally insisted that an entirely fresh administration should be formed, they finally agreed to the words "the Provisional Government now functioning in Poland should be reorganized." The only real difference between that formula and what Stalin had initially demanded was a change in verb; "enlarged" had become "reorganized." . . .

On that final Sunday morning at Livadia Palace neither the Americans nor the British suspected that the public communiqué and the secret protocol, so solemnly signed and endorsed with such expressions of mutual trust and goodwill, would soon be distorted and violated by their Soviet Allies, and that this process of distortion and violation would begin before the Prime Minister and the President had been able to report to their respective legislatures on the conference at which, they both asserted, the Great Powers were more closely united than ever before."

In the House of Commons on February 27th, the Prime Minister declared: "The impression I brought back from the Crimea . . . is that Marshal Stalin and the Soviet leaders wish to live in honorable friendship and equality with the Western democracies. I feel also that their word is their bond. I decline absolutely to embark here on a discussion about Russian good faith." That evening in Bucharest—despite the Yalta Declaration on Liberated Europe—Molotov's deputy (Andrei Vishinsky) issued to King Michael a two-hour ultimatum, demanding the dismissal of the Rumanian Prime Minister, General Radescu, the leader of an all-party Government.

Four days later, addressing a joint session of Congress, the President said: "The Crimea Conference . . . spells—and it ought to spell—the end of the system of unilateral action, exclusive alliances, and spheres of influence, and balances of power and all the other expedients which have been tried for centuries and have always failed. . . . I am sure that—under the agreement reached at Yalta—there will be a more stable political Europe than ever before." That evening in Bucharest, without any reference whatever to the Allied Control Commission, Vishinsky issued to King Michael a second ultimatum, demanding that he should appoint as Prime Minister Petru Groza, the leader of the Rumanian Communists. . . .

In strategy, as in diplomacy, Stalin's policy was always in tune with his post-war ambitions. Once military victory was assured, Stalin was less interested in bringing about Hitler's early downfall than he was in securing for the Soviet Union a commanding position in the heart of Europe. Although the timing of his various offensives in the last nine months of the war may have been governed very largely by tactical and logistic considerations, it is surprising how clearly these offensives fitted into the strategic pattern most likely to secure his political objectives. After reaching Warsaw, he concentrated on the drive up the Danube Valley through Bucharest and Belgrade to Budapest. Having thus gained control of the Balkans, he proceeded to complete the conquest of Poland by advancing from the Vistula to the Oder and then, though Berlin lay within his grasp, he turned his main attention to the capture of Vienna. The attack on the German capital was not resumed until it was in danger of being taken by the Americans. Finally, when the Red Army was unable to break through to Prague, Stalin bluffed Eisenhower into restraining the Allied advance so that Russia could enjoy the military honor and political advantage of liberating this capital also.

When the Second World War ended, therefore, of all the major political objectives which Stalin had sought to gain in Europe— either from Hitler or from Roosevelt and Churchill—the only one which had been denied him was control of the Black Sea Straits. The failure to secure access to warm-water ports in the Mediterranean represented the thwarting of one of Russia's traditional aims, but this was more than offset by the tremendous territorial gains she had made in Central and Eastern Europe. Since August 1939 the western frontiers of her power had been advanced 600 miles to the southwest, from the Dniester to the Adriatic, and 750 miles to the west, from the Pripet Marshes to the Thuringerwald, where the border of the Soviet Zone of Occupation ran within a hundred miles of the Rhine. With Germany destroyed, Britain and France exhausted, and the United States about to retire from active participation in European affairs, Russia could afford to go her own way, disregarding both the protests of her Allies and the provisions of the Yalta Agreement and the United Nations Charter.

There may have been a time when Stalin was prepared—as both Roosevelt and Churchill thought—to cooperate with the Western Allies on a friendly basis for the maintenance of postwar peace, but the records of the various conferences make it quite plain that the

Soviet leaders never placed any great trust in international pacts or organizations. In November 1940, when Ribbentrop presented the Führer's offer of a Four-Power Alliance for the division of the world, Molotov replied that "paper agreements would not suffice for the Soviet Union; rather she would have to insist on effective guarantees for her security." By "effective guarantees" Molotov meant physical possession of strategic areas related to Russia's defense. At Yalta, although Stalin never expressed himself so bluntly, the same point was implied. He agreed to join the United Nations—very much on Roosevelt's terms—but at the same time he expected to be given a free hand in what he regarded as Russia's proper sphere of influence, and especially in Poland.

In Stalin's mind this became the test of Anglo-American sincerity. Roosevelt and Churchill had both declared that they would not tolerate the establishment in Poland, or any other country on Russia's borders, of a government hostile to the Soviet Union. But they had also insisted upon "free and unfettered elections" with a secret ballot and universal suffrage. Stalin knew that these two principles were mutually exclusive, since any free election in any of the states of Eastern Europe would be certain to result in the return of a non-Communist Government suspicious of, if not openly antagonistic to, the Soviet Union. Consequently, in the months following Yalta when the American and British Governments made an issue of "free elections" in the Western sense, Stalin not unnaturally concluded that their real objective all along had been to set up a *cordon sanitaire* which would curtail his sphere of influence.

When the Polish question was discussed at Yalta, Potsdam and innumerable other conferences, Stalin persistently stressed the fact that Russia must have a "friendly" Government in Warsaw and that the Poles must be strong enough to hold the corridor by which the Germans had so often invaded Russia. While it was only natural that Stalin should be concerned about the security of his country, the treatment which Poland has received at the hands of the Soviet Union since the war indicates that Stalin's real concern was not security but expansion. For him Poland was the gateway *to* the West. Unless he were to control Poland, he would not have free access to Central Europe, and he needed to dominate Central Europe, and especially the Bohemian Mountains in order to protect not the Soviet

Union but her conquests in the Balkans. He was clearly determined to make certain that Russia secured for herself the fruits of victory. And why not? It was for these that she had fought. . . .

The "Unconditional Surrender" formula, though the President's brain-child, was the natural result of the American determination to wage the war to absolute victory without regard to the political consequences. Roosevelt certainly had noble and unselfish political aims—the winning of Russia's friendship and the setting up of a United Nations organization which would preserve peace and enforce throughout the world the principles of the Atlantic Charter. Carried away by this idealistic vision and convinced of his own ability to "handle" Stalin, Roosevelt failed to foresee that the immediate political situation arising out of the war might thwart the fulfillment of his ultimate political dream. The success of his policy really depended on his ability to maintain by personal contact over the conference table the spirit of "Big Three" cooperation which, he believed, he had established at Teheran and maintained at Yalta. But Roosevelt seems to have made no allowance for the possibility that one or more of the three leaders might be removed from the scene by death or political defeat. As it happened, he himself suffered the first of these fates and Churchill the second before the world struggle ended.

Roosevelt's death revealed the gap between his hopes and the realities of the situation, but it did not create that gap. This had been created already by his failure—and that of his Chiefs of Staff—to take account of post-war political factors in the determination of Allied strategy. That failure, the cause of so much of Europe's present suffering, had its origin partly in the immaturity of the Americans and partly in their history. At the risk of over-simplification, it may be said that the traditional attitude of the people of the United States to the recurrent conflicts of Europe is that war as a means of national policy is morally wrong. Consequently, the United States, if driven to war in self-defense or to uphold the right, should seek no national advantage or aggrandizement. Her sole purpose should be to bring about the defeat and punishment of the aggressor. Her aim should be Victory, nothing else. Since America fights for no political objective, except peace, no political directives should be given to American commanders in the field. They should be completely free to determine their strategy on military grounds alone, and the supreme military consideration is to bring hostilities to an end. To pursue a political aim is to practice Imperialism.

This was the doctrine applied by Marshall and his colleagues in the conduct of the war against Germany, although, with an ambivalence not uncharacteristic of the American people, it was not always applied in relation to the war against Japan. In the last eighteen months of the European conflict when Churchill became increasingly alarmed about Soviet policy, he sought to persuade the Americans that the military strength of the Western Allies should be employed in a manner calculated to achieve the double purpose of defeating Germany and preventing the Soviet Union from becoming too powerful. Only in Greece and Denmark was he successful, and in the former case his action provoked a public rebuke from Roosevelt's Secretary of State. Elsewhere he was repeatedly balked by American policy which stood on the twin pillars of Roosevelt's belief that Stalin had no aggressive ambitions and Marshall's determination to concentrate on victory in the field. . . .

The history of Europe reveals only too sharply the unhappy consequences of the policy which was pursued by the Americans and, until late in the war, by the British as well. Writing in 1941, Liddell Hart outlined these consequences in a statement which reads now like a prophecy:

> *If you concentrate exclusively on victory, with no thought for the after-effect, you may be too exhausted to profit by the peace, while it is almost certain that the peace will be a bad one, containing the germs of another war. This is a lesson supported by abundant experience. The risks become greater still in any war that is waged by a coalition, for in such a case a too complete victory inevitably complicates the problem of making a just and wise peace settlement. Where there is no longer the counterbalance of an opposing force to control the appetites of the victors, there is no check on the conflict of views and interests between the parties to the alliance. The divergence is then apt to become so acute as to turn the comradeship of common danger into the hostility of mutual dissatisfaction—so that the ally of one war becomes the enemy in the next.*

The two most serious miscalculations of the Second World War both concerned the Soviet Union: Hitler's miscalculation of Russia's military strength, and Roosevelt's miscalculation of Russia's political ambition. It was these two errors of judgment which gave Stalin the opportunity of establishing the Soviet Union as the dominant power in Europe. It is clear now that the Western democracies cannot afford to make another miscalculation about Russia's military power or political intentions. A third mistake might well be fatal to Western civilization. It is equally clear that, even though Stalin may have no intention of precipitating another world war, there is not likely to be any lessening of the tension in Europe or Asia. . . .

William Henry Chamberlin

THE MUNICH CALLED YALTA

One of the earliest and most common American complaints about the Yalta Conference holds that we appeased an aggressive ally and sacrificed the self-determination of Poland and China. The intellectual spearhead of this argument came from a group of long-time conservative students of communism, of whom William Henry Chamberlin was a leader. Author of a scholarly history of the Russian Revolution, Chamberlin presented, in the post-World War II period, an anti-Communist, "revisionist" critique of American foreign policy—from which this selection is taken.

The second conference of the Big Three, held at Yalta in February 1945, represented the high point of Soviet diplomatic success and correspondingly the low point of American appeasement. This conference took place under circumstances which were very disadvantageous to the western powers.

Roosevelt's mental and physical condition had disquieted Stimson at the time when the Morgenthau Plan was being approved. It certainly did not improve as a result of the strenuous presidential campaign and the long trip to the Crimean resort.

There has been no authoritative uninhibited analysis of the state of the President's health during the war. But there is a good deal of reliable testimony of serious deterioration, especially during the last year of Mr. Roosevelt's life. And it was during this year that decisions of the most vital moral and political importance had to be taken.

Among the symptoms of the President's bad health were liability to severe debilitating colds, extreme haggardness of appearance, occasional blackouts of memory, and loss of capacity for mental concentration. An extremely high authority who may not be identified described Roosevelt's condition at three of the principal conferences as follows:

"The President looked physically tired at Casablanca; but his mind worked well. At Teheran there were signs of loss of memory. At Yalta he could neither think consecutively nor express himself coherently. . . ."

It is certainly no exaggeration to say that Roosevelt was physically and mentally far less fit than Churchill and Stalin during the period when American military power was at its height and the supreme decisions which confronted the national leaders in the last phase of the war had to be taken. Had Roosevelt been able to delegate power and had there been a strong and capable Secretary of State, some of the unfortunate consequences of the President's incapacitation might have been averted and softened.

But Roosevelt clung to power with hands that were too weak to use it effectively. After his death it required much searching of files and ransacking of the memories of the participants to reconstruct what had occurred and to find out just what the President had or had not agreed to.

When Hull laid down his office on account of bad health in November 1944, his successor was Edward Stettinius. The ignorance and naiveté of the latter in foreign affairs soon became a byword to his associates in government service and to foreign diplomats. Stettinius was much better qualified to be master of ceremonies at the high jinks of some fraternal organization than to direct American foreign policy at a critical period.

Stettinius shared Roosevelt's harmful delusion that successful diplomacy was largely a matter of establishing friendly personal contacts. At the Dumbarton Oaks Conference which shaped the preliminary draft of the United Nations charter Stettinius made himself ridiculous by cheerfully shouting "Hi, Alex" and "Hiya, Andrei" at his partners in the negotiations, the correct and pained Sir Alexander Cadogan and the sullen and bored Andrei Gromyko.

The appointment of Stettinius was due to the influence of Hopkins. The latter's star as court favorite, after a temporary eclipse, was again in the ascendant at the time of the Yalta Conference. Hopkins was a very sick man and had to spend most of his time at Yalta in bed.

Roosevelt went to Yulta with no prepared agenda and no clearly defined purpose, except to get along with Stalin at any price. He had been provided with a very complete file of studies and recommendations, drawn up by the State Department, before he boarded the heavy cruiser *Quincy,* which took him to Malta, where there was a break in the journey to the Crimea. But these were never looked at. The President suffered from a cold and from sinus trouble and his appearance "disturbed" James F. Byrnes, who accompanied him on this trip.

The conference at Yalta lasted a week, from February 4 until February 11, 1945. The principal subjects discussed were Poland, German boundaries and reparations, the occupation regime for Germany, the conditions of Soviet participation in the war against Japan, procedure and voting rights in the future United Nations organization.

At the price of a few promises which were soon to prove worthless in practice, Stalin got what he wanted in Poland: a frontier that assigned to the Soviet Union almost half of Poland's prewar territory and the abandonment by America and Great Britain of the Polish government-in-exile in London. Roosevelt made a feeble plea that Lwow and the adjacent oil fields be included in Poland. Churchill appealed to Stalin's sense of generosity. Neither achieved any success. . . .

The protocol on reparations mentioned "the use of labor" as a possible source of reparations. Roosevelt observed that "the United States cannot take manpower as the Soviet Republic can." This gave implied American sanction to the large-scale exploitation of German war prisoners as slave labor in Britain and France, as well as in Russia, after the end of the war. The Morgenthau Plan, which Roosevelt and Churchill had approved at Quebec, recommended "forced labor outside Germany" as a form of reparations.

Procedure in the United Nations was discussed at some length. The records show that Roosevelt and Churchill were as unwilling as Stalin to forgo the right of veto in serious disputes, where the use of armed force was under discussion. There was a dispute, not settled at Yalta, as to whether the right of veto should apply to discussion of controversial matters. The Russians insisted that it should, the western representatives contended that it should not. Stalin conceded this minor point when Harry Hopkins visited Moscow in June 1945.

The Soviet Government received Roosevelt's consent to its proposal that Byelorussia and the Ukraine, two of the affiliated Soviet Republics, should be granted individual votes in the United Nations Assembly. When Brynes learned of this he raised vigorous objection, reminding Roosevelt that some of the opposition to America's entrance into the League of Nations was based on the argument that Britain would have five votes, one for each member of the Commonwealth. Roosevelt then asked for and obtained Stalin's consent to an arrangement which would give the United States three votes in the Assembly. This compensation was never pressed for and did not go into effect.

In reason and logic there was no case for giving separate votes to the Ukraine and Byelorussia. If the Soviet Union was a loose federation of independent states, like the British Commonwealth, each of its sixteen constitutent republics should have been entitled to a vote. If it was a centralized unitary state, it should have received only one vote. No one with an elementary knowledge of Soviet political realities could doubt that the Soviet Union belongs in the second category. It would cause no special shock or surprise to see Canada, South Africa, Australia, or India voting in opposition to Britain on some issues. It would be unthinkable for the Ukraine or Byelorussia to oppose the Soviet Union.

So far as the Assembly is concerned, Moscow's three votes have thus far been of little practical importance. The Assembly possesses little power and the Soviet satellites are in the minority. But, as Byrnes was to discover later during the arduous negotiation of the peace treaties with Italy, Hungary, Bulgaria, Rumania, and Finland, it was an advantage for the Soviet Union to start with three of the twenty-one votes of the participating nations in its pocket.

Contempt for the rights of smaller and weaker nations was conspicuous in the Soviet attitude at Yalta. At the first dinner Vishinsky declared that the Soviet Union would never agree to the right of the small nations to judge the acts of the great powers. Charles E. Bohlen,

American State Department expert on Russia, replied that the American people were not likely to approve of any denial of the small nation's right. Vishinsky's comment was that the American people should "learn to obey their leaders."

Churchill, discussing the same subject with Stalin, quoted the proverb: "The eagle should permit the small birds to sing and not care wherefore they sang." Stalin's low opinion of France, as a country that had been knocked out early in the war, was reflected in his remark: "I cannot forget that in this war France opened the gates to the enemy."

What Stalin did forget, and what no one reminded him of, was that while France was fighting the Germans, the Soviet Government was enthusiastically collaborating with the Nazi dictatorship, sending messages of congratulation after every new victory of the Wehrmacht. French Communists, acting under Stalin's orders, certainly contributed more than other Frenchmen to "opening the gates to the enemy."

Stalin was only willing to grant France a zone of occupation on condition that this should be carved out of territory assigned to the United States and Great Britain. For a time he held out against giving France a place on the Allied Control Council for Germany. In the end he yielded to Roosevelt on this point. The President's attitude toward General de Gaulle had always been strained and chilly. But, in Hopkin's words, "Winston and Anthony [Eden] fought like tigers" for France. They enlisted the aid of Hopkins, who persuaded Roosevelt to use his influence, in this case successfully, with Stalin. . . .

Another country was offered up as a sacrifice on the altar of appeasement at Yalta. This was China. Stalin had told Hull at Moscow and Roosevelt at Teheran that he would be on the side of the United States and Great Britain against Japan after the end of the war with Germany. At Yalta, with German military collapse clearly impending, the Soviet dictator set a price for his intervention in the Far East. The price was stiff. And it included items which it was not morally justifiable for the United States to accept. . . .

The Kurile Islands, a long chain of barren, volcanic islands extending into the North Pacific northeast of Japan proper, were to be handed over to the Soviet Union. The *status quo* was to be preserved in Outer Mongolia, a huge, sparsely populated, arid region which the Soviet Union took over without formal annexation in 1924.

South Sakhalin (which had belonged to Russia until 1905) and the Kurile Islands might be regarded as war booty, to be taken from Japan. And China had no prospect of upsetting *de facto* Soviet rule of Outer Mongolia by its own strength. But the concessions which Roosevelt and Churchill made to Stalin in Manchuria were of fateful importance for China's independence and territorial integrity.

Manchuria, because of its natural wealth in coal, iron, soya beans, and other resources, and because of the large investment of Japanese capital and technical skill, intensified after 1931, was the most industrially developed part of China. To give a strong foreign power control over its railways, a predominant interest in its chief port, Dairen, and a naval base at Port Arthur was to sign away China's sovereignty in Manchuria.

And this was done not only without consulting China but without informing China. The Chinese Government was prevented from even discussing Soviet claims in the future. For, at Stalin's insistence, the agreement to satisfy his annexationist claims was put in writing and contained this decisive assurance:

"The Heads of the three Great Powers have agreed that these claims of the Soviet Union shall be unquestioningly fulfilled after Japan has been defeated."

In the opinion of former Ambassador William C. Bullitt "no more unnecessary, disgraceful and potentially disastrous document has ever been signed by a President of the United States."

Severe as this judgment sounds, it has been borne out by the course of subsequent events. The Soviet intervention in the Far Eastern war was of no military benefit to the United States, because it took place only a few days before Japan surrendered. Politically this intervention was an unmitigated disaster.

During the Soviet occupation of Manchuria industrial equipment of an estimated value of two billion dollars was looted and carried off to Russia. This delayed for a long time any prospect of Chinese industrial self-sufficiency. As soon as Soviet troops occupied Manchuria, Chinese Communist forces, as if by a mysterious signal, began to converge on that area.

The Soviet military commanders shrewdly avoided direct, ostentatious cooperation with the Communists. After all, the Soviet Government had signed a treaty of friendship and alliance with the Nationalist Government of China on August 14, 1945. One clause of this treaty prescribed that "the Soviet Government is ready to render China moral support and assistance with military equipment and other material resources, this support and assistance to be given fully to the National Government as the central government of China."

This treaty was to prove about as valuable to the co-signatory as the nonaggression pacts which the Soviet Government concluded with Poland, Finland, Lativa, Lithuania, and Estonia. There is no indication that the Soviet Government gave the slightest "moral" or material support to the Chinese Nationalist Government. But Manchuria became an arsenal for the Chinese Communists, who were able to equip themselves with Japanese arms, obligingly stacked up for them by the Soviet occupation forces.

Soviet control of Dairen was used to block the use of this important port by Nationalist troops. Manchuria became the base from which the Chinese Communists could launch a campaign that led to the overrunning of almost all China.

Roosevelt's concessions at Yalta represented an abandonment of the historic policy of the United States in the Far East. This policy was in favor of the "open door," of equal commercial opportunity for all foreign nations, together with respect for Chinese independence. The American State Department had always been opposed to the "closed door" methods of Imperial Russia.

But at Yalta the "open door" was abandoned in a document that repeatedly referred to "the pre-eminent interests of the Soviet Union" in Manchuria. Those interests have now become pre-eminent in China. And the surrender of Manchuria to Stalin is not the least of the reasons for this development.

The Yalta concessions were a violation of the American pledge at Cairo that Manchuria should be restored to China. If New York State had been occupied by an enemy and was then handed back to the United States on condition that another alien power should have joint control of its railway systems, a predominant voice in the Port of New York Authority, and the right to maintain a naval base on Staten Island, most Americans would not feel that American sovereignty had been respected.

Whether considered from the standpoint of consistency with professed war aims or from the standpoint of serving American national interests, the record of Yalta is profoundly depressing. The large-scale alienation of Polish territory to the Soviet Union, of German territory to Poland, constituted an obvious and flagrant violation of the self-determination clauses of the Atlantic Charter. An offensive note of hypocrisy was added by inserting into the Yalta communiqué repeated professions of adherence to the Atlantic Charter.

The hopes of tens of millions of East Europeans for national independence and personal liberty were betrayed. The leaders of the Axis could scarcely have surpassed the cynicism of Roosevelt and Churchill in throwing over allies like Poland and China. The unwarranted concessions to Stalin in the Far East opened a Pandora's box of troubles for the United States, the end of which has not yet been seen.

There was not one positive, worthwhile contribution to European revival and stability in the sordid deals of Yalta, only imperialist power politics at its worst. The vindictive peace settlement, far worse than that of Versailles, which was being prepared promised little for European reconstruction. Roosevelt not long before had piously declared that "the German people are not going to be enslaved, because the United Nations do not traffic in human slavery." But at Yalta he sanctioned the use of the slave labor of German war prisoners, a throwback to one of the most barbarous practices of antiquity.

The agreements, published and secret, concluded at Yalta are defended mainly on two grounds. It is contended that military necessity forced the President to comply with Stalin's demands in Eastern Europe and East Asia. It is also argued that the source of difficulties in postwar Europe is to be found, not in the Yalta agreements, but in the Soviet failure to abide by these agreements.

Neither of these justifications stands up under serious examination. America in February 1945 was close to the peak of its military power. The atomic bomb still lay a few months in the future. But the United States possessed the most powerful navy in the world, the greatest aircraft production in quantity and quality, an army that, with its

British and other allies, had swept the Germans from North Africa, France, Belgium, and much of Italy.

The lumbering Soviet offensive in the East was dependent in no small degree on lend-lease American trucks and communication equipment. There was, therefore, no good reason for approaching Stalin with an inferiority complex or for consenting to a Polish settlement which sacrificed the friends of the West in that country and paved the way for the establishment of a Soviet puppet regime.

No doubt Stalin could have imposed such a regime by force. Only the Red Army in February 1945 was in a position to occupy Poland. How much better the outlook would have been if Churchill's repeated prodding for action in the Balkans had been heeded, if the Polish Army of General Anders, battle-hardened in Italy, had been able to reach Poland ahead of the Red Army!

But there would have been a great difference between a Soviet stooge regime set up by the naked force of the Red Army and one strengthened by the acquiescence and endorsement of the western powers. The former would have enjoyed no shred of moral authority. As it was, nationalist guerrilla resistance to the made-in-Moscow government was prolonged and embittered. Many thousands of lives were lost on both sides before the satellite regime, with a good deal of Russian military and police aid, clamped down its rule more or less effectively over the entire country. How much stronger this resistance would have been if the United States and Great Britain had continued to recognize the government-in-exile and insisted on adequate guarantees of free and fair elections!

There was equally little reason to give in to Stalin's Far Eastern demands. The desire to draw the Soviet Union into this war was fatuous, from the standpoint of America's interest in a truly independent China. Apparently Roosevelt was the victim of some extremely bad intelligence work. He was given to understand that the Kwantung Army, the Japanese occupation force in Manchuria, was a formidable fighting machine, which might be used to resist the American invasion of the Japanese home islands which was planned for the autumn.

But the Kwantung Army offered no serious resistance to the Soviet invasion in August. It had evidently been heavily depleted in numbers and lowered in fighting quality.

Apologists for the Yalta concessions maintain that Japan in February 1945 presented the aspect of a formidable, unbeaten enemy. Therefore, so the argument runs, Roosevelt was justified in paying a price for Soviet intervention, in the interest of ending the war quickly and saving American lives.

But Japanese resistance to American air and naval attacks on its own coasts was already negligible. American warships were able to cruise along the shores of Japan, bombarding at will. According to an account later published by Arthur Krock, of the *New York Times,* an Air Force general presented a report at Yalta pointing to the complete undermining of the Japanese capacity to resist. But the mistaken and misleading view that Japan still possessed powerful military and naval force prevailed.

Acceptance of this view by Roosevelt was especially unwarranted because two days before he left for Yalta Roosevelt received from General MacArthur a forty-page message outlining five unofficial Japanese peace overtures which amounted to an acceptance of unconditional surrender, with the sole reservation that the Emperor should be preserved. The other terms offered by the Japanese, who were responsible men, in touch with Emperor Hirohito, may be summarized as follows:

1. Complete surrender of all Japanese forces.
2. Surrender of all arms and munitions.
3. Occupation of the Japanese homeland and island possessions by Allied troops under American direction.
4. Japanese relinquishment of Manchuria, Korea, and Formosa, as well as all territory seized during the war.
5. Regulation of Japanese industry to halt present and future production of implements of war.
6. Turning over of any Japanese the United States might designate as war criminals.
7. Immediate release of all prisoners of war and internees in Japan and areas under Japanese control.

MacArthur recommended negotiations on the basis of the Japanese overtures. But Roosevelt brushed off this suggestion with the remark: "MacArthur is our greatest general and our poorest politician."

That the President, after receiving such a clear indication that Japan was on the verge of military collapse, should have felt it necessary to bribe Stalin into entering the Far Eastern war must surely be reckoned a major error of judgment, most charitably explained by Roosevelt's failing mental and physical powers.[1]

Captain Ellis M. Zacharias, Navy expert on Japan whose broadcasts in fluent Japanese hastened the surrender, asserts that intelligence reports indicating Japanese impending willingness to surrender were available at the time of the Yalta Conference.

One such report, communicated in the utmost secrecy to an American intelligence officer in a neutral capital, predicted the resignation of General Koiso as Premier in favor of the pacific Admiral Suzuki. The Admiral, in turn, according to the report, would turn over power to the Imperial Prince Higashi Kuni, who would possess sufficient authority and prestige, backed by a command from the Emperor, to arrange the surrender.

> *I am convinced that had this document, later proven to be correct in every detail, been brought to the attention of President Roosevelt and his military advisers, the war might have been viewed in a different light, both Iwo Jima and Okinawa might have been avoided, and different decisions could have been reached at Yalta.*[2]

Zacharias also believes that if the Japanese had been given a precise definition of what America understood by unconditional surrender as late as June, or even at the end of July 1945, both Soviet intervention and the dropping of atomic bombs on Hiroshima and Nagasaki could have been averted.[3]

Certainly there was a hopeful alternative to the policy, so disastrous in its results, of encouraging and bribing the Soviet Union to enter the Far Eastern picture. This was to aim at a quick peace with Japan, before the Soviet armies could have been transferred from the West to the East. There is every reason to believe that such a peace was attainable, if the Japanese had been assured of the right to keep

---

[1] The story of the Japanese peace overtures is told in a dispatch from Washington by Walter Trohan, correspondent of the *Chicago Tribune* and the *Washington Times-Herald*. It appeared in these two newspapers on August 19, 1945. Previous publication had been withheld because of wartime censorship regulations. Mr. Trohan personally gave me the source of his information, a man of unimpeachable integrity, very high in the inner circle of Roosevelt's wartime advisers.

[2] Captain Ellis M. Zacharias, U.S.N., *Secret Missions* (New York: Putnam, 1946), p. 335.

[3] Ibid., pp. 367–368.

the Emperor and perhaps given some assurance that their commercial interests in Manchuria and Korea would not be entirely wiped out.

There is little weight in the contention that the Yalta agreements, in themselves, were excellent, if the Soviet Government had only lived up to them. These agreements grossly violated the Atlantic Charter by assigning Polish territory to the Soviet Union and German territory to Poland without plebiscites. They violated the most elementary rules of humanity and civilized warfare by sanctioning slave labor as "reparations." And the whole historic basis of American foreign policy in the Far East was upset by the virtual invitation to Stalin to take over Japan's former exclusive and dominant role in Manchuria.

IV YALTA IN DOMESTIC POLITICS

Athan G. Theoharis

THE YALTA MYTHS

Athan Theoharis has written a blow-by-blow account of the partisan dispute over Yalta inside the United States from 1945–1955. An American historian, Theoharis describes what he calls a domestic cold war paralleling the international Cold War. This excerpt outlines his argument that many aspects of the controversy over the Yalta Conference must be understood as the by-products of a much older confrontation between our major political parties.

In 1945, the Yalta Conference was hailed as the dawn of a new era of peace and understanding. Five years later, it symbolized, for many people in the United States, the folly of trusting or seeking to reach accommodation with the Soviet Union; in fact, the postwar communization of Eastern Europe and China were directly attributed to Yalta agreements. Further, during the years from 1948 through 1955, those who wanted the United States to proceed with caution and from a position of strength in any negotiation with the Russians invoked the Yalta experience. Their unquestioned assumption was that Soviet leaders honored their pledges only when they found it expedient or when superior military force coerced them.

This image of Yalta resulted from postwar developments, both international and domestic. The intensification of the Cold War made the assumptions of Yalta suspect. During congressional debates and political campaigns, economic conservatives were able to raise doubts about New Deal and Fair Deal domestic policies by shifting their attack from domestic concerns to foreign policy and internal security matters. These conservatives also cited Yalta in their attempts to justify the need to restrict and investigate the use of executive authority.

Thus, during the late 1940s and early 1950s, they charged that Roosevelt's unilateral and secretive policy making at Yalta had permitted agreements and concessions that were detrimental to national security. Roosevelt's resort to secrecy and his abuse of executive authority, they further charged, was essential to his policy of "appeasing" the Soviet leaders, a policy that had created contemporary

THERE'S ONE BORN EVERY ADMINISTRATION

Reprinted courtesy of *The Chicago Tribune.* (Historical Pictures Service, Chicago)

problems. Then, centering on the loyalty of federal personnel, these conservatives attributed the conclusion of the specific Yalta agreements either to Communist infiltration of the U.S. delegation and the Roosevelt Administration or to the Administration's being "soft toward Communism."

This focus on national security broadened what had been an essentially conservative critique of the New Deal by providing a less direct, less partisan, or less overtly conservative mode of questioning federal personnel and reformist principles. In this sense, the post-

1945 charges of New Deal betrayal and executive abuse of authority differed in substance from the charges that conservatives directed against the Roosevelt Administration between 1933 and 1945. After 1948, these conservatives emphasized primarily international developments; their main criticism of federal personnel involved possible threats to internal security by foreign espionage or subversion.

During the 1930s and the war years, in contrast, their resort to anti-Communist, antiexecutive themes and charges had had a specific, distinctively antireformist purpose. Conservatives then had consistently questioned presidential authority and the advisability of federal reform. During the 1930s, by assailing New Deal priorities and personnel, economic conservatives had sought directly to stymie the enactment of legislation regulating the banks and the securities industry, providing for minimum wages and social security, and creating the Tennessee Valley Authority, the Rural Electrification Administration, and the National Recovery Administration. Anti-New Dealers had represented these measures as alien, subversive, and unconstitutional. Concentrating on Roosevelt's transformation of the office of the Presidency into an agency for initiating legislation and pressuring the Congress to act, they also had claimed that the ramifications of such measures might be dangerous to limited, representative government.

In the late 1930s, these conservatives were able to thwart Roosevelt's attempts to extend the New Deal. They successfully capitalized on the President's attempts to pack the Supreme Court, to purge conservative critics of the New Deal during the 1938 congressional elections, and to reorganize the federal government. The resultant stalemate between the Congress and the President derived from not only the failure of the New Deal to bring complete recovery, Roosevelt's shift in priorities after 1938 to foreign policy, and popular concern about the proliferation of federal agencies, but also the structure of the Congress. This structure guaranteed the conservatives a restrictive influence; they could use their congressional prerogatives and the committee system, which was dominated by chairmen whose power was based on seniority.

From 1939 through 1945, conservatives also raised these same criticisms about Roosevelt's methods in foreign policy matters. Challenging his use of executive agreements and powers to extend the United States' international commitments, anti-New Dealers specifically denounced Roosevelt's destroyer deal, his orders to naval vessels to "shoot on sight," the proposal of lend-lease, his assignment of U.S. convoy coverage to Iceland, and the drafting of the Atlantic Charter. The President had initiated these measures, they charged, in order to bypass congressional prerogatives and lead the United States to war. Roosevelt's subsequent wartime preferences for secrecy and summit diplomacy evoked charges that his actions were undemocratic and contrary to constitutional requirements. This critique, however, had a limited popular impact; the nature of the war undermined the force of these arguments, and Roosevelt's leadership seemingly justified these actions.

After 1945, particularly after 1949, conservative criticisms of New Deal reforms and presidential leadership had a distinctively different impact. Then, the debate concentrated directly on foreign policy and only indirectly involved questions of domestic reform. The subsequent reappraisal of the Yalta Conference and attention it received dramatized the conservatives' shift in tactics from domestic matters to national security and the public's shift in priorities from economic recovery to international peace and internal security. One basis for this interest in Yalta and the resultant spread of domestic conservatism had been the impact of the Cold War on domestic politics. Increasingly after 1947, U.S. politics and values assumed an anti-Communist orientation. An anti-Communist rhetoric that evolved to justify containment policies also served to immobilize reformist politics, to decrease tolerance for dissident ideals and controversial measures, and to legitimate conservative charges of subversion and betrayal. By concentrating on such past foreign policy decisions as the agreements made at the Yalta Conference, conservative critics of the Roosevelt Administration were able to increase their political following and establish the soundness of their earlier critique of New Deal principles and personnel.

Significantly, then, although criticisms of Yalta increased after 1945, and a more suspicious public became concerned about the people who attended the conference and the principles the conferees espoused, the change was not in the agreements. It was in the domestic political climate and the popular assumptions about what constituted a desirable course in foreign policy and the proper limits to executive authority and procedures. Yalta symbolized a policy approach based upon mutual trust and understanding between the United States and the Soviet Union, and with the postwar belief in the folly of trusting the Soviets came the critical reassessment of Yalta. Because Yalta also represented secretive, unilateral presidential diplomacy, this reassessment could directly assail Roosevelt's leadership in foreign affairs and indirectly question his methods in handling domestic problems. National security considerations that were connected with Roosevelt's approach to foreign policy provided the basis for partisan and conservative attacks on the Americanism of New Deal policy makers.

The Truman Administration's adoption of the containment policy amounted to a repudiation of Roosevelt's foreign policy approach; it provided a cover for these conservatives' attacks about Yalta's threat to national security and neutralized the Administration's defense of the conference. Formally, Truman and the other Democratic leaders might defend Yalta, but they did not support the spirit or the assumptions underlying its agreements. Their defense was essentially partisan.

Conservative and partisan Republicans most effectively exploited the symbolism of the conference and the political situation created with the intensification of the Cold War. The ensuing debate was politically irresponsible: Critics charged that past decisions at Yalta had created the Cold War. The implication was that, had the Administration been more forceful, a postwar world more in the U.S. image could have emerged. Although these criticisms and exploitation of the conference contributed to the evolution of a Yalta mythology, they did not follow a consistent pattern in the postwar decade. Domestic concerns determined the timing and nature of the Republican national and congressional leaders' becoming more openly critical of Yalta. Republican criticisms reflected two political phenomena: the factional split on questions of foreign and domestic policy within the Republican party, and the opportunities provided by the intensification of the Cold War for a more critical Republican response to Yalta.

The conflicting positions of different Republicans concerning Yalta and the direction of general foreign policy reflect, I would argue, a threefold factional division within the Republican party. I call these factions "extremists," "partisans," and "moderates." . . .

In 1945, only the "extremists" forthrightly criticized the conference.

THE TALLOW DOG THAT CHASED THE ASBESTOS CAT

Reprinted courtesy of *The Chicago Tribune.* (Historical Pictures Service, Chicago)

By 1949, although they had different reasons, the "moderates" and "partisans" also voiced this bitter criticism of Yalta. This post-1949 "alliance" between these three Republican factions was a hesitant, short-lived, and uneasy one. As critics, these Republicans shared only a common negativism and commitment: to defeat a Democratic Administration. Apart from this objective, the "moderates," "partisans," and "extremists" differed strikingly in their purposes for criticizing Yalta, however blurred these differences seemed between 1949 and 1952.

The "extremists" consistently depicted Yalta as the symbol of New Deal and Fair Deal appeasement or procommunism. Espousing a verbally assertive anticommunism, these conservatives demanded total victory, emphasized U.S. omnipotence, and thus generally opposed all of the Administration's foreign policy responses. Moreover, they usually attacked past policy decisions, partly for strictly political reasons. Because they were an opposition, they were not required to consider the responsibilities of power but could offer attractive, if unrealizable, alternatives. When advocating either retrenchment or confrontation, however, they assumed that the United States, by itself, could impose U.S. ideals on the postwar world. The "extremists," whose main goal was to discredit the New Deal, were either for isolation or indifferent to the possibly dismembering effect that their critique might have on popular support or understanding of the Truman Administration's allegedly internationalist foreign policy. Despite the aggressive tone of their rhetoric, the "extremists" opposed measures involving overseas military and economic commitments, even when those measures were anti-Soviet.

In contrast to the "extremists," both the "partisans" and "moderates" at least supported an internationalist foreign policy. In their critique of Administration policy, the "partisans" and "moderates" concentrated primarily on *past* Administration decisions, and thus on Yalta, while supporting the contemporary Administration's policy. The "moderates" tempered their criticisms and sought to avoid discrediting internationalism or bipartisanship. In addition, the "moderates" accepted some New Deal reforms but tried to prevent further changes. The "partisans," however, differed from both the "extremists" and "moderates" less over policies than politics. Their principal objective was to defeat the Democrats. Their post-1948 critique of Yalta and the bipartisan foreign policy was as guarded as their pre-1948 support of Yalta and the bipartisan foreign policy had been. . . .

From 1945 to 1949, the "extremists" were virtually the sole Republican critics of Yalta. The Republican party, they argued, should make the Democrats' foreign policy a campaign issue and support particularly the repudiation of Yalta. Republican congressional leaders, however unsympathetic they were to the Roosevelt Administration's policy toward the Soviet Union, did support the Truman Administration's containment policies. When they were critical of

Administration foreign policy, the leaders concentrated on present decisions and only obliquely referred to decisions made in the past. Accordingly, the "moderates" and "partisans" were sharply at odds with the "extremists." The "extremists'" reaction to the strategy adopted by Thomas Dewey, the Republican presidential nominee in 1948, dramatized this rift. Dewey had expressed support for the bipartisan foreign policy and had concentrated on arguments about domestic matters. The "extremists" denounced him for failing to condemn the foreign policy of past Democratic administrations, and after Truman's victory, they attributed Dewey's defeat to this failure.

After the 1948 election, the "moderates" and "partisans" changed their political strategy. They increasingly resorted to the "extremists'" concentration on past foreign policy decisions, which they termed erroneous, and the allegedly subversive personnel who were formulating policy. Despite this shift in tactics, both groups still disagreed fundamentally with the "extremists" and continued to espouse bipartisanship and internationalism. The "moderates'" and "partisans'" decision to stress foreign policy and anticommunism, however, indirectly helped to restore the "extremists'" respectability and to increase their influence in the Republican party and in the nation.

This post-1948 shift in Republican strategy profited from a series of significant international and domestic developments that occurred between 1948 and 1950. These included the Soviet explosion of an atomic bomb, Chiang Kai-shek's retreat to Formosa, Alger Hiss's trial and conviction for perjury, and the outbreak of the Korean War. These developments made more people doubt past policies and federal personnel.

Specifically by exploiting Yalta, Republican leaders sought to increase their national influence and following by discrediting Administration foreign policy makers. The 1948 presidential election had answered a critical, tactical question for the Republicans: Could the party defeat the Democrats nationally by ignoring foreign policy and concentrating solely on domestic issues? Thus, during the 1952 presidential campaign, the Republican party sought to gain popular support by pledging to repudiate Yalta, to eliminate from the State Department the men who had supported Yalta, and to preclude future Yaltas by curbing the use of executive authority in making foreign policy.

After the 1952 election, the "moderates" reverted to their pre-1949 position. The Eisenhower Administration, faced with the responsibilities of power, gradually broke with the "extremists" by overtly or tacitly rejecting their earlier charges and promises. Its 1953–1955 actions—House Joint Resolution 200, the Bohlen nomination, opposition to the Bricker Amendment, publication of the Yalta papers, and attendance at the Geneva Conference—indirectly renounced the "extremists'" tactics in order to restore a semblance of normality to U.S. partisan politics and the consideration of foreign policy.

By late 1954, the disparity between the "moderates'" and the "extremists'" positions on policy matters—and the "moderates'" effectiveness in undercutting the "extremists"—led even the "partisans" to reappraise the desirability of a negativist, simply anti-Communist stance. Senate censure of McCarthy dramatically reflected the "partisans'" attempts to distinguish their position from that of the "extremists." The basis for their disassociation from the "extremists," however, was expediency. The "partisans" realized that the "extremists," because of their rift with the Eisenhower Administration, had become a political liability.

In sum, gradually after 1945 Yalta had become an important issue in U.S. politics, a symbol of Cold War distrust and suspicions. . . .

* * *

The most prevalent criticism of Yalta cited the secrecy of the conference proceedings and the Administration's failure to disclose all the agreements immediately after the conference. Although military strategy was a successful justification for secrecy in 1945, it became a less meaningful explanation as the war became history and new secret agreements were disclosed. Critics could then effectively suggest that the Administration had intentionally kept these agreements from the public in order either to cover up errors in judgment or to set up an unalterable policy of appeasement.

The manner in which the Administration had represented the conference's commitment intensified these suspicions. The February, 1945, communiqué did not state or imply that additional understandings had been concluded. Roosevelt hinted during his March 1, 1945, report to the Congress that unpublished agreements had been reached, but he specifically denied that he had discussed the Far

'Maybe I Shouldn't Have Pulled
The Trigger'

"Maybe I Shouldn't Have Pulled the Trigger"—from *Herblock's Here and Now* (Simon & Schuster, 1955). © 1955 by the Washington Post Co. Used with permission. (Historical Pictures Service, Chicago)

East at Yalta. Moreover, following publication on March 29, 1945, of the "three votes" agreement, Secretary of State Stettinius assured the press that no further Yalta secret agreements remained undisclosed, "with the exception of military decisions and related matters." Roosevelt's and Stettinius' denials, with the subsequent disclosure of the Far Eastern agreements, enabled critics to rebut the Administration's contentions that no further agreements existed.

Conservative Republicans had instinctively distrusted Roosevelt's resort to executive agreements and secretive diplomacy. They opposed his transformation of the Presidency into an institution that made policy and attempted to form public opinion, and they suspected his motives and priorities. They also opposed in principle his attempt to commit the United States to collective security and internationalism, but they did not simply denounce his policy of cooperating with the Soviet Union and restricting German power and influence. Rather, they concentrated on the inherently elitist nature of his secret, personal diplomacy at Yalta.

The intimations about the Yalta Far Eastern agreements made by James F. Byrnes in January, 1946, buttressed this critique of executive procedures. At that time, Byrnes, who had attended Yalta as an adviser to the President, publicly expressed ignorance about both the existence of the Far Eastern agreements and the location of the formal text. Byrnes's role at Yalta had principally been that of an astute political adviser who was knowledgeable about congressional sensitivities and the possible partisan ramifications of decisions reached or considered at the conference. Because he had been a member of the delegation and because he had been Truman's Secretary of State since July 3, 1945, his remarks created the impression that Roosevelt had made far-reaching agreements at Yalta, agreements unknown to even his main advisers. Thus, a declaration of ignorance from a man of Byrnes's position seemed to document charges that additional secrets existed.

Security and loyalty considerations also called forth ghosts of Yalta. Since the late 1930s and early 1940s, opponents of the New Deal had charged that the Roosevelt Administration had been infiltrated by Communists. During the late 1940s and early 1950s, Senators McCarthy, Nixon, Mundt, and the Republican National Committee refined these charges, focusing on the existence of "Communists in

THE YALTA GHOST

Reprinted courtesy of *The Chicago Tribune.* (Historical Pictures Service, Chicago)

the State Department'' and other sensitive federal agencies. Alger Hiss's attendance at the Yalta Conference and his conviction of perjury in 1950 linked this concern about national security with Yalta and its agreements. Having attended Yalta as an adviser to Secretary of State Stettinius, having participated in the drafting and collating of position papers for the use of the U.S. delegation, and having served as secretary at the San Francisco Conference, Hiss seemingly represented a subversive who had risen to an important policy-making position. His attendance at the conference, in view of the secrecy surrounding the discussions and the agreements, could be exploited to confirm subversion and betrayal. Indeed, the Yalta mythmakers identified Hiss as one of the architects of the conference and its agreements.

Associated with this portrayal of Hiss's subversive influence at Yalta was a concern over Roosevelt's mental abilities. Roosevelt had appeared tired and worn during 1944. When addressing the Congress on March 1, 1945, he had delivered his report while seated. The President apologized, explaining that he was tired from the strains of a long trip. His death, one month later, provided one basis for subsequent charges that he had not been in command of his faculties at Yalta. Critics affirmed that a tired, enfeebled, and incompetent President, unduly sympathetic to leftist ideas, had been incapable of resisting the pressures of either Marshal Stalin or the "Communist" Alger Hiss at Yalta.

Other allegations of Roosevelt's presumed lack of mental alertness, which supposedly created the opportunity for Hiss and Stalin to determine policy, came from William Bullitt, a former ambassadorial appointee of the President, and James Farley, Roosevelt's campaign manager during the 1930s and Postmaster General from 1933 to 1940. In 1948, Bullitt questioned Roosevelt's health and mental competence at Yalta, and in 1951, Farley contended that since 1940 Roosevelt had not been in good health and could easily have been influenced by sycophants at Yalta. Their former policy-making positions, their association with Roosevelt, and, more importantly, Farley's Democratic credentials made their allegations effective material for anti-New Dealers to cite as supportive, objective confirmation of Roosevelt's incompetence.

The spirit of the conference further contributed to the evolution of the Yalta mythology. Postwar international developments—the communization of Eastern Europe and China, the confrontation with the Soviet Union, and the efforts to rebuild Germany and Japan—made more convincing the charges that the Yalta concessions were harmful, stupid, and possibly subversive. Critics then specifically denounced the Far Eastern and Eastern European concessions to the Soviet Union and the restrictions imposed on Germany and Japan.

The frustration and bitterness of ethnic groups, particularly the Polish-Americans, maximized the political impact of the mythmaking about Yalta. These groups accepted the charge that the conference had ceded Eastern Europe to the Russians. They were willing to believe that the communization of Eastern Europe had been the result of the leeway the Soviet Union received at Yalta. This frustration over the alleged sellout was effectively exploited by appeals to "liberate the satellite countries" and "repudiate Yalta."

Similarly, the development of the myth that the Far Eastern agreements had ceded China to the Russians happened only after the defeat of the Chinese Nationalists, the communization of China, the outbreak of the Korean War, and the subsequent Chinese Communist involvement. This accusation had not been popularly voiced, or accepted, in 1945 or 1946. The Truman Administration's later defense that these agreements had been based on the military importance of Soviet aid was unconvincing. The Yalta critics pointed to the Administration's awareness of the success of the atomic bomb, the timing between Soviet entrance on August 8, and Japanese surrender on August 14 as contradicting the need for Soviet involvement. They attributed the agreements either to Roosevelt's "softness toward Communism" or to the influence of "Communists in Government."

The acceptance of these myths about the nature of the Yalta agreements and the character of the personnel provided the foundation for a new political setting and new tactics. Increasingly after 1949, foreign policy and internal security became all-absorbing. The symbolism and mythology of Yalta provided seemingly conclusive support for charges that past decisions had caused contemporary difficulties and Communist infiltration of the Federal Government had caused the "sellout" and "betrayal" of Eastern Europe and China.

W. Averell Harriman

STATEMENT REGARDING OUR WARTIME RELATIONS WITH THE U.S.S.R., PARTICULARLY CONCERNING THE YALTA AGREEMENT

W. Averell Harriman was American Ambassador to Moscow at the time of Yalta, and has held a host of important governmental and advisory positions since then. He attended all eight formal plenary sessions at Livadia Palace and was privy to most of the bilateral negotiations concerning the Far East. He submitted, in 1951, a defense of the latter agreement to the congressional committees investigating the dismissal of General Douglas MacArthur and our Far Eastern policy generally. In this excerpt, he argues that Soviet–Chinese Nationalist relations after Yalta are more relevant to an assessment of Yalta than the agreements themselves.

To the Committees on Armed Services and Foreign Relations of the Senate: . . . The Yalta understanding provided a framework for negotiations between the Soviet Union and the Chinese National Government in the summer of 1945, looking toward a settlement of the long-standing difficulties between the two countries. . . .

In Washington on June 9, President Truman had discussed with T. V. Soong, Premier of the Chinese National Government, the provisions of the [Yalta] understanding, including the promise of Stalin to conclude a treaty of friendship with the National Government of China. On June 14, President Truman saw Soong again and told him of the renewed assurances Stalin had given Hopkins and myself in Moscow to support the National Government of China under Chiang. Soong expressed his gratification. On June 15 Ambassador Hurley informed Chiang of the Yalta understanding and also communicated to him Stalin's renewal of his assurances regarding China's sovereignty in Manchuria and his support of a unified and stable China and of the open-door policy.

By this time it had been agreed that negotiations would start

From *Hearings on the Military Situation in the Far East* before the Committees on Armed Services and Foreign Relations, U.S. Senate, 82nd Congress, 1st Session, 1951, excerpted material from pages 3328–3342.

promptly in Moscow between China and the Soviet Union regarding the matters dealt with in the Yalta understanding. T. V. Soong arrived in Moscow at the end of June 1945. Negotiations were conducted between Stalin and Molotov, on the one hand, and Soong, on the other. They were interrupted by the Potsdam Conference, but were resumed early in August, at which time Soong was joined by Wang Shi-chieh, the Foreign Minister of the Chinese National Government.

Stalin, at the outset, made demands that went substantially beyond the Yalta understanding. While Soong was not prepared to accede to all of these demands, he made it clear to me that his Government was anxious to reach an agreement with the Soviet Union, and to this end he was prepared to make concessions which we considered went beyond the Yalta understanding.

At no time did Soong give me any indication that he felt the Yalta understanding was a handicap in his negotiations. I repeatedly urged him not to give in to Stalin's demands. At the same time, during this period, I had several talks with Stalin and Molotov in which I insisted that the Soviet position was not justified. This action I took on instructions from Washington. Also, on instructions, I informed Soong that the United States would consider that any concessions which went beyond our interpretation of the Yalta understanding, would be made because Soong believed they would be of value in obtaining Soviet support in other directions. Soong told me that he thoroughly understood and accepted the correctness of this position. The fact is that, in spite of the position I took, Soong gave in on several points in order to achieve his objectives.

Events moved swiftly during the early days of August. On August 6, the first atomic bomb dropped on Hiroshima and on August 9 another on Nagasaki. On August 8, the Soviet Union entered the war against Japan. On August 10, Japan sued for peace through the Swiss Government and on August 14 an armistice was arranged. On that day a series of agreements between the Soviet Union and China including a Treaty of Friendship and Alliance, were concluded. They were ratified by the Chinese Government on August 24, 1945, and were made public at that time. The texts of these agreements are set forth on pages 585–596 of the volume entitled "United States Relations with China" and are summarized as follows on page 117:

The Treaty pledged mutual respect for their respective sovereignties and mutual noninterference in their respective internal affairs. In the exchange of notes the Soviet Union promised to give moral support and military aid entirely to the "National Government as the central government of China" and recognized Chinese sovereignty in Manchuria; and China agreed to recognize the independence of Outer Mongolia if a plebiscite after the defeat of Japan confirmed that that was the desire of the Outer Mongolian people. The agreement on Dairen committed China to declare Dairen a free port "open to the commerce and shipping of all nations" and provided for Chinese administration of the port; but it exceeded Yalta by granting the Soviet Union a lease of half of the port facilities free of charge. This agreement has not been put into effect, since Nationalist military and civil officials have been prevented from functioning in the Kwantung Peninsula area because of the attitude of the Russians and the Chinese Communists. The agreement on Port Arthur provided for the joint use of the area as a naval base by the two Powers and extended the boundary of that area farther than the United States expected, though not to the pre-1904 boundary which the U.S.S.R. would have preferred. The railway agreement provided for joint ownership and operation of the Chinese Eastern and South Manchurian Railways. The Treaty and the agreements regarding Dairen, Port Arthur, and the railroads were to run for thirty years.

Of prime importance is Article V of the Treaty of Friendship which reads as follows:

The High Contracting Parties, having regard to the interests of the security and economic development of each of them, agree to work together in close and friendly collaboration after the coming of peace and to act according to the principles of mutual respect for their sovereignty and territorial integrity and of noninterference in the internal affairs of the other contracting party.

Supplementing this provision an exchange of notes between Molotov and Wang specified.

In accordance with the spirit of the aforementioned Treaty, and in order to put into effect its aims and purposes, the Government of the U.S.S.R. agrees to render to China moral support and aid in military supplies and other material resources, such support and aid to be entirely given to the National Government as the central government of China.

Soong told me in Moscow he was gratified at the results obtained and expressed his gratitude for the active support the United States had given him in his negotiations. Ambassador Hurley informed the

Secretary of State on August 16 from Chungking that Chiang Kai-shek was "generally satisfied with the treaty." . . .

Nothing that was done at Yalta contributed to the loss of control over China by Chiang Kai-shek. The Yalta understanding was implemented by the Sino-Soviet agreements, which had they been carried out by Stalin, might have saved the Chinese National Government. The inability of the Chinese National Government to maintain control over China was due to the fact that the Sino-Soviet agreements were not honored by Stalin, and to other factors which have been dealt with before these Committees in great detail. . . .

In conclusion, I want to reemphasize the objectives that President Roosevelt and Prime Minister Churchill sought to achieve in their relations with the Soviet Union during the war.

Their primary ojective was to maintain Russia as an effective fighting ally. This problem in itself gave grave concern, not only as to the military capabilities of the Soviet forces, but also as to whether the Kremlin would make separate arrangements with Hitler and leave the Western Allies stranded. The building of mutual confidence in the conduct of the war was not an easy task. But the fact remains that Russia was an effective fighting ally, and carried out vital military undertakings against Hitler.

In addition, Roosevelt and Churchill sought to lay a foundation during the war for cooperation to maintain world peace by all nations, including the Soviet Union, and to find solutions to specific problems which would result from the war, particularly with regard to the treatment of those countries which would be occupied by the Red Army. No one was under any illusions about the difficulties that we would encounter. Nevertheless, step by step, Soviet leaders subscribed to principles which culminated in the formation of the United Nations. They entered into agreements designed to dispose of many specific problems. The carrying out of these commitments would have gone a long way toward achieving Roosevelt's objective of a peaceful world. The postwar difficulties stem from the fact that Stalin did not carry out his commitments and from the fact that the Soviet Union has failed to live up to the charter of the United Nations.

Some people claim that we "sold out" to the Soviet Union at Yalta. If this were true, it is difficult to understand why the Soviet Union has gone to such lengths to violate the Yalta understandings.

The fact is that these violations have been the basis of our protests against Soviet actions since the end of the war. There would have been a sell-out if Roosevelt and Churchill had failed to bend every effort to come to an understanding with the Soviet Union and had permitted the Red Army to occupy vast areas, without attempting to protect the interests of people in those areas.

Only by keeping our military forces in being after Germany and Japan surrendered could we have attempted to compel the Soviet Union to withdraw from the territory which it controlled and to live up to its commitments. The people of the United States and the war-weary people of Europe were in no mood to support such an undertaking. This country certainly erred in its rapid demobilization in 1945, but this is an error for which the entire American people must share the responsibility. I cannot believe that anyone seriously thinks that the move to bring the boys home could have been stopped. I still recall my grave concern when I was in Moscow at the cold reception the Congress gave to President Truman's recommendation for universal military training in the fall of 1945.

The most difficult question to answer is why Stalin took so many commitments which he subsequently failed to honor. There can be no clear answer to this question. I believe that the Kremlin had two approaches to their postwar policies, and in my many talks with Stalin I felt that he himself was of two minds. One approach emphasized reconstruction and development of Russia, and the other external expansion.

On the one hand, they were discussing possible understandings with us which would lead to peaceful relations and result in increased trade and loans from the West for the reconstruction of the terrible devastation left in the wake of the war. If they had carried out this program, they would have had to soft-pedal for the time at least the Communist designs for world domination—much along the lines of the policies they had pursued between the two wars.

On the other hand, we had constant difficulties with them throughout the war and they treated us with great suspicion. Moreover, there were indications that they would take advantage of the Red Army occupation of neighboring countries to be in a position to seize control in the postwar turmoil.

The Kremlin chose the second course. It is my belief that Stalin was influenced by the hostile attitude of the peoples of Eastern Europe toward the Red Army, and that he recognized that governments established by free elections would not be "friendly" to the Soviet Union. In addition, I believe he became increasingly aware of the great opportunities for Soviet expansion in the postwar economic chaos. After our rapid demobilization, I do not think that he conceived that the United States would take the firm stand against Soviet aggression that we have taken in the past five years.

The one great thing accomplished by our constant efforts during and since the war to reach a settlement with the Soviet Union is that we have firmly established our moral position before the world. Had these efforts not been made, many people of the free world would still be wondering whether we and not the Kremlin were to blame for the tensions that have developed. The fact that the Soviet Union did not live up to its undertakings made clear the duplicity and the aggressive designs of the Kremlin. This fact has provided the rallying point for the free world in their collective effort to build their defenses and to unite against aggression.

Charles E. Bohlen

TESTIMONY CONCERNING NOMINATION AS AMBASSADOR TO RUSSIA

As President Roosevelt's interpreter, Charles Bohlen was at his side during all meetings where the Russians were involved. An assistant to Secretary of State Edward Stettinius, Bohlen also kept the most complete and authoritative American set of minutes of Yalta Conference proceedings. When President Eisenhower nominated him as Ambassador to the Soviet Union in 1963, Republican Senators critical of Yalta took the occasion to question him at length on the subject. In Theoharis' categorization, Senator Hickenlooper (R. Iowa) is an "extremist," Senators Ferguson (R. Mich.) and Knowland (R. Calif.) are "partisans," and Senators Wiley (R. Wisc.) and Smith (R. N.J.) are "moderates."

From *Hearings on the Nomination of Charles E. Bohlen* before the Committee on Foreign Relations, U.S. Senate, 83rd Congress, 1st Session, 1953, excerpted material from pages 2–113.

The Chairman.   What was your position at Yalta?

Mr. Bohlen.   I was primarily an interpreter, but at the time of Yalta, I was an assistant to the Secretary of State and one of my duties was to serve as liaison officer with the White House.

I was appointed to that position in December 1944 by Mr. Stettinius when he became Secretary of State. At Yalta I served primarily in the capacity of an interpreter for President Roosevelt but was also an adviser to the delegation. . . .

Senator Smith.   In dealing with the disposition of Chinese property and Chinese issues at Yalta, Chiang Kai-shek definitely was not invited. I have heard that Mr. Stalin definitely objected to his being there because he wanted to talk with Messrs. Roosevelt and Churchill about this particular setup he was working for as the price of Russia entering the Japanese war. That probably is a true report.

Mr. Bohlen.   I had never heard that Stalin had objected to an invitation to Chiang Kai-shek being present at Yalta. I had never heard that it had ever been considered because the Soviet Union and Japan were not at war, and that was the reason why, for example, the Soviet Union was not represented at Cairo. In other words, there were two wars going on; there was the war in Europe in which the Soviet Union was a belligerent, and there was the war in the Pacific in which the Soviet Union was not involved. In fact, even diplomatic relations were maintained between the two countries, and I had heard—I cannot swear to this because I was not in on all these discussions—that if they were going to deal with the war in the Far East the Russians were not prepared to join in any such conference, that is, openly and officially, discussing a Far-Eastern war in which they were not involved.

My only background knowledge in regard to this Far-Eastern matter was that once the United States made the decision that we were going to invade the Japanese mainland, a decision which I believe, was made at the second Quebec Conference in the fall of 1944, certain things automatically followed in its wake. One of these was the importance of getting the Soviet Union into the Pacific war, not as is popularly supposed at any time, but in time to do some good, so to speak, in time to save American lives.

Now, clearly the agreement on the Far East was unnecessary. The estimates which were given to the President and to Mr. Churchill prior to Yalta proved to be erroneous. Whether the intelligence was faulty, in war you cannot take chances, and the estimate given to them officially and formally by their military staff was that the war in the Pacific would last 18 months after V-E Day.

In those circumstances the whole question of Russia's entry into it became a matter of considerable military importance, and the tragic thing about it was that it was unnecessary. There was no invasion of Japan; Russia's involvement was not in any sense necessary.

Another feature which, I think, no one would undertake to defend politically, as it were, was the fact that it was done behind the backs of the Chinese. My understanding then was that the reason for that was grounds of military security. If the Soviet Union was coming into the war 2 or 3 months after the end of V-E Day, obviously it would be of great advantage for Japan to know that well in advance of the events. She might have been disposed herself to make some military move involving Russia. Those were the reasons given, sir. . . .

Senator Hickenlooper. . . . Getting back to the Yalta and the Cairo agreements, it is understandable that under certain theories Mr. Stalin did not attend the Cairo Conference at Cairo because he was not at war with Japan, and at Cairo President Roosevelt and Chiang Kai-shek discussed Japanese affairs. They did not at Cairo discuss the disposition of any Russian property. But at Yalta, when Mr. Roosevelt and Mr. Churchill and Mr. Stalin talked, they did discuss the disposition of Chinese property—

Mr. Bohlen. That is true.

Senator Hickenlooper (continuing). And General Chiang was not present.

Mr. Bohlen. That is true.

Senator Hickenlooper. I mean in one case, one might excuse or one might see a reason for the absence of Stalin, because nothing affecting him particularly as to his property or claimed property was discussed. At Yalta, however, they whacked up some property that China thought basically hers.

Mr. Bohlen. It is true that Chinese representatives were not present.

Senator Hickenlooper. Yes. It runs in my mind that evidence was disclosed that the Air Force and the Navy and a substantial number of important Army people advanced the idea at Yalta and before that Japan was practically on her knees at that time; that 75 or 80 percent of her shipping had been destroyed and it would not be actually necessary for a large-scale invasion of Japan and, therefore, not necessary for Russia to come in. Do you have any knowledge of that?

Mr. Bohlen. No, sir; I have no knowledge. But I believe that the decision reached by our military authorities was to invade the Japanese Islands; I think the date had even been tentatively fixed as November 1, 1945. The decision had been made at the second Quebec conference; that is all I know of it. . . .

I think there was the belief that Russia's entry into the war before we hit the islands would save hundreds of thousands of American casualties. Such was the opinion which, I think, was the reason and, I think, the justification or excuse—it was the reason why it was considered of such overriding importance to get the Soviet Union into the war. The disposition of Chinese territories, as you know, was subsequently embodied in the Soviet-Chinese Treaty of August 1945, which was almost universally hailed in this country, as well as, I believe, in China, as a great event, because this treaty involved the recognition by the Soviet Union of the sovereignty of the Chinese Nationalist Government over Manchuria.

Now, the fact that they did not abide by that treaty is another matter; but when it was concluded it was very widely acclaimed as a great omen for the future, and an intelligent and common-sense disposition of the problems between Russia and China.

The first reaction from the Chinese was not one that they had been sold, as it were, down the river. Mr. T.V. Soong in his negotiations in Moscow found the Yalta agreement of considerable use to him as a backstop.

There are now, in retrospect, two valid criticisms of the argument: First it was unnecessary, the war did not take the course predicted; and, secondly, it was done without the participation of the Chinese Government, . . .

Senator Hickenlooper. To make historic facts current here, there was some evidence that Mr. Roosevelt was told before he went to Yalta—the words, I think, were 99 percent a certainty—by a colonel from the Manhattan district who was sent especially to the

Mediterranean, and who got on a gunboat to tell Mr. Stettinius on the way to Yalta that the atomic bomb was a practical certainty, and that with it the Japanese could be brought completely to heel without the necessity of a larger-scale invasion. But in those matters I assume you had no knowledge?

Mr. Bohlen. I had no knowledge at all of the atom bomb until the late Spring of 1945, just before the test was made, but I think in this connection, just from the point of view of the historical record, that on January 23, 1945, there was a memorandum for President Roosevelt from the Joint Chiefs of Staff which states that Russia's entry at as early a date as possible consistent with her ability to engage in offensive operations was necessary to provide maximum assistance to our Pacific operation.

Senator Ferguson. What is the date of that?

Mr. Bohlen. January 23, 1945. It is quoted in Mr. Harriman's statement to the committees.

Senator Humphrey. Senator Hickenlooper, what was the first explosion in the flats?

Senator Hickenlooper. August 5 or 6, 1945.

Senator Sparkman. No. August 6 was the date it was dropped. It was exploded out here in May.

Senator Humphrey. Alamogordo was in May 1945. And yet, a colonel, in 1944, said it was a certainty?

Senator Hickenlooper. Yes.

Mr. Bohlen. Senator, I think the date was July 16, 1945; it was at Potsdam that the notification came to President Truman of the success at Alamogordo.

Senator Hickenlooper. It was the middle of the year.

Senator Humphrey. Who was this colonel?

Senator Hickenlooper. Colonel Considine. He met Mr. Stettinius on a cruiser just outside of Malta. Mr. Stettinius was on his way from Malta to the Yalta conference. That testimony is on the record. . . .

Senator Sparkman. . . . Now, a minute ago you said that, if I understood you correctly, the Yalta decision was wrong because, first, it was not necessary to get Russia into the war. You are speaking now from hindsight rather than what was actually true at that time, are you not?

Mr. Bohlen. That is right, and I would like to make that very clear, that I do not consider that the men who made the agreement at Yalta considered that they were playing a low trick on Nationalist China. They did not look upon it in that way.

As I say, the embodiment of this agreement in a treaty was, so far as I am aware, welcomed in China. There was certainly no belief at Yalta on the part of President Roosevelt and Mr. Hopkins that they were selling out an ally.

And, as I say, the thing turned out to be unnecessary because the military estimate of the course of the war in the Pacific was not borne out by facts. But I am convinced—

Senator Sparkman. Of course, the military estimate was naturally changed with the great success of the atomic bomb—

Mr. Bohlen. Why, certainly.

Senator Sparkman (continuing). Which had not even had its preliminary explosion.

Mr. Bohlen. That is correct.

Senator Sparkman. They did not even know the mechanism would work at the time of Yalta.

Mr. Bohlen. That is right.

Senator Sparkman. Mr. Bohlen, I was a member of the Military Affairs Committee of the House, and I remember very clearly General Marshall's discussion before our committee of affairs at the time Germany collapsed, and after Yalta, in which he was preparing us for the terrific losses which we would sustain when we invaded Japan. . . .

Senator Ferguson. Mr. Bohlen, you said that you were an assistant to the Secretary of State at Yalta?

Mr. Bohlen. Yes, sir.

Senator Ferguson. I note that Mr. Alger Hiss was the Deputy Director, Office of Special Political Affairs, Department of State—

Mr. Bohlen. Yes, sir.

Senator Ferguson (continuing). At Yalta.

Mr. Bohlen. That is true, sir.

Senator Ferguson. Would you tell us what his job entailed, what his duties were?

Mr. Bohlen. Hiss was present in the delegation at the plenary sessions of the conference but took no part in them, because no one spoke except the President, or on occasion the Secretary of State. I am absolutely certain that Hiss never saw President Roosevelt in a capacity of adviser to him and never had any interviews with him except that first one when the President met the whole delegation before the opening of the Conference.

Mr. Hiss was not present at any of these discussions on the Far East between President Roosevelt and Stalin, and was at none of the private meetings with Stalin.

Senator Ferguson. Do you know whether or not he prepared any data or obtained any information upon which the agreements were had?

Mr. Bohlen. If he had, it was for Mr. Stettinius, because he was attached to the State Department delegation. I was sort of betwixt and between in that I had to be with the President for interpreting purposes.

But from what I saw of Mr. Hiss' activities at Yalta, he confined himself to problems of the United Nations, the voting formula, and to matters pertaining to the establishment of the United Nations.

Senator Ferguson. You have indicated that you believed that the Yalta agreement was not necessary, so far as the Far East was concerned.

Mr. Bohlen. What I meant, sir, was—what Senator Sparkman is quite right about—were the advantages of hindsight, and I might almost add the advantages of hindmyopia, because the terrific compulsions of the war are absent when you look at it 10 years afterward. The agreement at Yalta on the Far East was, as I understood it, based upon the military estimate that we were going to have to invade the Japanese Islands, which would involve very large American casualties, and that Russia's entry into the war before the landing would result in the elimination or containment, in its proper military sense, of the Kwantung Army.

Senator Ferguson. Yes.

Mr. Bohlen. I say it was unnecessary, because the military development did not turn out as foreseen, but I think that in the course of a war the men who were responsible for its conduct cannot afford to underestimate the enemy, and there is a healthy and natural tendency to overestimate him because to underestimate is to court catastrophe.

Senator Ferguson. The other criticism, if it was a criticism, was that Chiang Kai-shek or anyone connected with the Chinese Government was not present.

Mr. Bohlen. Yes, sir. I think that, in general, it is distasteful, to put it mildly, to do things involving another country without the representative of that country present; but there the major considerations were secrecy, and security. . . .

Senator Ferguson. Was not this agreement in relation to the Far East, as far as it gave other people's rights and liberties and lands away, in violation of the Atlantic Charter?

Mr. Bohlen. I think I have answered that in saying, Senator, that the Yalta agreement in itself was not a final definitive international instrument. The definite instrument was the treaty between China and the Soviet Union of August 1945.

Senator Ferguson. Yes; but we are talking about the agreement, whether it was morally right or wrong, or whether it was just a misinterpretation of the agreement that was wrong; what I want to know is whether or not the giving of this land of another power, another nation, was not in violation of the Atlantic Charter?

Did we not say there that there would be no aggrandizement? Was it not a violation of that?

Mr. Bohlen. I do not consider that the Yalta agreement, in effect, did that.

Senator Ferguson. What did it do? It agreed that we would use our influence.

Mr. Bohlen. That we would support that position.

Senator Ferguson. We would support that position, which was in violation of the Atlantic Charter, was it not?

Mr. Bohlen. Well, sir, I do not think that the Atlantic Charter was against any territorial adjustments between countries. Perhaps my understanding of it is erroneous. . . .

Senator Ferguson. Do you know how we agreed to, as is indicated by Sherwood on Roosevelt and Hopkins when he states:

> The conclusions from the foregoing are obvious: Since Russia is the decisive factor in the war she must be given every assistance, and every effort must be made to obtain her friendship. Likewise, since without question she will dominate Europe on the defeat of the Axis, it is even more essential to develop and maintain the most friendly relations with Russia.

Did you ever hear of that before?

Mr. Bohlen. No sir; I never had until I read it in the book. I have no idea who prepared that memorandum. I think there is something in the book that says it was prepared by a military adviser for Quebec or something of that nature.

Senator Ferguson. Do you know whether or not that was the basis of the agreements at Yalta and Teheran?

Mr. Bohlen. Nothing that I saw would support it that that was the basis.

Senator Ferguson. Well, looking at the agreements, do you not think that is exactly what they were doing? Were they not treating Russia as being the dominant figure after the war, and were not these concessions being made to her for the purpose of allowing her to become the dominant figure?

Mr. Bohlen. No, sir; I would not say that that was the general purpose as I saw it. I think that it is, perhaps, necessary for me here to give a little background, which requires an act of memory and some imagination to put yourself back into the circumstances of the greatest war that has ever been fought.

At the time of Yalta, the Russian armies were in virtually full occupation of Poland; they were very close to the German border; offensives which had been undertaken in the latter part of January or the middle of January had brought them almost up to the German Silesian border, and there was only a small part of northeast Poland that was not under Soviet occupation.

I think the Soviet armies were very near Vienna, and were well across Hungary at the time of Yalta.

I think most of the agreements relating to Europe, therefore, were agreements which, in effect, dealt with areas which were under Soviet control, and I would like to say here that in all my experience at these conferences, the Russians were most reluctant to discuss any of the problems of Eastern Europe. They clearly would have preferred no agreement whatsoever in regard to Poland and those matters. They had physical possession by that time of Poland through their armies. They had installed their own government, which grew out of the so-called Lublin Committee in Poland, and I know that those of us who worked on Poland—and I did, myself—felt that we were trying to do everything we could to lay down some ground rules for developments in these countries and if they had been lived up to, sir, I think Eastern Europe would not now be in the enslaved condition that we find it.

Senator Ferguson.   Did that not bring you to the conclusion that any agreements that you made would be interpreted so as to give her absolute control of Europe, as it was indicated in the Quebec agreement that we knew that she was going to be the dominant power, and we were playing to give her the dominant power?

Mr. Bohlen.   I would not from what I saw, Senator, agree with that statement. I do not know who prepared that document that is quoted in the book, but it is the first time I had ever heard of it or seen it.

Senator Ferguson.   Is it part of the State Department—

Mr. Bohlen.   Not that I know of, sir. I think that the map of Europe, as we look at it today, and what we call the Iron Curtain is the line roughly where the armies of the Soviet Union and the armies of the western allies met, which were set by the zonal limits. . . .

Senator Ferguson.   Well, wouldn't you say that the Yalta agreement, the Teheran agreement, is now the basis of the situation in Europe?

Mr. Bohlen.   No sir; I would not.

Senator Ferguson.   Both East and West?

Mr. Bohlen.   I would not.

Senator Ferguson.   You would not?

Mr. Bohlen.   I would not, sir. I believe that the map of Europe would look very much the same if there had never been the Yalta Conference at all.

Senator Ferguson.   You don't say then that these agreements are the cause of this enslavement?

Mr. Bohlen.   I don't, sir. I say it is the violation of them.

Senator Ferguson.   That is what I say.

Mr. Bohlen.   What I am saying, sir, I think in this business just because a policy failed doesn't mean it was a wrong one. In other words, I don't think the men who backed the League of Nations were necessarily wrong, despite the fact that the League of Nations failed to prevent World War II. . . .

The Chairman. Senator Ferguson, you mentioned Hiss. Is the record clear as to what part he played, if any, according to this witness?

Mr. Bohlen. As I said earlier this morning, Hiss at that time was in charge of the section of the Department of State dealing with the United Nations. As far as I personally know, he dealt with that at Yalta and confined his activities to that.

He may have done some other things for Secretary Stettinius at the Foreign Ministers' meeting, at which I was not present. I can testify under any form of oath necessary that he was not present at any of these meetings between Stalin and President Roosevelt, and as far as I am aware, he knew nothing whatsoever about this Far-Eastern matter.

The Chairman. Will the Senator yield? I want to get the record clear there.

Do I understand that according to your recollection, while you acted as interpreter for President Roosevelt, between Stalin, Molotov, and Roosevelt, at no time was Hiss present?

Mr. Bohlen. He was not present, sir, at any of these private meetings. Hiss would be present when you had the large plenary sessions of the conference, at which maybe 10 or 15 or more people from the United States delegation were present.

As I explained this morning, I think possibly an explanation of the way the conference was organized might be helpful. At 4 o'clock in the afternoon the top three would meet, the President, Mr. Churchill, and Stalin, with their advisers, with their Foreign Ministers, and then the people sitting in the back row with the other members of the delegation.

In the mornings the Foreign Ministers would meet, and I did not attend those meetings as a regular thing. Then occasionally—I think there were three such meetings during the Yalta Conference—the President alone with Stalin. When I say alone, I mean without Mr. Churchill.

At those meetings there were the President and Mr. Harriman, and Stalin, Molotov, and the two interpreters. I have no recollection or no record of the President's meetings with Mr. Churchill, which occurred somewhat more frequently I would say; nor of any of Mr. Churchill's private meetings with Stalin, so I can testify that at these private meetings between the President and Stalin, Alger Hiss was not present.

Senator Knowland. Mr. Chairman, at that point will the Senator yield?

Senator Ferguson. Yes; I yield.

Senator Knowland. Pardon this interruption. I have here the book by Stettinius called *Roosevelt and the Russians: The Yalta Conference,* and on page 83 he says:

> This Saturday night dinner was the last leisurely social gathering at the Yalta Conference. The pressure of the next few days was most exhausting. My usual daily schedule, for instance, was to confer with Matthews, Bohlen, and Hiss, just after I got up in the morning. I next discussed the conference problems with the President.

That is on page 83. Then a little farther down on page 83 he says:

> After these dinners, I usually conferred with Matthews, Bohlen, Hiss, and Foote, read cables from Acting Secretary of State through to Washington, drafted cables to the Department, and then went to bed.

Then on Page 84, Secretary Stettinius says:

> The next morning at 10:30, Harriman, Matthews, Hiss, Bohlen, and I met with the President on the sun porch overlooking the sea to review our proposals for the conference agenda. We arrived just before the President's meeting with the military chiefs broke up. Since the military chiefs were about to leave, I suggested that they remain in order that they might be fully informed of the diplomatic position of the State Department, and thus be in a position to correlate this with the secret military conferences that were to take place within the Chiefs of Staff of the three countries.

Now there are other references to Mr. Hiss, but that at least to me would seem to indicate that he did more than merely sit in on these large plenary meetings.

Mr. Bohlen. I thought the question was whether Hiss had been present at these private meetings between President Roosevelt and Stalin.

Senator Knowland. As I understood Senator Ferguson, what he was trying to get at was what kind of a part did Mr. Hiss play at these Yalta conferences.

Now, we recognize, as you have testified, and I think all the books on the subject rather indicate that the actual discussions with Mr.

Stalin and Mr. Churchill were carried on either by the President or, in rare instances, perhaps by Mr. Stettinius, but what we are trying to find out, I assume from the line of questioning, is what influence, if any, Mr. Hiss may have played which he could have done either at preliminary meetings or at other gatherings that were outside of the plenary sessions.

Mr. Bohlen. What Mr. Stettinius is talking about is meetings that are always held in conferences of that kind. Hiss was there as an adviser to the Secretary of State, not there as an adviser to President Roosevelt direct, and at these meetings my recollection is that Hiss' part in it dealt virtually exclusively with the United Nations business, which was, of course, a very big subject. . . .

The Chairman.[1] I would like to ask one question. With respect to what Senator Knowland read from Mr. Stettinius' book about Stettinius starting the day by consulting with you and Hiss at the Yalta Conference, I think it would be very interesting if you could tell us what the subjects were that you talked about.

Mr. Bohlen. Senator, since that has been read, I have been trying to rack my memory to figure out exactly what we did discuss and whether these meetings actually took place every morning.

Insofar as my memory serves me, they were more or less means to find out where we stood, what had happened the day before, and for the orderly conduct of business to take place.

What had been referred to the Foreign Ministers from the previous day's meeting, what was expected of them, what they were to report on for the forthcoming day, I would say my recollection is they were almost exclusively procedural, rather than policy decisions. As I say, with respect to most of these agreements, with the exception of the Far-Eastern one, the United States policy had been well established before we went to Yalta. There were some changes that occurred in negotiations.

The Chairman. What part of the discussion did Hiss take part in?

Mr. Bohlen. As I say, I can't recall Hiss expressing an opinion on anything about Poland, the Far East, or anything. I do recall his

[1] A portion of page 58 is included here out of place so as to put it in topical order. —Ed.

expressing his opinion about the United Nations matters. But I wouldn't trust my memory to the extent of saying he never did.

But, by and large, my picture of what happened is that when the subject of discussion came around to—let's say the voting formula in the United Nations, that he was the man who spoke to that. That was his particular job at this conference.

Senator Ferguson. But he heard what was going on.

Mr. Bohlen. Oh, yes; he heard what was going on. . . .

Senator Ferguson. Well, as it turned out now, it [Yalta Agreement] has had a great influence on what has happened in China.

Mr. Bohlen. I think that is a matter of opinion, Senator.

Senator Ferguson. You don't think so?

Mr. Bohlen. I don't think it did; no, sir.

Senator Ferguson. You don't think it had anything to do with what happened in China?

Mr. Bohlen. Well, everything has something to do with something, but I don't believe that it was the cause of what subsequently happened in China insofar as this treaty between the Chinese and the Soviets went, in its intended effect.

I say "intended effect" advisedly; that on the whole I think that that was a help to Chiang Kai-shek rather than a hindrance in the major business of establishing his sovereignty over China.

Now, that is a matter of opinion, and I am just giving you mine.

Senator Ferguson. Did Russia agree to do anything in this agreement other than to come into the war?

Mr. Bohlen. Well, recognition of Chiang Kai-shek's sovereignty over Manchuria was the important element embodied in the treaty. I have not the text of the treaty here, but I think it says that the Soviet Government recognizes as the sole supreme authority in Manchuria the Nationalist Chinese Government, and that the representatives of that Government should be permitted to go up into that area even while the Soviet armies are in occupation.

Senator Ferguson. Now, didn't this agreement in regard to Japan make the course easier for the Soviet Union in northeast Asia, especially in Manchuria and Korea, after the defeat of Japan, and thus facilitate the Communist conquest of China, and after that the Communist armed invasion of South Korea?

Mr. Bohlen. These are purely matters of opinion, Senator.

Senator Ferguson. What is your opinion on it?

Mr. Bohlen. My opinion is that they did not, in this sense. I am not a Far East expert. I have no firsthand knowledge of China. I have not been engaged in that end of the business.

In this testimony, I don't want to divest myself of the slightest responsibility that I have for these matters. On the other hand, in the interest of accuracy, I don't think that I should take on responsibilities that were not mine. So, when I give you an opinion on this point, it is an opinion of a non-expert in Oriental matters.

I think the Communist conquest of China is one thing, and the terms of the treaty another. . . .

Senator Ferguson. Now, do you know that after the Teheran Conference the Polish general headquarters became aware of the fact that military responsibility over Poland had been shifted to Soviet Russia? . . .

Mr. Bohlen. With regard to the question of the relief for dropping supplies to the Warsaw garrison in August 1944, we had a considerable row with the Russians over that. Mr. Harriman was Ambassador, and he had several knockdown, drag-out fights and finally they allowed one flight to go in and drop the supplies. Some flights were made there and back—

Senator Ferguson. Wasn't that before Yalta?

Mr. Bohlen. Yes, sir, it was.

Senator Ferguson. And, therefore, shouldn't we have understood that Russia was dominating the situation in Poland and intended to do so?

Mr. Bohlen. Yes; their armies were in Poland.

Senator Ferguson. And then why would we make an agreement providing for free elections when we knew that they wouldn't carry out free elections, and that their idea of free elections was no elections at all really?

Mr. Bohlen. Do you consider, Senator, If I might, myself, ask a question, that it would have been better to have made no agreement about Poland?

Senator Ferguson. It would have been better to make an agreement whereby we would have had something to say about the elections.

Mr. Bohlen. How would you do that, Senator?

Senator Ferguson. Then why did you make any when you knew the Russians wouldn't carry them out?

Mr. Bohlen. I don't think you knew that for certain.

Senator Ferguson. Why did we have to surrender the rights of these people and be a party to the surrender?

Mr. Bohlen. I don't consider that the agreement of Yalta involved a surrender. It involved the opposite.

Whether or not the Russians carried out, sir, is to my mind a very different question. I think the agreement on that part of the Polish agreement is about the best you could put down on paper as to what you hoped the Russians would do and they put their signature to.

The fact that they violated it I don't think means that the agreement was bad.

Senator Ferguson. Then you wouldn't have been a party to an agreement that you knew or should have known was not going to be carried out.

Mr. Bohlen. I think this is an important problem.

If agreements made as written are all right and provide for the things that this country believes in, such as free elections, universal suffrage, if you have doubts as to whether the other party is going to carry them out, it still seems to me that it is worthwhile to set your opinion of what ought to happen, and if you are able to get the other fellow to agree to it, I think in the parlance of diplomacy, that that is what it is all about.

Senator Ferguson. In other words, you would favor a settlement in Korea, even when anticipating that it wouldn't be carried out. In other words you want to get an agreement that would look good on paper.

Mr. Bohlen. No, sir; I don't think that is the point.

Senator Ferguson. Isn't that what happened in these agreements?

Mr. Bohlen. No, sir. The point is that you were confronted at Yalta on the question of Poland which had been the subject of intense correspondence over a period of years between the Soviet, American, and British Governments. . . .

. . . The problem you were faced with at Yalta was what were you really going to do about Poland. There were three courses of action that were open.

1. You could have, by just accepting the total *fait accompli,* let it go and do nothing about it, which is what I think Stalin would have preferred by all indications.
2. To stick completely with the London government in exile, which would have meant that no member of it would have been in Poland. There wouldn't have been any entry into Poland on the part of anybody.
3. To attempt to get as many members of the Polish group in London as possible into the reorganized government.

Yes, but the other alternative was this. You had the country, Poland, which the Russians were in occupation of. The alternatives were leaving, washing your hands, so to speak, of the whole business, and leaving this complete Communist government, which would be worse.

The other alternative of just sticking with the London government amounted to almost the same thing, because you would have had an exile government in London and you would have had nothing in Poland, and they would have had nothing. . . .

Senator Ferguson.   And Poland was not present at these divisions.

Mr. Bohlen.   That is true, but it was not possible to have Polish representatives present.

Senator Ferguson.   Well, no one representing Poland was present. It was just like the case of Chiang Kai-shek. No one representing China was present.

Mr. Bohlen.   Well, the question is what do you do about a situation, Senator? And I think nothing would be easier if you had to do them all over again, you would probably do them with greater perfection, although in many ways under the compulsions of the times I don't know what you would have done that would have a great improvement over this. I will say this. I think more care could have been used in all of these agreements as to how they looked, that is to say, from the point of view of the record. I don't know if you were thinking of what you could do to assist Poland, which I can assure you was the major motivation in the minds as I saw it of the President and Winston Churchill—they had no other interests than that; they felt very strongly on this subject.

I think the tragic fact is that by the progress of the war, which short of some drastic revision of strategy, the map of Europe as we see it today was almost made by the war itself. I think very few people have any illusions.

Senator Ferguson.　We were making political agreements of division prior to the ending of the war.

Mr. Bohlen.　It is true in this sense.

Senator Ferguson.　And we did it without consultation with our allies who were fighting in the war.

Mr. Bohlen.　I think the President felt, and so did Mr. Churchill, that they were in effect trying to fight the battles for the Poles which the Poles were not able to do themselves.

Now I don't know whether these judgments were mistaken, whether there were better ways to do it, but I am utterly and totally convinced that that was the main thought. That the British had very strong feelings about Poland, had gone to war over Poland—

Senator Ferguson.　That is the sad part of it. They went to war over Poland, and there is no Poland today. We went to war over China and China is gone today. . . .

Mr. Bohlen.　What I am saying in one sense is that a possible course of action would have been to have stuck by the government in London, that is to say we recognize no other government.

Senator Ferguson.　But you don't have to sacrifice all principle.

Mr. Bohlen.　I don't think that this is a sacrifice of principle insofar as this agreement goes. I think it was an attempt to do just the opposite. I think it was an attempt to produce a Polish Government in national unity.

Senator Ferguson.　Isn't it true at Yalta, so far as Poland is concerned, so far as international law is concerned, that the sovereign rights of an allied country were violated, according to what we envisaged when we signed the Atlantic Charter? Isn't that true?

Mr. Bohlen.　I don't quite see—

Senator Ferguson.　We divided Poland without Poland being present. We broke off recognition of the London government.

We, Great Britain, and France recognized the present Polish Government, which is nothing more or less than a satellite of the Soviet Union, and wasn't that all in violation of the principles of the Atlantic Charter?

Mr. Bohlen.　I just don't read the Atlantic Charter to indicate there should be no territorial adjustments of any kind, and I would like to call your attention to the fact that this arrangement specifically says:

> . . . *expresses the view of three heads of the governments consider the eastern frontier of Poland should follow the Curzon line. They recognize that Poland must receive substantial accessions of territory in the north and west.*

That is an expression of view. It is perfectly possible to quarrel with the expression of view, but the map of Poland is not as a result thereof, and I will give you an illustration to show you how little, unfortunately, any of these things mattered in Eastern Europe. Neither the United States Government nor the British Government nor the French Government were ever consulted about a certain part of Czechoslovakia. The Czech Government ceded that part to the Soviet Union, and it is now just as much a part of the Soviet Union as anything else.

Senator Ferguson. We didn't consent to that. We, through a lack of interest, haven't recognized the governments in the Baltic States, but they are gone.

Mr. Bohlen. It seems to me almost everything you can think of has been tried in relation to the areas which the Russians ended the war in control of, and I would say that there would be a really serious charge against any of these agreements if they handed over to Russia something that she did not have.

I look upon them as exactly the opposite. You were faced with the fact and not a theory, and what you were attempting to do through diplomatic instruments was to try and express what you hoped to see in those countries through the medium of these instrumentalities which have been violated.

Senator Ferguson. And we also entered into them.

Mr. Bohlen. Well, sir, if the wording of these agreements in places here reflect in your opinion things that were improper. I think your criticism is correct.

Senator Ferguson. I think it is as far as the Curzon line is concerned.

Mr. Bohlen. The Curzon line I think is a legitimate case. President Roosevelt told Mikolajczyk our position was that there should be no territorial settlements until the peace treaty. I think what began to happen, and it was particularly true in the British mind, was that by the time you came to the peace settlement the game might be totally up. There wouldn't have been any need to settle. . . .

Senator Ferguson. You put men in the State Department. You put them there on the assumption that as advisors to the President they will use judgment. We all talk about hindsight. Good judgment doesn't require you to use hindsight.

Mr. Bohlen. This supposition that this particular treaty [1945 U.S.S.R-China Treaty] was instrumental in bringing about the downfall of Chiang Kai-shek I do not think is the case.

Was it suggested that it would have been preferable to have had no treaty between the Soviet Union and China, to have left that a wide-open breach, or is it meant that the treaty could have been better than it is? Everything could be better, Senator, but it seems to me that every country must learn through its own mistakes, and I think the first task is to identify those mistakes correctly.

Senator Ferguson. I think the saddest thing of all in relation to history is that we don't learn from history.

Mr. Bohlen. One of the things I have felt is these Yalta agreements obviously show imperfections, and I can assure you many of them, the one on Poland was not a happy agreement for anybody connected with it. The President spoke on that point I believe before Congress after Yalta. He was very unhappy about it.

Senator Ferguson. But we agreed to it.

Mr. Bohlen. We felt it was the best we could do. The alternative of doing nothing was worse. That was the judgment.

I would like to say this: A great deal of the moral position of the United States in the leadership accepted by the free world is due to the fact that an honest attempt was made to see if any form of arrangement with the Soviet Union could be arrived at that would have any value for the future of the world. Without that attempt, it would seem to me you would have a much more divided opinion throughout the free world as to who was to blame.

People would say, "How do you know? You didn't try it." These things are all very complicated. History will deal with it and I would not undertake to say that these agreements couldn't have been done better, but I do know this much: that if there had been no Yalta Conference, I sincerely doubt very much if the map of the world would look very different.

I do not think Yalta was the cause. I think Yalta was more a result of certain matters affecting the conduct of the war, certain realities that existed in the world which cannot be changed by wishing they were not there.

Senator Ferguson. But it places our government in the position of having consented to this map of the world.

Mr. Bohlen. No, sir; I don't think so. I don't think that is true. If you wish to say the Iron Curtain stopped at the Curzon line, I think we would all be very, very much happier. The Iron Curtain is on the Elbe, which had nothing whatsoever to do with Yalta. . . .

The Chairman. Looking at it from circumstances as they exist today, what would you say?

Mr. Bohlen. That is very hard today. As I testified before, I think from a technical point of view there could always have been improvements in the texts of these arguments, but given the circumstances, I have never been able to see afterward that you could have done much more that would have been of benefit to Poland or the Polish people.

I will testify to my deep conviction that what was animating President and Prime Minister Churchill was a desire to do the very best that they could for Poland.

The Chairman. I would like to get this matter plainly before us. As I understand it, your position is that in spite of the promises made in the Atlantic Charter, conditions at that time as they appeared to Roosevelt and the others were such that this was the best arrangement that could be made. Is that correct?

Mr. Bohlen. That is my opinion, sir. . . .

V YALTA, REVISIONISM, AND THE COLD WAR

William Appleman Williams

THE NIGHTMARE OF DEPRESSION AND THE VISION OF OMNIPOTENCE

William Appleman Williams is the acknowledged dean of the newer revisionist school of American historians. This group views American foreign policy as a logical outgrowth of our internal economic system and finds our pretensions to world power to be at least as responsible for the Cold War as the actions of the Soviet Union. Typically, their research interest begins in the period immediately after Yalta. This selection from Williams' seminal work is one of the most direct, explicit treatments of Yalta from the revisionist viewpoint.

Though there were various shades of opinion as to how the central issue of reconstruction should be dealt with, the Russians divided into three broad groups. One of them, occasionally called "our softies" by their Russian opponents, held that it was necessary and desirable to undertake reconstruction at a relatively moderate tempo, obtaining assistance from the United States. The softies stressed the need and desirability of relaxing the pervasive and extensive controls that had been exercised over Soviet life ever since the first Five-Year Plan and the wisdom of revising, decentralizing, and rationalizing the industrial system that had been built. They also emphasized the danger of deteriorating relations with the United States. Perhaps most significant of all, they advanced the thesis that Western capitalism could probably avoid another serious depression, and hence the appeal and the safety of the Soviet Union depended upon its ability to improve the quality of life in Russia and thereby induce other peoples to accept communism by the force and persuasiveness of example.

Others within Russia argued that the softies were wrong in theory or in fact. Some of these men, who may be called the conservatives, agreed with the softies that it was desirable to ease up at home and were half convinced by the more favorable analysis of foreign capitalism, but they doubted that the Western nations, and in particular the United States, would help the Soviet Union solve its reconstruction problems. Hence they concluded that Russia would have to establish a basic security perimeter in Europe, the Middle East, and Asia and once again pull itself up by its own bootstraps. Opposed to the softies and the conservatives was a group which may be called the doctrinaire revolutionaries. The die-hards scoffed at the analysis and proposals advanced by the moderates and asserted that the only practical and realistic program was to secure a base for militant revolutionary activity throughout the world. Such doctrinaires stressed the need to force the pace of reconstruction while doing all that was possible to export revolutions.

Stalin's temperament and experience inclined him toward resolving the dilemma posed by the problem of reconstruction and the tradition of revolution by supporting the conservatives. But that approach depended on two things for success: (1) limiting and controlling revolutionary action by foreign communists, which otherwise would antagonize the United States, and (2) reaching an economic and political understanding with America, an agreement that would enable Russia to handle the problem of recovery and at the same time relax certain controls and pressures inside the country. To use the language of Wall Street, Stalin was a bull on communism. He was confident that if given a peaceful opportunity to develop its program in Russia, communism would gradually appeal to more and more countries of the world. He felt this was particularly likely in the underdeveloped areas and in poorer industrialized nations. If this could be managed by getting aid from America and by restraining foreign communists from seizing power through revolutions, then the movement toward socialism and communism would move slowly enough to avoid frightening the United States into retaliation against the Soviet Union itself.

Several developments in the winter of 1942–1943 encouraged Stalin to embark upon an effort to resolve the dilemma in this fashion. One was the Western landing in North Africa, which took the edge off his suspicion and anger over the failure to make an assault on the European continent. More important, however, was an American approach concerning postwar economic relations with Russia which seemed to suggest that the Soviet Union could get help in dealing with its reconstruction problems. Stalin responded quickly and decisively. But as he was ultimately forced to conclude, the American overture concerning postwar economic ties did not represent a changed outlook on the part of the majority of the leaders of America's corporate system.

In its origins, indeed, the plan was a continuation of the open-door idea that America's economic system had to have a constantly expanding foreign market if it was to survive and prosper. At bottom, therefore, it was the fear of another depression (or the resumption of the old one) that prompted a few American leaders such as Donald M. Nelson to think of large-scale exports to Russia. They also worried about America's depletion of certain raw materials and thought that Russia could continue to supply such items as manganese after the war. To some extent, moreover, this small minority of American leaders began to realize that, whatever his many faults, Stalin was not another Hitler and that the Soviet Union had not developed by the same dynamic as Nazi Germany.

During 1943, therefore, Nelson and a few other Americans pushed the idea of a large loan to Russia. Stalin told Nelson that he was very much in favor of the plan and even gave him a list of priority needs as a first step in working out a specific program. Their negotiations had much to do with the improvement in political relations between the two countries, exemplified by Stalin's voluntary promise to Secretary of State Hull in October, 1943, that Russia would enter the war against Japan. A bit later, in November, the conversations at the Teheran Conference also reflected the improved atmosphere.

For his part, Roosevelt exhibited more awareness of the importance of including Russia as a full partner in any plans for the postwar world. He also appeared to enjoy a broader recognition of the need to undertake basic modifications at home if America was to avoid a serious crisis after the war. In a similar way, he apparently grasped the fact that Stalin was "most deeply interested" in Russian recovery problems and indicated some understanding of the idea that improvement at home depended upon an "economic bill of rights" as well as upon political liberty. He seemed to be realizing, in short, that "America's own rightful place in the world depends in large part upon" such domestic considerations. "For unless there is security here at home," he explained, "there cannot be lasting peace in the world."

It may be that these words indicated Roosevelt's awareness that

America's traditional policy of open-door expansion had contributed significantly to its domestic and international difficulties. But while he said he was "sorry" that he did not have time to discuss Russia's postwar recovery problems with Stalin at Teheran, the fact is that he never took—or made—time to do so during the remaining sixteen months of his life. He did not even see to it that his subordinates prepared themselves to discuss the issue with Stalin. Roosevelt's declining health may account in part for this, but in that event it is clear that such an approach to the Russians was very low on the President's list of priorities. In short, it is not possible to account for the continuance of the Open Door Policy simply by blaming Roosevelt's successors, for the President did not carry through the implications of his remarks in the winter of 1943–1944.

Had Roosevelt done this, it would be more meaningful to charge his successors—or the Russians—with sabotaging his plan for the future; for it is quite true that the small group around Nelson which favored some *rapprochement* with the Russians was opposed by a much larger number of America's corporate leaders who did not favor that approach to the postwar world. It seems likely that Averell Harriman, one of the many wealthy industrial and banking leaders who supported Roosevelt, and who was one of the President's top advisors, was one of the more influential leaders of the anti-Russian group.

Harriman's natural antagonism to the Soviets was reinforced by his vigorous belief in the necessity of open-door expansion, a belief that may have been heightened even more by an unhappy experience with the Russians in the 1920s, when his attempt to control a sizable segment of the world's manganese market by developing Russian supplies ended in mutual dissatisfaction. Harriman was but one of many corporate leaders, however, who had gone into the Roosevelt Administration with anti-Russian views. Others included James B. Forrestal and Bernard Baruch. All of these men were skeptical of Nelson's approach to dealing with the Soviets and were supported in their view by State Department experts such as George Frost Kennan (who was in Russia much of the time with Harriman).

These men shared Harriman's extremely reserved reaction, early in 1944, to the news that the Russians "were anxious to come to a prompt understanding" about postwar economic relations. His view became even clearer when, a bit later that year, Stalin made a formal request for a loan of six billion dollars. Harriman advised cutting the initial amount under discussion to one-tenth of that sum and proposed that the project should be defined as a credit, rather than as a loan, so that if it ever actually went through, the United States could exercise extensive controls over Russia's use of the money. Thus, while he agreed with the Nelson group that "the question of long-term credits represents the key point in any negotiations with the Soviet Government," he also shared the State Department's view that the lever provided by Russian weakness and devastation could and should be used to insure a predominant role for America in all decisions about the postwar world.

Harriman and the majority of American leaders knew precisely what kind of choice they made. In one of his official reports, Harriman candidly acknowledged "that the sooner the Soviet Union can develop a decent life for its people the more tolerant they will become." Turning his back on that analysis, which implied a basic policy of helping the Russians recover from the devastation of the war, Harriman instead proposed that Russia "should be given to understand that our willingness to cooperate wholeheartedly with them in their vast reconstruction problems will depend upon their behavior in international matters." In such fashion did the leaders of the New and Fair Deals reassert a Russian policy established by Woodrow Wilson and sustained by Herbert Hoover and Charles Evans Hughes.

From the very beginning of the discussions with Stalin in 1943, Roosevelt was aware of the Soviet overtures for economic aid and of the importance Stalin attached to them, yet he neither took the lead himself nor directed the State Department (or other advisors) to open actual negotiations with the Russians. Indeed, the President's whole attitude and approach reinforced the position of the Harriman group. He declined, furthermore, to undertake any serious planning for Germany, even halting that which was in progress, and did nothing to remedy the lack of serious research and analysis concerning American and world economic problems.

His attitude, so clearly reflecting the traditional outlook of open-door expansion, was revealed even more vividly in the spring of 1944, when the Soviet Army began to advance into eastern Europe. Confronted by Churchill with the need to come to some clear understanding with the Russians, Roosevelt at first agreed to the idea of a clear and precise division of authority. Then, in an abrupt turnabout, he asserted that he must have "complete freedom of action," whatever the agreement arranged by Churchill and Stalin. After considerable effort, Churchill and Stalin worked out an understanding—"a good guide," said Churchill, "for the conduct of our affairs"—whereby Russia would exercise predominant authority in southeastern Europe, Great Britain would do so in Greece, and the Allies would share responsibility in Yugoslavia. Roosevelt reluctantly accepted this division of power on the basis of a three-month trial.

During subsequent months, the British intervened to crush a revolution in Greece and prepare the way for the installation of a government they wanted and could control. Though he urged the British to take a more liberal line, Roosevelt went along with Churchill on the need to control affairs in Greece and acquiesced in the Prime Minister's action. Both in fact and in the eyes of the Russians, that committed Roosevelt on the eve of the Yalta Conference to the agreement worked out between Churchill and Stalin. For his part, Stalin refrained from attacking or blocking the British move in Greece. Churchill reported that Stalin "adhered very strictly to this understanding." Stalin also initiated his efforts to forestall trouble with the Western Allies arising from foreign communist agitation and revolution. He advised, and apparently even warned, Tito and Mao Tse-tung to abstain from revolutionary action in their nations and instead to accept subordinate positions in coalition governments led by pro-Western parties.

Against this background, and in the context of Germany's imminent defeat, Roosevelt met Churchill and Stalin at Yalta in February, 1945. In addition to their knowledge of the Churchill-Stalin agreement, and of Stalin's self-containment during the Greek episode, American leaders were aware that the Chinese communists, after a long debate, had concluded in September, 1944, that they preferred to work with the United States rather than with Russia in the future development of China. Thus it is absolutely clear that Roosevelt and his advisors knew that the Soviet Union was prepared to negotiate seriously about the character of postwar relations with the United States and that America had an equally fruitful opportunity in Asia. But it became apparent during the conference that American leaders were not concerned to push such negotiations. They were not prepared to abandon, or even seriously to modify, the traditional policy for American expansion.

Disturbed by America's ambivalence and Churchill's growing open opposition, which increased the difficulty he had in controlling the doctrinaire revolutionaries within his own camp, Stalin went to Yalta with two approaches to the postwar world. One was based on receiving a large loan from the United States. His overtures in this direction were answered with vague and unrewarding replies. Stalin's alternative was to obtain, by agreement or by self-exertion, economic reparations from Germany and a strong strategic position in eastern Europe, the Black Sea area, and the Far East. America went to Yalta, on the other hand, guided by little except a sense of mission to reform the world, a growing fear of postwar economic crisis, and an increasing confidence that Russian weakness would enable America to exercise its freedom and solve its problems by further open-door expansion.

The conflict over affairs in eastern Europe, and particularly Poland, which stemmed from these contrasting outlooks is usually stressed in discussing the origins of the cold war. Yet it may be that the issues of German reparations and American expansion in the Middle East were equally important as determining factors. Failing to obtain a loan from America, Stalin faced three possible courses of action. He could give way and accept the American interpretation of all disputed points, abandoning foreign communists to their fate and attempting to control the extremists in his own nation. He could respond with an orthodox revolutionary program throughout the world. Or, relying on large economic reparations from Germany, he could continue the effort to resolve his dilemma in a conservative manner. This approach would also do much to keep Germany from becoming a threat to Russia in the immediate future. It left him, however, with the need to effect some basic settlement concerning eastern Europe, the Far East, and the Black Sea region.

Stalin was able to reach such an understanding with the United States in but one of those areas. This was in Asia where he traded American predominance in China (and Japan) for stategic and economic rights in Manchuria. Concerning eastern Europe, however, Stalin accepted an ambivalent proposal on the Polish issue which represented America's unwillingness to acknowledge his agreement with Churchill as much as it did Russia's security needs. He was no more successful in the Middle East, where American oil companies had moved back into Iran in 1943. Supported by the State Department and special emissaries, the companies were well along in their efforts to obtain extensive concessions. Roosevelt was "thrilled" by the chance to work along with the oil companies and make Iran an example of what America could do for underdeveloped areas of the world, an attitude which helps explain why the United States was not willing to allow the Russians to obtain oil rights in northern Iran. Stalin gave way on the issue at Yalta and also refrained from pushing his desire to gain more security for Russia in the Black Sea area.

Despite his failure to get any positive response from the United States on the question of a postwar loan, or a clear understanding on other vital issues, Stalin still hoped to effect a conservative resolution of his dilemma. Throughout the first half of 1945, for example, *Izvestia* stressed the vitality of the American economy (in striking contrast to fears being expressed in Congressional hearings), emphasized the importance of resolving outstanding issues by negotiation, and re-iterated the fruitfulness of economic cooperation. The British press attaché in Russia reported that Soviet comment remained restrained and hopeful until America initiated a campaign of vigorous criticism and protest aimed at Soviet predominance in eastern Europe. Stalin grew more and more skeptical about the possibility of active coopera-tion with the United States, but he did not adopt an attitude of fatalism toward a clash with the United States. Indeed, he never did, although the softies in the party were later subjected to vigorous and extensive attack and an anti-American campaign in the Soviet press became ex-tremely embittered late in 1947 and early in 1948.

Stalin's effort to solve Russia's problem of security and recovery short of widespread conflict with the United States was not matched by American leaders who acceded to power upon the death of Roosevelt. The President bequeathed them little, if anything, beyond the traditional outlook of open-door expansion, and they proceeded rapidly and with a minimum of debate to translate that conception of America and the world into a series of actions and policies which closed the door to any result but the cold war.

The various themes which went into America's conception of the freedom and the necessity of open-door expansion, from the doctrine of the elect to the frontier thesis, had been synthesized into an ideology before Roosevelt's death. Once that occurred, it became very difficult—and perhaps artificial, even then—to assign priorities to the various facets of the *Weltanschauung*. Even a single man, let alone a group, emphasized different themes at various times. Yet the open-door outlook was based on an economic definition of the world, and this explanation of reality was persistently stressed by America's corporate leadership as it developed its policy toward the Soviet Union and other nations. It was not the possession of the atomic bomb which prompted American leaders to get tough with Russia but rather their open-door outlook which interpreted the bomb as the final guarantee that they could go further faster down that path to world predominance.

Long before anyone knew that the bomb would work, most American leaders were operating on the basis of three assumptions or ideas which defined the world in terms of a cold war. The first specified Russia as being evil but weak. This attitude, predominant among American leaders from the first days of the Bolshevik Revolution in 1917, was reinforced and deepened by the nonaggression pact signed by Russia with Nazi Germany in 1939. There is little evidence to support the oft-asserted claim that Americans changed their basic attitude toward the Soviet Union during the war. Most of them welcomed Russian help against Germany, and some of them mitigated their antagonisms and suspicions, but several careful studies make it clear that large and crucial segments of the American public remained "dubious about the prospects of building the peace together with Russia." Even before the end of the war in Europe, many Americans were again comparing Stalin with Hitler and stressing the importance of avoiding any repetition of the appeasement of Nazi Germany. Others, like John Foster Dulles, who had sought persistently and until a very late date to reach a broad compromise with Hitler and Japan, changed their approach when it came to dealing with Russia. They made no such efforts to reach an understanding with Stalin. And by the time of the San Francisco Conference on the United Nations, such leaders as Averell Harriman were publicly expressing their view that there was an "irreconcilable difference" between Russia and the Western powers.

At the same time, however, very few—if any—American leaders

thought that Russia would launch a war. Policy-makers were quite aware of the "pitiful" conditions in western Russia, of the nation's staggering losses and its general exhaustion, of its "simply enormous" need for outside help "to repair the devastation of war," and of Stalin's stress on firm economic and political agreements with the United States to provide the basis for that reconstruction. Far from being concerned about a Russian attack, American leaders emphasized the importance of denying any and all Soviet requests or overtures for a revised strategic agreement in the Middle East and stressed the importance of pushing the Russians back to their traditional boarders in eastern Europe. The first overt skirmishes of the cold war concerned American protests, initiated on August 18, 1945, over what had happened in eastern Europe as a consequence of the Red Army's advance and the Stalin-Churchill agreement of October, 1944. Such protests were not prompted by the fear that Russia was about to overwhelm Europe or the world in general, but rather by the traditional outlook of the open door and the specific desire to get the Russians out of eastern Europe.

Another basic attitude held by American leaders defined the United States as the symbol and the agent of positive good as opposed to Soviet evil and assumed that the combination of American strength and Russian weakness made it possible to determine the future of the world in accordance with that judgment. One important Congressional leader, for example, remarked in 1943 that lend-lease provided the United States with a "wonderful opportunity" to bring the United States to "a greater degree of determining authority" in the world. He was quite aware that his view was "shared by some of the members of the President's Cabinet" and that important State Department officials were "fully in accord" with the same outlook. Another key congressman was thinking in terms of the "United States seeking world power as a trustee for civilization." Following the even earlier lead of publisher Henry R. Luce, who had announced in 1941 that it was high noon of the American Century, various business spokesmen began stressing the need to become "missionaries of capitalism and democracy." Shortly thereafter, a leading oil-industry leader asserted that America "must set the pace and assume the responsibility of the majority stockholder in this corporation known as the world." Such remarks were not unique; they merely represented the increasing verbalization of one aspect of America's traditional policy.

The third essential aspect of the open-door outlook, which also made its appearance before the end of the war, was the fear that America's economic system would suffer a serious depression if it did not continue to expand overseas. Stressing the fact that there remained roughly nine million unemployed in 1940, one leading New Deal senator warned in 1943 that the danger of another depression could not be overemphasized. A government economic expert promptly supported this view with his own report that "it unfortunately is a fact that for the majority of the people in the United States the thing we have liked to refer to as the American standard of living is only possible in situations where two people in the family are working."

Impressed by such testimony that the problem of avoiding a depression posed "quite a challenge," American leaders agreed in 1944 on the vital importance of overseas expansion. Labor leader William Green thought that the issue of foreign markets "ought to be dealt with at the peace conference." His conception of world trade was that other nations "ought to be able to purchase here and we ought to be able to produce here what they need." Undersecretary of State Dean Acheson, however, provided the fullest statement of the attitude. In order to assure social stability, he explained, it was essential to maintain and expand the wartime level of employment. "If we do not," he warned, "it seems clear that we are in for a very bad time . . . having the most far-reaching consequences upon our economic and social system."

"We may say," he continued, that "it is a problem of markets. . . . We have got to see that what the country produces is used and is sold under financial arrangements which make its production possible." "You must look to foreign markets," he advised his government colleagues. He admitted (in an aside very similar to a comment made by Brooks Adams in 1900, when he was proposing such expansion) "that under a different system in this country you could use the entire production of the country in the United States." Acheson depreciated such an approach: "That would completely change our

Constitution, our relation to property, human liberty, our very conception of law. And nobody contemplates that. Therefore, you must look to other markets and those markets are abroad."

Acheson's "contention [was] that we cannot have full employment and prosperity in the United States without the foreign markets," and his Congressional audience "agreed on that." Hence the only remaining issue concerned the means to be employed; and again all policy-making branches of the government accepted the need to provide loans to underwrite the necessary sales and the importance of writing the appropriate guarantees of this American approach to prosperity into the peace treaties. Acheson assured the congressmen that he "would not dream" of following any other course.

Arthur Schlesinger, Jr.

ORIGINS OF THE COLD WAR

Arthur Schlesinger, Jr. is one of the most prolific and best-known American historians. In this selection, he challenges the revisionist critique of America's Cold War behavior. Schlesinger devotes little direct attention to Yalta, but his twin emphasis on the American strategy of "universalism" and Soviet expansionist ideology places him close to the "orthodox" defenders of the Yalta Conference. He devotes most of his attention to detailing the diplomatic moves and counter-moves which preceded and succeeded Yalta—thus placing the conference in a context which pre-revisionist historians had not been prodded to do.

The Cold War in its original form was a presumably mortal antagonism, arising in the wake of the Second World War, between two rigidly hostile blocs, one led by the Soviet Union, the other by the United States. For nearly two somber and dangerous decades this antagonism dominated the fears of mankind; it may even, on occasion, have come close to blowing up the planet. In recent years, however, the once implacable struggle has lost its familiar clarity

Reprinted by permission from *Foreign Affairs* (October 1967). Copyright © 1967 by the Council on Foreign Relations, Inc.

of outline. With the passing of old issues and the emergence of new conflicts and contestants, there is a natural tendency, especially on the part of the generation which grew up during the Cold War, to take a fresh look at the causes of the great contention between Russia and America.

Some exercises in reappraisal have merely elaborated the orthodoxies promulgated in Washington or Moscow during the boom years of the Cold War. But others, especially in the United States (there are no signs, alas, of this in the Soviet Union), represent what American historians call "revisionism"—that is, a readiness to challenge official explanations. No one should be surprised by this phenomenon. Every war in American history has been followed in due course by skeptical reassessments of supposedly sacred assumptions. So the War of 1812, fought at the time for the freedom of the seas, was in later years ascribed to the expansionist ambitions of Congressional war hawks; so the Mexican War became a slaveholders' conspiracy. So the Civil War has been pronounced a "needless war," and Lincoln has even been accused of maneuvering the rebel attack on Fort Sumter. So too the Spanish-American War and the First and Second World Wars have, each in its turn, undergone revisionist critiques. It is not to be supposed that the Cold War would remain exempt.

In the case of the Cold War, special factors reinforce the predictable historiographical rhythm. The outburst of polycentrism in the communist empire has made people wonder whether communism was ever so monolithic as official theories of the Cold War supposed. A generation with no vivid memories of Stalinism may see the Russia of the forties in the image of the relatively mild, seedy and irresolute Russia of the sixties. And for this same generation the American course of widening the war in Viet Nam—which even non-revisionists can easily regard as folly—has unquestionably stirred doubts about the wisdom of American foreign policy in the sixties which younger historians may have begun to read back into the forties.

It is useful to remember that, on the whole, past exercises in revisionism have failed to stick. Few historians today believe that the war hawks caused the War of 1812 or the slaveholders the Mexican War, or that the Civil War was needless, or that the House of Morgan brought America into the First World War or that Franklin Roosevelt schemed to produce the attack on Pearl Harbor. But this does not mean that one should deplore the rise of Cold War revisionism.[1] For revisionism is an essential part of the process by which history, through the posing of new problems and the investigation of new possibilities, enlarges its perspectives and enriches its insights.

More than this, in the present context, revisionism expresses a deep, legitimate and tragic apprehension. As the Cold War has begun to lose its purity of definition, as the moral absolutes of the fifties become the moralistic clichés of the sixties, some have begun to ask whether the appalling risks which humanity ran during the Cold War were, after all, necessary and inevitable; whether more restrained and rational policies might not have guided the energies of man from the perils of conflict into the potentialities of collaboration. The fact that such questions are in their nature unanswerable does not mean that it is not right and useful to raise them. Nor does it mean that our sons and daughters are not entitled to an accounting from the generation of Russians and Americans who produced the Cold War.

The orthodox American view, as originally set forth by the American government and as reaffirmed until recently by most American scholars, has been that the Cold War was the brave and essential response of free men to communist aggression. Some have gone back well before the Second World War to lay open the sources of Russian expansionism. Geopoliticians traced the Cold War to imperial Russian strategic ambitions which in the nineteenth century led to the Crimean War, to Russian penetration of the Balkans and the Middle East and to Russian pressure on Britain's "lifeline" to India. Ideologists traced it to the Communist Manifesto of 1848 ("the violent overthrow of the bourgeoisie lays the foundation for the sway of the proletariat"). Thoughtful observers (a phrase meant to exclude those who speak in Dullese about the unlimited evil of godless, atheistic, militant communism) concluded that classical Russian imperialism and Pan-Slavism, compounded after 1917 by Leninist messianism, confronted the West at the end of the Second World War with an inexorable drive for domination.

The revisionist thesis is very different. In its extreme form, it is that, after the death of Franklin Roosevelt and the end of the Second

[1] As this writer somewhat intemperately did in a letter to *The New York Review of Books,* October 20, 1966.

World War, the United States deliberately abandoned the wartime policy of collaboration and, exhilarated by the possession of the atomic bomb, undertook a course of aggression of its own designed to expel all Russian influence from Eastern Europe and to establish democratic-capitalist states on the very border of the Soviet Union. As the revisionists see it, this radically new American policy—or rather this resumption by Truman of the pre-Roosevelt policy of insensate anti-communism—left Moscow no alternative but to take measures in defense of its own borders. The result was the Cold War.

These two views, of course, could not be more starkly contrasting. It is therefore not unreasonable to look again at the half-dozen critical years between June 22, 1941, when Hitler attacked Russia, and July 2, 1947, when the Russians walked out of the Marshall Plan meeting in Paris. Several things should be borne in mind as this re-examination is made. For one thing, we have thought a great deal more in recent years, in part because of writers like Roberta Wohlstetter and T. C. Schelling, about the problems of communication in diplomacy—the signals which one nation, by word or by deed, gives, inadvertently or intentionally, to another. Any honest reappraisal of the origins of the Cold War requires the imaginative leap—which should in any case be as instinctive for the historian as it is prudent for the statesman—into the adversary's viewpoint. We must strive to see how, given Soviet perspectives, the Russians might conceivably have misread our signals, as we must reconsider how intelligently we read theirs.

For another, the historian must not overindulge the man of power in the illusion cherished by those in office that high position carries with it the easy ability to shape history. Violating the statesman's creed, Lincoln once blurted out the truth in his letter of 1864 to A. G. Hodges: "I claim not to have controlled events, but confess plainly that events have controlled me." He was not asserting Tolstoyan fatalism but rather suggesting how greatly events limit the capacity of the statesman to bend history to his will. The physical course of the Second World War—the military operations undertaken, the position of the respective armies at the war's end, the momentum generated by victory and the vacuums created by defeat—all these determined the future as much as the character of individual leaders and the substance of national ideology and purpose.

Nor can the historian forget the conditions under which decisions are made, especially in a time like the Second World War. These were tired, overworked, aging men: in 1945, Churchill was 71 years old, Stalin had governed his country for 17 exacting years, Roosevelt his for 12 years nearly as exacting. During the war, moreover, the importunities of military operations had shoved postwar questions to the margins of their minds. All—even Stalin, behind his screen of ideology—had became addicts of improvisation, relying on authority and virtuosity to conceal the fact that they were constantly surprised by developments. Like Eliza, they leaped from one cake of ice to the next in the effort to reach the other side of the river. None showed great tactical consistency, or cared much about it; all employed a certain ambiguity to preserve their power to decide big issues; and it is hard to know how to interpret anything any one of them said on any specific occasion. This was partly because, like all princes, they designed their expressions to have particular effects on particular audiences; partly because the entirely genuine intellectual difficulty of the questions they faced made a degree of vacillation and mind-changing eminently reasonable. If historians cannot solve their problems in retrospect, who are they to blame Roosevelt, Stalin and Churchill for not having solved them at the time?

Peacemaking after the Second World War was not so much a tapestry as it was a hopelessly raveled and knotted mess of yarn. Yet, for purposes of clarity, it is essential to follow certain threads. One theme indispensable to an understanding of the Cold War is the contrast between two clashing views of world order: the "universalist" view, by which all nations shared a common interest in all the affairs of the world, and the "sphere-of-influence" view, by which each great power would be assured by the other great powers of an acknowledged predominance in its own area of special interest. The universalist view assumed that national security would be guaranteed by an international organization. The sphere-of-interest view assumed that national security would be guaranteed by the balance of power. While in practice these views have by no means been incompatible (indeed, our shaky peace has been based on a combination of the two), in the abstract they involved sharp contradictions. The tradition of American thought in these matters was universalist

—i.e. Wilsonian. Roosevelt had been a member of Wilson's sub-cabinet; in 1920, as candidate for Vice President, he had campaigned for the League of Nations. It is true that, within Roosevelt's infinitely complex mind, Wilsonianism warred with the perception of vital strategic interests he had imbibed from Mahan. Moreover, his temperamental inclination to settle things with fellow princes around the conference table led him to regard the Big Three—or Four—as trustees for the rest of the world. On occasion, as this narrative will show, he was beguiled into flirtation with the sphere-of-influence heresy. But in principle he believed in joint action and remained a Wilsonian. His hope for Yalta, as he told the Congress on his return, was that it would "spell the end of the system of unilateral action, the exclusive alliances, the spheres of influence, the balances of power, and all the other expedients that have been tried for centuries—and have always failed."

Whenever Roosevelt backslid, he had at his side that Wilsonian fundamentalist, Secretary of State Cordell Hull, to recall him to the pure faith. After his visit to Moscow in 1943, Hull characteristically said that, with the Declaration of Four Nations on General Security (in which America, Russia, Britain and China pledged "united action . . . for the organization and maintenance of peace and security"), "there will no longer be need for spheres of influence, for alliances, for balance of power, or any other of the special arrangements through which, in the unhappy past, the nations strove to safeguard their security or to promote their interests."

Remembering the corruption of the Wilsonian vision by the secret treaties of the First World War, Hull was determined to prevent any sphere-of-influence nonsense after the Second World War. He therefore fought all proposals to settle border questions while the war was still on and, excluded as he largely was from wartime diplomacy, poured his not inconsiderable moral energy and frustration into the promulgation of virtuous and spacious general principles.

In adopting the universalist view, Roosevelt and Hull were not indulging personal hobbies. Sumner Welles, Adolf Berle, Averell Harriman, Charles Bohlen—all, if with a variety of nuances, opposed the sphere-of-influence approach. And here the State Department was expressing what seems clearly to have been the predominant mood of the American people, so long mistrustful of European power politics. The Republicans shared the true faith. John Foster Dulles argued that the great threat to peace after the war would lie in the revival of sphere-of-influence thinking. The United States, he said, must not permit Britain and Russia to revert to these bad old ways; it must therefore insist on American participation in all policy decisions for all territories in the world. Dulles wrote pessimistically in January 1945, "The three great powers which at Moscow agreed upon the 'closest cooperation' about European questions have shifted to a practice of separate, regional responsibility."

It is true that critics, and even friends, of the United States sometimes noted a discrepancy between the American passion for universalism when it applied to territory far from American shores and the pre-eminence the United States accorded its own interests nearer home. Churchill, seeking Washington's blessing for a sphere-of-influence initiative in Eastern Europe, could not forbear reminding the Americans, "We follow the lead of the United States in South America"; nor did any universalist of record propose the abolition of the Monroe Doctrine. But a convenient myopia prevented such inconsistencies from qualifying the ardency of the universalist faith.

There seem only to have been three officials in the United States Government who dissented. One was the Secretary of War, Henry L. Stimson, a classical balance-of-power man, who in 1944 opposed the creation of a vacuum in Central Europe by the pastoralization of Germany and in 1945 urged "the settlement of all territorial acquisitions in the shape of defense posts which each of these four powers may deem to be necessary for their own safety" in advance of any effort to establish a peacetime United Nations. Stimson considered the claim of Russia to a preferred position in Eastern Europe as not unreasonable: as he told President Truman, "he thought the Russians perhaps were being more realistic than we were in regard to their own security." Such a position for Russia seemed to him comparable to the preferred American position in Latin America; he even spoke of "our respective orbits." Stimson was therefore skeptical of what he regarded as the prevailing tendency "to hang on to exaggerated views of the Monroe Doctrine and at the same time butt into every question that comes up in Central Europe." Acceptance of spheres of influence seemed to him the way to avoid "a head-on collision."

A second official opponent of universalism was George Kennan, an eloquent advocate from the American Embassy in Moscow of "a prompt and clear recognition of the division of Europe into spheres of influence and of a policy based on the fact of such division." Kennan argued that nothing we could do would possibly alter the course of events in Eastern Europe; that we were deceiving ourselves by supposing that these countries had any future but Russian domination; that we should therefore relinquish Eastern Europe to the Soviet Union and avoid anything which would make things easier for the Russians by giving them economic assistance or by sharing moral responsibility for their actions.

A third voice within the government against universalism was (at least after the war) Henry A. Wallace. As Secretary of Commerce, he stated the sphere-of-influence case with trenchancy in the famous Madison Square Garden speech of September 1946 which led to his dismissal by President Truman:

> *On our part, we should recognize that we have no more business in the political affairs of Eastern Europe than Russia has in the political affairs of Latin America, Western Europe, and the United States. . . . Whether we like it or not, the Russians will try to socialize their sphere of influence just as we try to democratize our sphere of influence. . . . The Russians have no more business stirring up native Communists to political activity in Western Europe, Latin America, and the United States than we have in interfering with the politics of Eastern Europe and Russia.*

Stimson, Kennan and Wallace seem to have been alone in the government, however, in taking these views. They were very much minority voices. Meanwhile universalism, rooted in the American legal and moral tradition, overwhelmingly backed by contemporary opinion, received successive enshrinements in the Atlantic Charter of 1941, in the Declaration of the United Nations in 1942 and in the Moscow Declaration of 1943.

The Kremlin, on the other hand, thought *only* of spheres of interest; above all, the Russians were determined to protect their frontiers, and especially their border to the west, crossed so often and so bloodily in the dark course of their history. These western frontiers lacked natural means of defense—no great oceans, rugged mountains, steaming swamps or impenetrable jungles. The history of Russia had been the history of invasion, the last of which was by now horribly killing up to twenty million of its people. The protocol of Russia therefore meant the enlargement of the area of Russian influence. Kennan himself wrote (in May 1944): "Behind Russia's stubborn expansion lies only the age-old sense of insecurity of a sedentary people reared on an exposed plain in the neighborhood of fierce nomadic peoples," and he called this "urge" a "permanent feature of Russian psychology."

In earlier times the "urge" had produced the tsarist search for buffer states and maritime outlets. In 1939 the Soviet-Nazi pact and its secret protocol had enabled Russia to begin to satisfy in the Baltic states, Karelian Finland and Poland, part of what it conceived as its security requirements in Eastern Europe. But the "urge" persisted, causing the friction between Russia and Germany in 1940 as each jostled for position in the area which separated them. Later it led to Molotov's new demands on Hitler in November 1940—a free hand in Finland, Soviet predominance in Rumania and Bulgaria, bases in the Dardanelles—the demands which convinced Hitler that he had no choice but to attack Russia. Now Stalin hoped to gain from the West what Hitler, a closer neighbor, had not dared yield him.

It is true that, so long as Russian survival appeared to require a second front to relieve the Nazi pressure, Moscow's demand for Eastern Europe was a little muffled. Thus the Soviet government adhered to the Atlantic Charter (though with a significant if obscure reservation about adapting its principles to "the circumstances, needs, and historic peculiarities of particular countries"). Thus it also adhered to the Moscow Declaration of 1943, and Molotov then, with his easy mendacity, even denied that Russia had any desire to divide Europe into spheres of influence. But this was guff, which the Russians were perfectly willing to ladle out if it would keep the Americans, and especially Secretary Hull (who made a strong personal impression at the Moscow conference) happy. "A declaration," as Stalin once observed to Eden, "I regard as algebra, but an agreement as practical arithmetic. I do not wish to decry algebra, but I prefer practical arithmetic."

The more consistent Russian purpose was revealed when Stalin offered the British a straight sphere-of-influence deal at the end of 1941. Britain, he suggested, should recognize the Russian absorption of the Baltic states, part of Finland, eastern Poland and Bessarabia; in return, Russia would support any special British need for bases or security arrangements in Western Europe. There was nothing specifically communist about these ambitions. If Stalin achieved them, he would be fulfilling an age-old dream of the tsars. The British reaction was mixed. "Soviet policy is amoral," as Anthony Eden noted at the time; "United States policy is exaggeratedly moral, at least where non-American interests are concerned." If Roosevelt was a universalist with occasional leanings toward spheres of influence and Stalin was a sphere-of-influence man with occasional gestures toward universalism, Churchill seemed evenly poised between the familiar realism of the balance of power, which he had so long recorded as an historian and manipulated as a statesman, and the hope that there must be some better way of doing things. His 1943 proposal of a world organization divided into regional councils represented an effort to blend universalist and sphere-of-interest conceptions. His initial rejection of Stalin's proposal in December 1941 as "directly contrary to the first, second and third articles of the Atlantic Charter" thus did not spring entirely from a desire to propitiate the United States. On the other hand, he had himself already reinterpreted the Atlantic Charter as applying only to Europe (and thus not to the British Empire), and he was, above all, an empiricist who never believed in sacrificing reality on the altar of doctrine.

So in April 1942 he wrote Roosevelt that "the increasing gravity of the war" had led him to feel that the Charter "ought not to be construed so as to deny Russia the frontiers she occupied when Germany attacked her." Hull, however, remained fiercely hostile to the inclusion of territorial provisions in the Anglo-Russian treaty; the American position, Eden noted, "chilled me with Wilsonian memories." Though Stalin complained that it looked "as if the Atlantic Charter was directed against the U.S.S.R.," it was the Russian season of military adversity in the spring of 1942, and he dropped his demands.

He did not, however, change his intentions. A year later Ambassador Standley could cable Washington from Moscow: "In 1918 Western Europe attempted to set up a *cordon sanitaire* to protect it from the influence of bolshevism. Might not now the Kremlin envisage the formation of a belt of pro-Soviet states to protect it from the influences the West?" It well might; and that purpose became increasingly clear as the war approached its end. Indeed, it derived sustenance from Western policy in the first area of liberation.

The unconditional surrender of Italy in July 1943 created the first major test of the Western devotion to universalism. America and Britain, having won the Italian war, handled the capitulation, keeping Moscow informed at a distance. Stalin complained:

> The United States and Great Britain made agreements but the Soviet Union received information about the results . . . just as a passive third observer. I have to tell you that it is impossible to tolerate the situation any longer. I propose that the [tripartite military-political commission] be established and that Sicily be assigned . . . as its place of residence.

Roosevelt, who had no intention of sharing the control of Italy with the Russians, suavely replied with the suggestion that Stalin send an officer "to General Eisenhower's headquarters in connection with the commission." Unimpressed, Stalin continued to press for a tripartite body; but his Western allies were adamant in keeping the Soviet Union off the Control Commission for Italy, and the Russians in the end had to be satisfied with a seat, along with minor Allied states, on a meaningless Inter-Allied Advisory Council. Their acquiescence in this was doubtless not unconnected with a desire to establish precedents for Eastern Europe.

Teheran in December 1943 marked the high point of three-power collaboration. Still, when Churchill asked about Russian territorial interests, Stalin replied a little ominously, "There is no need to speak at the present time about any Soviet desires, but when the time comes we will speak." In the next weeks, there were increasing indications of a Soviet determination to deal unilaterally with Eastern Europe—so much so that in early February 1944 Hull cabled Harriman in Moscow:

> Matters are rapidly approaching the point where the Soviet Government will have to choose between the development and extension of the foundation of international cooperation as the guiding principle of the postwar world as against the continuance of a unilateral and arbitrary method of dealing with its special problems even though these problems are admittedly of more direct interest to the Soviet Union than to other great powers.

As against this approach, however, Churchill, more tolerant of sphere-of-influence deviations, soon proposed that, with the impending liberation of the Balkans, Russia should run things in Rumania, and Britain in Greece. Hull strongly opposed this suggestion but made the mistake of leaving Washington for a few days; and Roosevelt, momentarily free from his Wilsonian conscience, yielded to Churchill's plea for a three-months' trial. Hull resumed the fight on his return, and Churchill postponed the matter.

The Red Army continued its advance into Eastern Europe. In August the Polish Home Army, urged on by Polish-language broadcasts from Moscow, rose up against the Nazis in Warsaw. For 63 terrible days, the Poles fought valiantly on, while the Red Army halted on the banks of the Vistula a few miles away, and in Moscow Stalin for more than half this time declined to cooperate with the Western effort to drop supplies to the Warsaw Resistance. It appeared a calculated Soviet decision to let the Nazis slaughter the anti-Soviet Polish underground; and, indeed, the result was to destroy any substantial alternative to a Soviet solution in Poland. The agony of Warsaw caused the most deep and genuine moral shock in Britain and America and provoked dark forebodings about Soviet postwar purposes.

Again history enjoins the imaginative leap in order to see things for a moment from Moscow's viewpoint. The Polish question, Churchill would say at Yalta, was for Britain a question of honor. "It is not only a question of honor for Russia," Stalin replied, "but one of life and death. . . . Throughout history Poland had been the corridor for attack on Russia." A top postwar priority for any Russian regime must be to close that corridor. The Home Army was led by anti-communists. It clearly hoped by its action to forestall the Soviet occupation of Warsaw and, in Russian eyes, to prepare the way for an anti-Russian Poland. In addition, the uprising from a strictly operational viewpoint was premature. The Russians, it is evident in retrospect, had real military problems at the Vistula. The Soviet attempt in September to send Polish units from the Red Army across the river to join forces with the Home Army was a disaster. Heavy German shelling thereafter prevented the ferrying of tanks necessary for an assault on the German position. The Red Army itself did not take Warsaw for another three months. Nonetheless, Stalin's indifference to the human tragedy, his effort to blackmail the London Poles during the ordeal, his sanctimonious opposition during five precious weeks to aerial resupply, the invariable coldness of his explanations ("the Soviet command has come to the conclusion that it must dissociate itself from the Warsaw adventure") and the obvious political benefit to the Soviet Union from the destruction of the Home Army—all these had the effect of suddenly dropping the mask of wartime comradeship and displaying to the West the hard face of Soviet policy. In now pursuing what he grimly regarded as the minimal requirements for the postwar security of his country, Stalin was inadvertently showing the irreconcilability of both his means and his ends with the Anglo-American conception of the peace.

Meanwhile Eastern Europe presented the Alliance with still another crisis that same September. Bulgaria, which was not at war with Russia, decided to surrender to the Western Allies while it still could; and the English and Americans at Cairo began to discuss armistice terms with Bulgarian envoys. Moscow, challenged by what it plainly saw as a Western intrusion into its own zone of vital interest, promptly declared war on Bulgaria, took over the surrender negotiations and, invoking the Italian precedent, denied its Western Allies any role in the Bulgarian Control Commission. In a long and thoughtful cable, Ambassador Harriman meditated on the problems of communication with the Soviet Union. "Words," he reflected, "have a different connotation to the Soviets than they have to us. When they speak of insisting on 'friendly governments' in their neighboring countries, they have in mind something quite different from what we would mean." The Russians, he surmised, really believed that Washington accepted "their position that although they would keep us informed they had the right to settle their problems with their western neighbors unilaterally." But the Soviet position was still in flux: "the Soviet Government is not one mind." The problem, as Harriman had earlier told Harry Hopkins, was "to strengthen the hands of those around Stalin who want to play the game along our lines." The way to do this, he now told Hull, was to

be understanding of their sensitivity, meet them much more than half way,
encourage them and support them wherever we can, and yet oppose them

promptly with the greatest of firmness where we see them going wrong. . . . The only way we can eventually come to an understanding with the Soviet Union on the question of non-interference in the internal affairs of other countries is for us to take a definite interest in the solution of the problems of each individual country as they arise.

As against Harriman's sophisticated universalist strategy, however, Churchill, increasingly fearful of the consequences of unrestrained competition in Eastern Europe, decided in early October to carry his sphere-of-influence proposal directly to Moscow. Roosevelt was at first content to have Churchill speak for him too and even prepared a cable to that effect. But Hopkins, a more rigorous universalist, took it upon himself to stop the cable and warn Roosevelt of its possible implications. Eventually Roosevelt sent a message to Harriman in Moscow emphasizing that he expected to "retain complete freedom of action after this conference is over." It was now that Churchill quickly proposed—and Stalin as quickly accepted—the celebrated division of southeastern Europe: ending (after further haggling between Eden and Molotov) with 90 percent Soviet predominance in Rumania, 80 percent in Bulgaria and Hungary, fifty-fifty in Jugoslavia, 90 percent British predominance in Greece.

Churchill in discussing this with Harriman used the phrase "spheres of influence." But he insisted that these were only "immediate wartime arrangements" and received a highly general blessing from Roosevelt. Yet, whatever Churchill intended, there is reason to believe that Stalin construed the percentages as an agreement, not a declaration; as practical arithmetic, not algebra. For Stalin, it should be understood, the sphere-of-influence idea did not mean that he would abandon all efforts to spread communism in some other nation's sphere; it did mean that, if he tried this and the other side cracked down, he could not feel he had serious cause for complaint. As Kennan wrote to Harriman at the end of 1944:

As far as border states are concerned the Soviet government has never ceased to think in terms of spheres of interest. They expect us to support them in whatever action they wish to take in those regions, regardless of whether that action seems to us or to the rest of the world to be right or wrong. . . . I have no doubt that this position is honestly maintained on their part, and that they would be equally prepared to reserve moral judgment on any actions which we might wish to carry out, i.e., in the Caribbean area.

In any case, the matter was already under test a good deal closer to Moscow than the Caribbean. The communist-dominated resistance movement in Greece was in open revolt against the effort of the Papandreou government to disarm and disband the guerrillas (the same Papandreou whom the Greek colonels have recently arrested on the claim that he is a tool of the communists). Churchill now called in British Army units to crush the insurrection. This action produced a storm of criticism in his own country and in the United States; the American Government even publicly dissociated itself from the intervention, thereby emphasizing its detachment from the sphere-of-influence deal. But Stalin, Churchill later claimed, "adhered strictly and faithfully to our agreement of October, and during all the long weeks of fighting the Communists in the streets of Athens not one word of reproach came from *Pravda* or *Izvestia*," though there is no evidence that he tried to call off the Greek communists. Still, when the communist rebellion later broke out again in Greece, Stalin told Kardelj and Djilas of Jugoslavia in 1948, "The uprising in Greece must be stopped, and as quickly as possible."

No one, of course, can know what really was in the minds of the Russian leaders. The Kremlin archives are locked; of the primary actors, only Molotov survives, and he has not yet indicated any desire to collaborate with the Columbia Oral History Project. We do know that Stalin did not wholly surrender to sentimental illusion about his new friends. In June 1944, on the night before the landings in Normandy, he told Djilas that the English "find nothing sweeter than to trick their allies. . . . And Churchill? Churchill is the kind who, if you don't watch him, will slip a kopeck out of your pocket. Yes, a kopeck out of your pocket! . . . Roosevelt is not like that. He dips in his hand only for bigger coins." But whatever his views of his colleagues it is not unreasonable to suppose that Stalin would have been satisfied at the end of the war to secure what Kennan has called "a protective glacis along Russia's western border," and that, in exchange for a free hand in Eastern Europe, he was prepared to give the British and Americans equally free hands in their zones of vital interest, including in nations as close to Russia as Greece (for the British) and, very probably—or at least so the Jugoslavs believe—China (for the United States). In other words, his initial objectives were very probably not world conquest but Russian security.

It is now pertinent to inquire why the United States rejected the idea of stabilizing the world by division into spheres of influence and insisted on an East European strategy. One should warn against rushing to the conclusion that it was all a row between hard-nosed, balance-of-power realists and starry-eyed Wilsonians. Roosevelt, Hopkins, Welles, Harriman, Bohlen, Berle, Dulles and other universalists were tough and serious men. Why then did they rebuff the sphere-of-influence solution?

The first reason is that they regarded this solution as containing within itself the seeds of a third world war. The balance-of-power idea seemed inherently unstable. It had always broken down in the past. It held out to each power the permanent temptation to try to alter the balance in its own favor, and it built this temptation into the international order. It would turn the great powers of 1945 away from the objective of concerting common policies toward competition for postwar advantage. As Hopkins told Molotov at Teheran, "The President feels it essential to world peace that Russia, Great Britain and the United States work out this control question in a manner which will not start each of the three powers arming against the others." "The greatest likelihood of eventual conflict," said the Joint Chiefs of Staff in 1944 (the only conflict which the J.C.S., in its wisdom, could then glimpse "in the foreseeable future" was between Britain and Russia), ". . . would seem to grow out of either nation initiating attempts to build up its strength, by seeking to attach to herself parts of Europe to the disadvantage and possible danger of her potential adversary." The Americans were perfectly ready to acknowledge that Russia was entitled to convincing assurance of her national security—but not this way. "I could sympathize fully with Stalin's desire to protect his western borders from future attack," as Hull put it. "But I felt that this security could best be obtained through a strong postwar peace organization."

Hull's remark suggests the second objection: that the sphere-of-influence approach would, in the words of the State Department in 1945, "militate against the establishment and effective functioning of a broader system of general security in which all countries will have their part." The United Nations, in short, was seen as the alternative to the balance of power. Nor did the universalists see any necessary incompatibility between the Russian desire for "friendly governments" on its frontier and the American desire for self-determination in Eastern Europe. Before Yalta the State Department judged the general mood of Europe as "to the left and strongly in favor of far-reaching economic and social reforms, but not, however, in favor of a left-wing totalitarian regime to achieve these reforms." Governments in Eastern Europe could be sufficiently to the left "to allay Soviet suspicions" but sufficiently representative "of the center and *petit bourgeois* elements" not to seem a prelude to communist dictatorship. The American criteria were therefore that the government "should be dedicated to the preservation of civil liberties" and "should favor social and economic reforms." A string of New Deal states—of Finlands and Czechoslovakias—seemed a reasonable compromise solution.

Third, the universalists feared that the sphere-of-interest approach would be what Hull termed "a haven for the isolationists," who would advocate America's participation in Western Hemisphere affairs on condition that it did not participate in European or Asian affairs. Hull also feared that spheres of interest would lead to "closed trade areas or discriminatory systems" and thus defeat his cherished dream of a low-tariff, freely trading world.

Fourth, the sphere-of-interest solution meant the betrayal of the principles for which the Second World War was being fought—the Atlantic Charter, the Four Freedoms, the Declaration of the United Nations. Poland summed up the problem. Britain, having gone to war to defend the independence of Poland from the Germans, could not easily conclude the war by surrendering the independence of Poland to the Russians. Thus, as Hopkins told Stalin after Roosevelt's death in 1945, Poland had "become the symbol of our ability to work out problems with the Soviet Union." Nor could American liberals in general watch with equanimity while the police state spread into countries which, if they had mostly not been real democracies, had mostly not been tyrannies either. The execution in 1943 of Ehrlich and Alter, the Polish socialist trade union leaders, excited deep concern. "I have particularly in mind," Harriman cabled in 1944, "objection to the institution of secret police who may become involved in the persecution of persons of truly democratic convictions who may not be willing to conform to Soviet methods."

Fifth, the sphere-of-influence solution would create difficult domestic problems in American politics. Roosevelt was aware of the six million or more Polish votes in the 1944 election; even more acutely, he was aware of the broader and deeper attack which would follow if, after going to war to stop the Nazi conquest of Europe, he permitted the war to end with the communist conquest of Eastern Europe. As Archibald MacLeish, then Assistant Secretary of State for Public Affairs, warned in January 1945, "The wave of disillusionment which has distressed us in the last several weeks will be increased if the impression is permitted to get abroad that potentially totalitarian provisional governments are to be set up without adequate safeguards as to the holding of free elections and the realization of the principles of the Atlantic Charter." Roosevelt believed that no administration could survive which did not try everything short of war to save Eastern Europe, and he was the supreme American politician of the century.

Sixth, if the Russians were allowed to overrun Eastern Europe without argument, would that satisfy them? Even Kennan, in a dispatch of May 1944, admitted that the "urge" had dreadful potentialities: "If initially successful, will it know where to stop? Will it not be inexorably carried forward, by its very nature, in a struggle to reach the whole—to attain complete mastery of the shores of the Atlantic and the Pacific?" His own answer was that there were inherent limits to the Russian capacity to expand—"that Russia will not have an easy time in maintaining the power which it has seized over other people in Eastern and Central Europe unless it receives both moral and material assistance from the West." Subsequent developments have vindicated Kennan's argument. By the late forties, Jugoslavia and Albania, the two East European states farthest from the Soviet Union and the two in which communism was imposed from within rather than from without, had declared their independence of Moscow. But, given Russia's success in maintaining centralized control over the international communist movement for a quarter of a century, who in 1944 could have had much confidence in the idea of communist revolts against Moscow?

Most of those involved therefore rejected Kennan's answer and stayed with his question. If the West turned its back on Eastern Europe, the higher probability, in their view, was that the Russians would use their security zone, not just for defensive purposes, but as a springboard from which to mount an attack on Western Europe, now shattered by war, a vacuum of power awaiting its master. "If the policy is accepted that the Soviet Union has a right to penetrate her immediate neighbors for security," Harriman said in 1944, "penetration of the next immediate neighbors becomes at a certain time equally logical." If a row with Russia were inevitable, every consideration of prudence dictated that it should take place in Eastern rather than Western Europe.

Thus idealism and realism joined in opposition to the sphere-of-influence solution. The consequence was a determination to assert an American interest in the postwar destiny of all nations, including those of Eastern Europe. In the message which Roosevelt and Hopkins drafted after Hopkins had stopped Roosevelt's initial cable authorizing Churchill to speak for the United States at the Moscow meeting of October 1944, Roosevelt now said, "There is in this global war literally no question, either military or political, in which the United States is not interested." After Roosevelt's death Hopkins repeated the point to Stalin: "The cardinal basis of President Roosevelt's policy which the American people had fully supported had been the concept that the interests of the U.S. were worldwide and not confined to North and South America and the Pacific Ocean."

For better or worse, this was the American position. It is now necessary to attempt the imaginative leap and consider the impact of this position on the leaders of the Soviet Union who, also for better or for worse, had reached the bitter conclusion that the survival of their country depended on their unchallenged control of the corridors through which enemies had so often invaded their homeland. They could claim to have been keeping their own side of the sphere-of-influence bargain. Of course, they were working to capture the resistance movements of Western Europe; indeed, with the appointment of Oumansky as Ambassador to Mexico they were even beginning to enlarge underground operations in the Western Hemisphere. But, from their viewpoint, if the West permitted this, the more fools they; and, if the West stopped it, it was within their right to do so. In overt political matters the Russians were scrupulously playing the game. They had watched in silence while the British shot down communists in Greece. In Jugoslavia Stalin was urging Tito (as Djilas later revealed) to keep King Peter. They had not only acknowledged

Western pre-eminence in Italy but had recognized the Badoglio regime; the Italian Communists had even voted (against the Socialists and the Liberals) for the renewal of the Lateran Pacts.

They would not regard anti-communist action in a Western zone as a *casus belli;* and they expected reciprocal license to assert their own authority in the East. But the principle of self-determination was carrying the United States into a deeper entanglement in Eastern Europe than the Soviet Union claimed as a right (whatever it was doing underground) in the affairs of Italy, Greece or China. When the Russians now exercised in Eastern Europe the same brutal control they were prepared to have Washington exercise in the American sphere of influence, the American protests, given the paranoia produced alike by Russian history and Leninist ideology, no doubt seemed not only an act of hyprocrisy but a threat to security. To the Russians, a stroll into the neighborhood easily became a plot to burn down the house: when, for example, damaged American planes made emergency landings in Poland and Hungary Moscow took this as attempts to organize the local resistance. It is not unusual to suspect one's adversary of doing what one is already doing oneself. At the same time, the cruelty with which the Russians executed their idea of spheres of influence—in a sense, perhaps, an unwitting cruelty, since Stalin treated the East Europeans no worse than he had treated the Russians in the thirties—discouraged the West from accepting the equation (for example, Italy = Rumania) which seemed so self-evident to the Kremlin.

So Moscow very probably, and not unnaturally, perceived the emphasis on self-determination as a systematic and deliberate pressure on Russia's western frontiers. Moreover, the restoration of capitalism to countries freed at frightful cost by the Red Army no doubt struck the Russians as the betrayal of the principles for which *they* were fighting. "That they, the victors," Isaac Deutscher has suggested, "should now preserve an order from which they had experienced nothing but hostility, and could expect nothing but hostility . . . would have been the most miserable anti-climax to their great 'war of liberation.' " By 1944 Poland was the critical issue: Harriman later said that "under instructions from President Roosevelt, I talked about Poland with Stalin more frequently than any other subject." While the West saw the point of Stalin's demand for a "friendly government" in Warsaw, the American insistence on the sovereign virtues of free elections (ironically in the spirit of the 1917 Bolshevik decree of peace, which affirmed "the right" of a nation "to decide the forms of its state existence by a free vote, taken after the complete evacuation of the incorporating or, generally, of the stronger nation") created an insoluble problem in those countries, like Poland (and Rumania) where free elections would almost certainly produce anti-Soviet governments.

The Russians thus may well have estimated the Western pressures as calculated to encourage their enemies in Eastern Europe and to defeat their own minimum objective of a protective glacis. Everything still hung, however, on the course of military operations. The wartime collaboration had been created by one thing, and one thing alone: the threat of Nazi victory. So long as this threat was real, so was the collaboration. In late December 1944, von Rundstedt launched his counter-offensive in the Ardennes. A few weeks later, when Roosevelt, Churchill and Stalin gathered in the Crimea, it was in the shadow of this last considerable explosion of German power. The meeting at Yalta was still dominated by the mood of war.

Yalta remains something of an historical perplexity—less, from the perspective of 1967, because of a mythical American deference to the sphere-of-influence thesis than because of the documentable Russian deference to the universalist thesis. Why should Stalin in 1945 have accepted the Declaration on Liberated Europe and an agreement on Poland pledging that "the three governments will jointly" act to assure "free elections of governments responsive to the will of the people"? There are several probable answers: that the war was not over and the Russians still wanted the Americans to intensify their military effort in the West; that one clause in the Declaration premised action on "the opinion of the three governments" and thus implied a Soviet veto, though the Polish agreement was more definite; most of all that the universalist algebra of the Declaration was plainly in Stalin's mind to be construed in terms of the practical arithmetic of his sphere-of-influence agreement with Churchill the previous October. Stalin's assurance to Churchill at Yalta that a proposed Russian amendment to the Declaration would not apply to Greece makes it clear that Roosevelt's pieties did not, in Stalin's mind, nullify Churchill's percentages. He could well have been strengthened in this supposition by the fact that *after* Yalta, Churchill himself repeatedly reasserted the terms of the October agreement as if he regarded it, despite Yalta, as controlling.

Harriman still had the feeling before Yalta that the Kremlin had "two approaches to their postwar policies" and that Stalin himself was "of two minds." One approach emphasized the internal reconstruction and development of Russia; the other its external expansion. But in the meantime the fact which dominated all political decisions—that is, the war against Germany—was moving into its final phase. In the weeks after Yalta, the military situation changed with great rapidity. As the Nazi threat declined, so too did the need for cooperation. The Soviet Union, feeling itself menaced by the American idea of self-determination and the borderlands diplomacy to which it was leading, skeptical whether the United Nations would protect its frontiers as reliably as its own domination in Eastern Europe, began to fulfill its security requirements unilaterally.

In March Stalin expressed his evaluation of the United Nations by rejecting Roosevelt's plea that Molotov come to the San Francisco conference, if only for the opening sessions. In the next weeks the Russians emphatically and crudely worked their will in Eastern Europe, above all in the test country of Poland. They were ignoring the Declaration on Liberated Europe, ignoring the Atlantic Charter, self-determination, human freedom and everything else the Americans considered essential for a stable peace. "We must clearly recognize," Harriman wired Washington a few days before Roosevelt's death, "that the Soviet program is the establishment of totalitarianism, ending personal liberty and democracy as we know and respect it."

At the same time, the Russians also began to mobilize communist resources in the United States itself to block American universalism. In April 1945 Jacques Duclos, who had been the Comintern official responsible for the Western communist parties, launched in *Cahiers du Communisme* an uncompromising attack on the policy of the American Communist Party. Duclos sharply condemned the revisionism of Earl Browder, the American communist leader, as "expressed in the concept of a long-term class peace in the United States, of the possibility of the suppression of the class struggle in the postwar period and of establishment of harmony between labor and capital." Browder was specifically rebuked for favoring the "self-determination" of Europe "west of the Soviet Union" on a bourgeois-democratic basis. The excommunication of Browderism was plainly the Politburo's considered reaction to the impending defeat of Germany; it was a signal to the communist parties of the West that they should recover their identity; it was Moscow's alert to communists everywhere that they should prepare for new policies in the postwar world.

The Duclos piece obviously could not have been planned and written much later than the Yalta conference—that is, well before a number of events which revisionists now cite in order to demonstrate American responsibility for the Cold War: before Allen Dulles, for example, began to negotiate the surrender of the German armies in Italy (the episode which provoked Stalin to charge Roosevelt with seeking a separate peace and provoked Roosevelt to denounce the "vile misrepresentations" of Stalin's informants); well before Roosevelt died; many months before the testing of the atomic bomb; even more months before Truman ordered that the bomb be dropped on Japan. William Z. Foster, who soon replaced Browder as the leader of the American Communist Party and embodied the new Moscow line, later boasted of having said in January 1944, "A post-war Roosevelt administration would continue to be, as it is now, an imperialist government." With ancient suspicions revived by the American insistence on universalism, this was no doubt the conclusion which the Russians were reaching at the same time. The Soviet canonization of Roosevelt (like their present-day canonization of Kennedy) took place after the American President's death.

The atmosphere of mutual suspicion was beginning to rise. In January 1945 Molotov formally proposed that the United States grant Russia a $6 billion credit for postwar reconstruction. With characteristic tact he explained that he was doing this as a favor to save America from a postwar depression. The proposal seems to have been diffidently made and diffidently received. Roosevelt requested that the matter "not be pressed further" on the American side until he had a chance to talk with Stalin; but the Russians did not follow it up either at Yalta in February (save for a single glancing reference) or during the Stalin-Hopkins talks in May or at Potsdam. Finally the proposal was renewed in the very different political atmosphere of

August. This time Washington inexplicably mislaid the request during the transfer of the records of the Foreign Economic Administration to the State Department. It did not turn up again until March 1946. Of course this was impossible for the Russians to believe; it is hard enough even for those acquainted with the capacity of the American government for incompetence to believe; and it only strengthened Soviet suspicions of American purposes.

The American credit was one conceivable form of Western contribution to Russian reconstruction. Another was lend-lease, and the possibility of reconstruction aid under the lend-lease protocol had already been discussed in 1944. But in May 1945 Russia, like Britain, suffered from Truman's abrupt termination of lend-lease shipments— "unfortunate and even brutal," Stalin told Hopkins, adding that, if it was "designed as pressure on the Russians in order to soften them up, then it was a fundamental mistake." A third form was German reparations. Here Stalin in demanding $10 billion in reparations for the Soviet Union made his strongest fight at Yalta. Roosevelt, while agreeing essentially with Churchill's opposition, tried to postpone the matter by accepting the Soviet figure as a "basis for discussion"— a formula which led to future misunderstanding. In short, the Russian hope for major Western assistance in postwar reconstruction foundered on three events which the Kremlin could well have interpreted respectively as deliberate sabotage (the loan request), blackmail (lend-lease cancellation) and pro-Germanism (reparations).

Actually the American attempt to settle the fourth lend-lease protocol was generous and the Russians for their own reasons declined to come to an agreement. It is not clear, though, that satisfying Moscow on any of these financial scores would have made much essential difference. It might have persuaded some doves in the Kremlin that the U.S. government was genuinely friendly; it might have persuaded some hawks that the American anxiety for Soviet friendship was such that Moscow could do as it wished without inviting challenge from the United States. It would, in short, merely have reinforced both sides of the Kremlin debate; it would hardly have reversed deeper tendencies toward the deterioration of political relationships. Economic deals were surely subordinate to the quality of mutual political confidence; and here, in the months after Yalta, the decay was steady.

The Cold War had now begun. It was the product not of a decision but of a dilemma. Each side felt compelled to adopt policies which the other could not but regard as a threat to the principles of the peace. Each then felt compelled to undertake defensive measures. Thus the Russians saw no choice but to consolidate their security in Eastern Europe. The Americans, regarding Eastern Europe as the first step toward Western Europe, responded by asserting their interest in the zone the Russians deemed vital to their security. The Russians concluded that the West was resuming its old course of capitalist encirclement; that it was purposefully laying the foundation for anti-Soviet regimes in the area defined by the blood of centuries as crucial to Russian survival. Each side believed with passion that future international stability depended on the success of its own conception of world order. Each side, in pursuing its own clearly indicated and deeply cherished principles, was only confirming the fear of the other that it was bent on aggression.

Very soon the process began to acquire a cumulative momentum. The impending collapse of Germany thus provoked new troubles: the Russians, for example, sincerely feared that the West was planning a separate surrender of the German armies in Italy in a way which would release troops for Hitler's eastern front, as they subsequently feared that the Nazis might succeed in surrendering Berlin to the West. This was the context in which the atomic bomb now appeared. Though the revisionist argument that Truman dropped the bomb less to defeat Japan than to intimidate Russia is not convincing, this thought unquestionably appealed to some in Washington as at least an advantageous side-effect of Hiroshima.

So the machinery of suspicion and counter-suspicion, action and counter-action, was set in motion. But, given relations among traditional national states, there was still no reason, even with all the postwar jostling, why this should not have remained a manageable situation. What made it unmanageable, what caused the rapid escalation of the Cold War and in another two years completed the division of Europe, was a set of considerations which this account has thus far excluded.

Up to this point, the discussion has considered the schism within the wartime coalition as if it were entirely the result of disagreements

among national states. Assuming this framework, there was unquestionably a failure of communication between America and Russia,
a misperception of signals and, as time went on, a mounting tendency
to ascribe ominous motives to the other side. It seems hard, for
example, to deny that American postwar policy created genuine difficulties for the Russians and even assumed a threatening aspect for
them. All this the revisionists have rightly and usefully emphasized.

But the great omission of the revisionists—and also the fundamental explanation of the speed with which the Cold War escalated
—lies precisely in the fact that the Soviet Union was *not* a traditional
national state. This is where the "mirror image," invoked by some
psychologists, falls down. For the Soviet Union was a phenomenon
very different from America or Britain: it was a totalitarian state,
endowed with an all-explanatory, all-consuming ideology, committed
to the infallibility of government and party, still in a somewhat messianic mood, equating dissent with treason, and ruled by a dictator
who, for all his quite extraordinary abilities, had his paranoid
moments.

Marxism-Leninism gave the Russian leaders a view of the world
according to which all societies were inexorably destined to proceed
along appointed roads by appointed stages until they achieved the
classless nirvana. Moreover, given the resistance of the capitalists
to this development, the existence of any non-communist state was
by definition a threat to the Soviet Union. "As long as capitalism and
socialism exist," Lenin wrote, "we cannot live in peace: in the end,
one or the other will triumph—a funeral dirge will be sung either
over the Soviet Republic or over world capitalism."

Stalin and his associates, whatever Roosevelt or Truman did or
failed to do, were bound to regard the United States as the enemy,
not because of this deed or that, but because of the primordial fact
that America was the leading capitalist power and thus, by Leninist
syllogism, unappeasably hostile, driven by the logic of its system to
oppose, encircle and destroy Soviet Russia. Nothing the United
States could have done in 1944–45 would have abolished this mistrust, required and sanctified as it was by Marxist gospel—nothing
short of the conversion of the United States into a Stalinist despotism; and even this would not have sufficed, as the experience of
Jugoslavia and China soon showed, unless it were accompanied by

total subservience to Moscow. So long as the United States remained a capitalist democracy, no American policy, given Moscow's theology, could hope to win basic Soviet confidence, and every American action was poisoned from the source. So long as the Soviet Union remained a messianic state, ideology compelled a steady expansion of communist power.

It is easy, of course, to exaggerate the capacity of ideology to control events. The tension of acting according to revolutionary abstractions is too much for most nations to sustain over a long period: that is why Mao Tse-tung has launched his Cultural Revolution, hoping thereby to create a permanent revolutionary mood and save Chinese communism from the degeneration which, in his view, has overtaken Russian communism. Still, as any revolution grows older, normal human and social motives will increasingly reassert themselves. In due course, we can be sure, Leninism will be about as effective in governing the daily lives of Russians as Christianity is in governing the daily lives of Americans. Like the Ten Commandments and the Sermon on the Mount, the Leninist verities will increasingly become platitudes for ritual observance, not guides to secular decision. There can be no worse fallacy (even if respectable people practiced it diligently for a season in the United States) than that of drawing from a nation's ideology permanent conclusions about its behavior.

A temporary recession of ideology was already taking place during the Second World War when Stalin, to rally his people against the invader, had to replace the appeal of Marxism by that of nationalism. ("We are under no illusions that they are fighting for us," Stalin once said to Harriman. "They are fighting for Mother Russia.") But this was still taking place within the strictest limitations. The Soviet Union remained as much a police state as ever; the regime was as infallible as ever; foreigners and their ideas were as suspect as ever. "Never, except possibly during my later experience as ambassador in Moscow," Kennan has written, "did the insistence of the Soviet authorities on isolation of the diplomatic corps weigh more heavily on me . . . than in these first weeks following my return to Russia in the final months of the war. . . . [We were] treated as though we were the bearers of some species of the plague"—which, of course, from the Soviet viewpoint, they were: the plague of skepticism.

Paradoxically, of the forces capable of bringing about a modification of ideology, the most practical and effective was the Soviet dictatorship itself. If Stalin was an ideologist, he was also a pragmatist. If he saw everything through the lenses of Marxism-Leninism, he also, as the infallible expositor of the faith, could reinterpret Marxism-Leninism to justify anything he wanted to do at any given moment. No doubt Roosevelt's ignorance of Marxism-Leninism was inexcusable and led to grievous miscalculations. But Roosevelt's efforts to work on and through Stalin were not so hopelessly naive as it used to be fashionable to think. With the extraordinary instinct of a great political leader, Roosevelt intuitively understood that Stalin was the *only* lever available to the West against the Leninist ideology and the Soviet system. If Stalin could be reached, then alone was there a chance of getting the Russians to act contrary to the prescriptions of their faith. The best evidence is that Roosevelt retained a certain capacity to influence Stalin to the end; the nominal Soviet acquiescence in American universalism as late as Yalta was perhaps an indication of that. It is in this way that the death of Roosevelt was crucial—not in the vulgar sense that his policy was then reversed by his successor, which did not happen, but in the sense that no other American could hope to have the restraining impact on Stalin which Roosevelt might for a while have had.

Stalin alone could have made any difference. Yet Stalin, in spite of the impression of sobriety and realism he made on Westerners who saw him during the Second World War, was plainly a man of deep and morbid obsessions and compulsions. When he was still a young man, Lenin had criticized his rude and arbitrary ways. A reasonably authoritative observer (N. S. Khrushchev) later commented, "These negative characteristics of his developed steadily and during the last years acquired an absolutely insufferable character." His paranoia, probably set off by the suicide of his wife in 1932, led to the terrible purges of the mid-thirties and the wanton murder of thousands of his Bolshevik comrades. "Everywhere and in everything," Khrushchev says of this period, "he saw 'enemies,' 'double-dealers' and 'spies.' " The crisis of war evidently steadied him in some way, though Khrushchev speaks of his "nervousness and hysteria . . . even after the war began." The madness, so rigidly controlled for a time, burst out with new and shocking intensity in the postwar years. "After the war," Khrushchev testifies,

> the situation became even more complicated. Stalin became even more capricious, irritable and brutal; in particular, his suspicion grew. His persecution mania reached unbelievable dimensions. . . . He decided everything, without any consideration for anyone or anything.
> Stalin's wilfulness showed itself . . . also in the international relations of the Soviet Union. . . . He had completely lost a sense of reality; he demonstrated his suspicion and haughtiness not only in relation to individuals in the USSR, but in relation to whole parties and nations.

A revisionist fallacy has been to treat Stalin as just another Realpolitik statesman, as Second World War revisionists see Hitler as just another Stresemann or Bismarck. But the record makes it clear that in the end nothing could satisfy Stalin's paranoia. His own associates failed. Why does anyone suppose that any conceivable American policy would have succeeded?

An analysis of the origins of the Cold War which leaves out these factors—the intransigence of Leninist ideology, the sinister dynamics of a totalitarian society and the madness of Stalin—is obviously incomplete. It was these factors which made it hard for the West to accept the thesis that Russia was moved only by a desire to protect its security and would be satisfied by the control of Eastern Europe; it was these factors which charged the debate between universalism and spheres of influence with apocalyptic potentiality.

Leninism and totalitarianism created a structure of thought and behavior which made postwar collaboration between Russia and America—in any normal sense of civilized intercourse between national states—inherently impossible. The Soviet dictatorship of 1945 simply could not have survived such a collaboration. Indeed, nearly a quarter-century later, the Soviet regime, though it has meanwhile moved a good distance, could still hardly survive it without risking the release inside Russia of energies profoundly opposed to communist despotism. As for Stalin, he may have represented the only force in 1945 capable of overcoming Stalinism, but the very traits which enabled him to win absolute power expressed terrifying instabilities of mind and temperament and hardly offered a solid foundation for a peaceful world.

The difference between America and Russia in 1945 was that some Americans fundamentally believed that, over a long run, a modus vivendi with Russia was possible; while the Russians, so far as one can tell, believed in no more than a short-run modus vivendi with the United States.

Harriman and Kennan, this narrative has made clear, took the lead in warning Washington about the difficulties of short-run dealings with the Soviet Union. But both argued that, if the United States developed a rational policy and stuck to it, there would be, after long and rough passages, the prospect of eventual clearing. "I am, as you know," Harriman cabled Washington in early April, "a most earnest advocate of the closest possible understanding with the Soviet Union so that what I am saying relates only to how best to attain such understanding." Kennan has similarly made it clear that the function of his containment policy was "to tide us over a difficult time and bring us to the point where we could discuss effectively with the Russians the dangers and drawbacks this status quo involved, and to arrange with them for its peaceful replacement by a a better and sounder one." The subsequent careers of both men attest to the honesty of these statements.

There is no corresponding evidence on the Russian side that anyone seriously sought a modus vivendi in these terms. Stalin's choice was whether his long-term ideological and national interests would be better served by a short-run truce with the West or by an immediate resumption of pressure. In October 1945 Stalin indicated to Harriman at Sochi that he planned to adopt the second course— that the Soviet Union was going isolationist. No doubt the succession of problems with the United States contributed to this decision, but the basic causes most probably lay elsewhere: in the developing situations in Eastern Europe, in Western Europe and in the United States.

In Eastern Europe, Stalin was still for a moment experimenting with techniques of control. But he must by now have begun to conclude that he had underestimated the hostility of the people to Russian dominion. The Hungarian elections in November would finally convince him that the Yalta formula was a road to anti-Soviet governments. At the same time, he was feeling more strongly than ever a sense of his opportunities in Western Europe. The other half of the Continent lay unexpectedly before him, politically demoralized, economically prostrate, militarily defenseless. The hunting would be better and safer than he had anticipated. As for the United States, the alacrity of postwar demobilization must have recalled Roosevelt's offhand remark at Yalta that "two years would be the limit" for keeping American troops in Europe. And, despite Dr. Eugene Varga's doubts about the imminence of American economic breakdown, Marxist theology assured Stalin that the United States was heading into a bitter postwar depression and would be consumed with its own problems. If the condition of Eastern Europe made unilateral action seem essential in the interests of Russian security, the condition of Western Europe and the United States offered new temptations for communist expansion. The Cold War was now in full swing.

It still had its year of modulations and accommodations. Secretary Byrnes conducted his long and fruitless campaign to persuade the Russians that America only sought governments in Eastern Europe "both friendly to the Soviet Union and representative of all the democratic elements of the country." Crises were surmounted in Trieste and Iran. Secretary Marshall evidently did not give up hope of a modus vivendi until the Moscow conference of foreign secretaries of March 1947. Even then, the Soviet Union was invited to participate in the Marshall Plan.

The point of no return came on July 2, 1947, when Molotov, after bringing 89 technical specialists with him to Paris and evincing initial interest in the project for European reconstruction, received the hot flash from the Kremlin, denounced the whole idea and walked out of the conference. For the next fifteen years the Cold War raged unabated, passing out of historical ambiguity into the realm of good versus evil and breeding on both sides simplifications, stereotypes and self-serving absolutes, often couched in interchangeable phrases. Under the pressure even America, for a deplorable decade, forsook its pragmatic and pluralist traditions, posed as God's appointed messenger to ignorant and sinful man and followed the Soviet example in looking to a world remade in its own image.

In retrospect, if it is impossible to see the Cold War as a case of

American aggression and Russian response, it is also hard to see it as a pure case of Russian aggression and American response. "In what is truly tragic," wrote Hegel, "there must be valid moral powers on both the sides which come into collision. . . . Both suffer loss and yet both are mutually justified." In this sense, the Cold War had its tragic elements. The question remains whether it was an instance of Greek tragedy—as Auden has called it, "the tragedy of necessity," where the feeling aroused in the spectator is "What a pity it had to be this way"—or of Christian tragedy, "the tragedy of possibility," where the feeling aroused is "What a pity is was this way when it might have been otherwise."

Once something has happened, the historian is tempted to assume that it had to happen; but this may often be a highly unphilosophical assumption. The Cold War could have been avoided only if the Soviet Union had not been possessed by convictions both of the infallibility of the communist word and of the inevitability of a communist world. These convictions transformed an impasse between national states into a religious war, a tragedy of possibility into one of necessity. One might wish that America had preserved the poise and proportion of the first years of the Cold War and had not in time succumbed to its own forms of self-righteousness. But the most rational of American policies could hardly have averted the Cold War. Only today, as Russia begins to recede from its messianic mission and to accept, in practice if not yet in principle, the permanence of the world of diversity, only now can the hope flicker that this long, dreary, costly contest may at last be taking on forms less dramatic, less obsessive and less dangerous to the future of mankind.

Christopher Lasch

THE COLD WAR, REVISITED
AND RE-VISIONED

Christopher Lasch is an American historian and a partisan of the revisionist position. In this summary article on the revisionist controversy, he draws attention to one of revisionism's important proponents, Gar Alperovitz. After summarizing the various positions on the origins of the Cold War, citing George Kennan's work as the most influential orthodox interpretation, Lasch pushes the logic of revisionism to raise questions of American Foreign policy that have taken on fresh meaning in the context of the Vietnam War.

More than a year has passed since Arthur Schlesinger, Jr. announced that the time had come "to blow the whistle before the current outburst of revisionism regarding the origins of the cold war goes much further." Yet the outburst of revisionism shows no signs of subsiding. On the contrary, a growing number of historians and political critics, judging from such recent books as Ronald Steel's *Pax Americana* and Carl Oglesby's and Richard Shaull's *Containment and Change,* are challenging the view, once so widely accepted, that the cold war was an American response to Soviet expansionism, a distasteful burden reluctantly shouldered in the face of a ruthless enemy bent on our destruction, and that Russia, not the United States, must therefore bear the blame for shattering the world's hope that two world wars in the twentieth century would finally give way to an era of peace.

"Revisionist" historians are arguing instead that the United States did as much as the Soviet Union to bring about the collapse of the wartime coalition. Without attempting to shift the blame exclusively to the United States, they are trying to show, as Gar Alperovitz puts it, that "the cold war cannot be understood simply as an American response to a Soviet challenge, but rather as the insidious interaction of mutual suspicions, blame for which must be shared by all."

Not only have historians continued to re-examine the immediate origins of the cold war—in spite of attempts to "blow the whistle" on

From *The New York Times Magazine*, January 14, 1968. © 1968 by The New York Times Company. Reprinted by permission.

their efforts—but the scope of revisionism has been steadily widening. Some scholars are beginning to argue that the whole course of American diplomacy since 1898 shows that the United States has become a counterrevolutionary power committed to the defense of a global status quo. . . .

Even Schlesinger has now admitted, in a recent article in *Foreign Affairs,* that he was "somewhat intemperate," a year ago, in deploring the rise of cold-war revisionism. Even though revisionist interpretations of earlier wars "have failed to stick," he says, "revisionism is an essential part of the process by which history . . . enlarges its perspectives and enriches its insights." Since he goes on to argue that "postwar collaboration between Russia and America [was] . . . inherently impossible" and that "the most rational of American policies could hardly have averted the cold war," it is not clear what Schlesinger thinks revisionism has done to enlarge our perspective and enrich our insights; but it is good to know, nevertheless, that revisionists may now presumably continue their work (inconsequential as it may eventually prove to be) without fear of being whistled to a stop by the referee.

The orthodox interpretation of the cold war, as it has come to be regarded, grew up in the late forties and early fifties—years of acute international tension, during which the rivalry between the United States and the Soviet Union repeatedly threatened to erupt in a renewal of global war. Soviet-American relations had deteriorated with alarming speed following the defeat of Hitler. At Yalta, in February, 1945, Winston Church had expressed the hope that world peace was nearer the grasp of the assembled statesmen of the great powers "than at any time in history." It would be "a great tragedy," he said, "if they, through inertia or carelessness, let it slip from their grasp. History would never forgive them if they did."

Yet the Yalta agreements themselves, which seemed at the time to lay the basis of postwar cooperation, shortly provided the focus of bitter dissension, in which each side accused the other of having broken its solemn promises. In Western eyes, Yalta meant free elections and parliamentary democracies in Eastern Europe, while the Russians construed the agreements as recognition of their demand for governments friendly to the Soviet Union.

The resulting dispute led to mutual mistrust and to a hardening of positions on both sides. By the spring of 1946 Churchill himself, declaring that "an iron curtain has descended" across Europe, admitted, in effect, that the "tragedy" he had feared had come to pass. Europe split into hostile fragments, the eastern half dominated by the Soviet Union, the western part sheltering nervously under the protection of American arms. NATO, founded in 1949 and countered by the Russian-sponsored Warsaw Pact, merely ratified the existing division of Europe.

From 1946 on, every threat to the stability of this uneasy balance produced an immediate political crisis—Greece in 1947, Czechoslovakia and the Berlin blockade in 1948—each of which, added to existing tensions, deepened hostility on both sides and increased the chance of war. When Bernard Baruch announced in April, 1947, that "we are in the midst of a cold war," no one felt inclined to contradict him. The phrase stuck, as an accurate description of postwar political realities.

Many Americans concluded, moreover, that the United States, was losing the cold war. Two events in particular contributed to this sense of alarm—the collapse of Nationalist China in 1949, followed by Chiang Kai-shek's flight to Taiwan, and the explosion of an atomic bomb by the Russians in the same year. These events led to the charge that American leaders had deliberately or unwittingly betrayed the country's interests. The Alger Hiss case was taken by some people as proof that the Roosevelt Administration had been riddled by subversion.

Looking back to the wartime alliance with the Soviet Union, the American Right began to argue that Roosevelt, by trusting the Russians, had sold out the cause of freedom. Thus Nixon and McCarthy, aided by historians like Stefan J. Possony, C. C. Tansill and others, accused Roosevelt of handing Eastern Europe to the Russians and of giving them a preponderant interest in China which later enabled the Communists to absorb the entire country.

The liberal interpretation of the cold war—what I have called the orthodox interpretation—developed partly as a response to these charges. In liberal eyes, the right-wingers made the crucial mistake of assuming that American actions had been decisive in shaping the postwar world. Attempting to rebut this devil theory of postwar politics, liberals relied heavily on the argument that the shape of postwar politics had already been dictated by the war itself, in which the Western democracies had been obliged to call on Soviet help in defeating Hitler. These events, they maintained, had left the Soviet Union militarily dominant in Eastern Europe and generally occupying a position of much greater power, relative to the West, than the position she had enjoyed before the war.

In the face of these facts, the United States had very little leeway to influence events in what were destined to become Soviet spheres of influence, particularly since Stalin was apparently determined to expand even if it meant ruthlessly breaking his agreements—and after all it was Stalin, the liberals emphasized, and not Roosevelt or Truman, who broke the Yalta agreement on Poland, thereby precipitating the cold war.

These were the arguments presented with enormous charm, wit, logic and power in George F. Kennan's *American Diplomacy* (1951), which more than any other book set the tone of cold-war historiography. For innumerable historians, but especially for those who were beginning their studies in the fifties, Kennan served as the model of what a scholar should be—committed yet detached—and it was through the perspective of his works that a whole generation of scholars came to see not only the origins of the cold war, but the entire history of twentieth-century diplomacy.

It is important to recognize that Kennan's was by no means an uncritical perspective—indeed, for those unacquainted with Marxism it seemed the only critical perspective that was available in the fifties. While Kennan insisted that the Russians were primarily to blame for the cold war, he seldom missed an opportunity to criticize the excessive moralism, the messianic vision of a world made safe for democracy, which he argued ran "like a red skein" through American diplomacy. . . .

* * *

Like Kennan, . . . [liberal] writers saw containment as a necessary response to Soviet expansionism and to the deterioration of Western power in Eastern Europe. At the same time, they were critical, in varying degrees, of the legalistic-moralistic tradition which kept American statesmen from looking at foreign relations in the light of balance-of-power considerations.

Some of them tended to play off Churchillian realism against the idealism of Roosevelt and Cordell Hull, arguing, for instance, that the Americans should have accepted the bargain made between Churchill and Stalin in 1944, whereby Greece was assigned to the Western sphere of influence and Rumania, Bulgaria and Hungary to the Soviet sphere, with both liberal and Communist parties sharing in the control of Yugoslavia.

These criticisms of American policy, however, did not challenge the basic premise of American policy, that the Soviet Union was a ruthlessly aggressive power bent on world domination. They assumed, moreover, that the Russians were in a position to realize large parts of this program, and that only counter-pressure exerted by the West, in the form of containment and the Marshall Plan, prevented the Communists from absorbing all of Europe and much of the rest of the world as well.

It is their criticism of these assumptions that defines the revisionist historians and distinguishes them from the "realists." What impresses revisionists is not Russia's strength but her military weakness following the devastating war with Hitler, in which the Russians suffered much heavier losses than any other member of the alliance. . . .

. . . The historian who has done most to promote a revisionist interpretation of the cold war, and of American diplomacy in general, is William Appleman Williams of the University of Wisconsin . . . William's works, particularly *The Tragedy of American Diplomacy* (1959), not only challenge the orthodox interpretation of the cold war, they set against it an elaborate counterinterpretation which, if valid, forces one to see American policy in the early years of the cold war as part of a larger pattern of American globalism reaching as far back as 1898.

According to Williams, American diplomacy has consistently adhered to the policy of the "open door"—that is, to a policy of commercial, political and cultural expansion which seeks to extend American influence into every corner of the earth. This policy was consciously and deliberately embarked upon, Williams argues, because American statesmen believe that American capitalism needed ever-expanding foreign markets in order to survive, the closing of the frontier having put an end to its expansion on the continent of North America. Throughout the twentieth century, the makers of American foreign policy, he says, have interpreted the national interest in this light.

The cold war, in William's view, therefore has to be seen as the latest phase of a continuing effort to make the world safe for democracy—read liberal capitalism, American style—in which the United States finds itself increasingly cast as the leader of a world-wide counter-revolution.

After World War II, Williams maintains, the United States had "a vast proportion of actual as well as potential power vis-à-vis the Soviet Union." The United States "cannot with any real warrant or meaning claim that it has been *forced* to follow a certain approach or policy." (Compare this with a statement by Arthur Schlesinger: "The cold war could have been avoided only if the Soviet Union had not been possessed by convictions both of the infallibility of the Communist word and of the inevitability of a Communist world.")

The Russians, by contrast, Williams writes, "viewed their position in the 1940s as one of weakness, not offensive strength." One measure of Stalin's sense of weakness, as he faced the enormous task of rebuilding the shattered Soviet economy, was his eagerness to get a large loan from the United States. Failing to get such loan—instead, the United States drastically cut back lend-lease payments to Russia in May, 1945—Stalin was faced with three choices, according to Williams:

> He could give way and accept the American peace program at every point—which meant, among other things, accepting governments in Eastern Europe hostile to the Soviet Union.
>
> He could follow the advice of the doctrinaire revolutionaries in his own country who argued that Russia's best hope lay in fomenting world-wide revolution.
>
> Or he could exact large-scale economic reparations from Germany while attempting to reach an understanding with Churchill and Roosevelt on the need for governments in Eastern Europe not necessarily Communist but friendly to the Soviet Union.

His negotiations with Churchill in 1944, according to Williams, showed that Stalin had already committed himself, by the end of the war, to the third of these policies—a policy, incidentally, which required him to withdraw support from Communist revolutions in

Greece and in other countries which under the terms of the Churchill-Stalin agreement had been conceded to the Western sphere of influence.

But American statesmen, the argument continues, unlike the British, were in no mood to compromise. They were confident of America's strength and Russia's weakness (although later they and their apologists found it convenient to argue that the contrary had been the case). Furthermore, they believed that "we cannot have full employment and prosperity in the United States without the foreign markets," as Dean Acheson told a special Congressional committee on post-war economic policy and planning in November, 1944. These considerations led to the conclusion, as President Truman put it in April, 1945, that the United States should "take the lead in running the world in the way that the world ought to be run"; or more specifically, in the words of Foreign Economic Administrator Leo Crowley, that "if you create good governments in foreign countries, automatically you will have better markets for ourselves." Accordingly, the United States pressed for the "open door" in Eastern Europe and elsewhere.

In addition to these considerations, there was the further matter of the atomic bomb, which first became a calculation in American diplomacy in July, 1945. The successful explosion of an atomic bomb in the New Mexico desert, Williams argues, added to the American sense of omnipotence and led the United States "to overplay its hand" —for in spite of American efforts to keep the Russians out of Eastern Europe, the Russians refused to back down.

Nor did American pressure have the effect, as George Kennan hoped, of promoting tendencies in the Soviet Union "which must eventually find their outlet in either the break-up or the gradual mellowing of Soviet power." Far from causing Soviet policy to mellow, American actions, according to Williams, stiffened the Russians in their resistance to Western pressure and strengthened the hand of those groups in the Soviet Union which had been arguing all along that capitalist powers could not be trusted.

Not only did the Russians successfully resist American demands in Eastern Europe, they launched a vigorous counterattack in the form of the Czechoslovakian coup of 1948 and the Berlin blockade. Both East and West thus found themselves committed to the policy of cold war, and for the next 15 years, until the Cuban missile crisis led to a partial detente, Soviet-American hostility was the determining fact of international politics. . . .

* * *

Next to William's *Tragedy of American Diplomacy,* the most important attack on the orthodox interpretation of the cold war is Alperovitz's *Atomic Diplomacy.* A young historian trained at Wisconsin, Berkeley and King's College, Cambridge, and currently a research fellow at Harvard, Alperovitz adds very little to the interpretation formulated by Williams, but he provides William's insights with a mass of additional documentation. By doing so, he has made it difficult for conscientious scholars any longer to avoid the challenge of revisionist interpretations. Unconventional in its conclusions, *Atomic Diplomacy* is thoroughly conventional in its methods. That adds to the book's persuasiveness. Using the traditional sources of diplomatic history—official records, memoirs of participants, and all the unpublished material to which scholars have access—Alperovitz painstakingly reconstructs the evolution of American policy during the six-month period March to August, 1945. He proceeds with a thoroughness and caution which, in the case of a less controversial work, would command the unanimous respect of the scholarly profession. His book is no polemic. It is a work in the best—and most conservative—traditions of historical scholarship. Yet the evidence which Alperovitz has gathered together challenges the official explanation of the beginnings of the cold war at every point.

What the evidence seems to show is that as early as April, 1945, American officials from President Truman on down had decided to force a "symbolic showdown" with the Soviet Union over the future of Eastern Europe. Truman believed that a unified Europe was the key to European recovery and economic stability, since the agricultural southeast and the industrial northwest depended on each other. Soviet designs on Eastern Europe, Truman reasoned, threatened to disrupt the economic unity of Europe and therefore had to be resisted. The only question was whether the showdown should take place immediately or whether it should be delayed until the bargaining position of the United States had improved.

At first it appeared to practically everybody that delay would only weaken the position of the United States. Both of its major bargaining counters, its armies in Europe and its lend-lease credits to

Russia, could be more effectively employed at once, it seemed, than at any future time. Accordingly, Truman tried to "lay it on the line" with the Russians. He demanded that they "carry out their [Yalta] agreements" by giving the pro-Western elements in Poland an equal voice in the Polish Government (although Roosevelt, who made the Yalta agreements, believed that "we placed, as clearly shown in the agreement, somewhat more emphasis" on the Warsaw [pro-Communist] Government than on the pro-Western leaders). When Stalin objected that Poland was "a country in which the U.S.S.R. is interested first of all and most of all," the United States tried to force him to give in by cutting back lend-lease payments to Russia.

At this point, however—in April, 1945—Secretary of War Henry L. Stimson convinced Truman that "we shall probably hold more cards in our hands later than now." He referred to the atomic bomb, and if Truman decided to postpone the showdown with Russia, it was because Stimson and other advisers persuaded him that the new weapon would "put us in a position," as Secretary of State James F. Byrnes argued, "to dictate our own terms at the end of the war."

To the amazement of those not privy to the secret, Truman proceeded to take a more conciliatory attitude toward Russia, an attitude symbolized by Harry Hopkins's mission to Moscow in June, 1945. Meanwhile, Truman twice postponed the meeting with Churchill and Stalin at Potsdam. Churchill complained, "Anyone can see that in a very short space of time our armed power on the Continent will have vanished."

But when Truman told Churchill that an atomic bomb had been successfully exploded at Alamogordo, exceeding all expectations, Churchill immediately understood and endorsed the strategy of delay. "We were in the presence of a new factor in human affairs," he said, "and possessed of powers which were irresistible." Not only Germany but even the Balkans, which Churchill and Roosevelt had formerly conceded to the Russian sphere, now seemed amenable to Western influence. That assumption, of course, had guided American policy (though not British policy) since April, but it could not be acted upon until the bombing of Japan provided the world with an unmistakable demonstration of American military supremacy.

Early in September, the foreign ministers of the Big Three met in London. Byrnes—armed, as Stimson noted, with "the presence of the bomb in his pocket, so to speak, as a great weapon to get through" the conference—tried to press the American advantage. He demanded that the Governments of Bulgaria and Rumania re-organize themselves along lines favorable to the West. In Bulgaria, firmness won a few concessions; in Rumania, the Russians stood firm. The American strategy had achieved no noteworthy success. Instead—as Stimson, one of the architects of that strategy, rather belatedly observed—it had "irretrievably embittered" Soviet American relations.

The revisionist view of the origins of the cold war, as it emerges from the works of Williams, Alperovitz, . . . and others, can be summarized as follows. The object of American policy at the end of World War II was not to defend Western or even Central Europe but to force the Soviet Union out of Eastern Europe. The Soviet menace to the "free world," so often cited as the justification of the containment policy, simply did not exist in the minds of American planners. They believed themselves to be negotiating not from weakness but from almost unassailable superiority.

Nor can it be said that the cold war began because the Russians "broke their agreements." The general sense of the Yalta agreements—which were in any case very vague—was to assign to the Soviet Union a controlling influence in Eastern Europe. Armed with the atomic bomb, American diplomats tried to take back what they had implicitly conceded at Yalta.

The assumption of American moral superiority, in short, does not stand up under analysis.

The opponents of this view have yet to make a very convincing reply. Schlesinger's recent article in *Foreign Affairs,* referred to at the outset of this article, can serve as an example of the kind of arguments which historians are likely to develop in opposition to the revisionist interpretation. Schlesinger argues that the cold war came about through a combination of Soviet intransigence and mis-understanding. There were certain "problems of communication" with the Soviet Union, as a result of which "the Russians might con-ceivably have misread our signals." Thus the American demand for self-determination in Poland and other East European countries "very probably" appeared to the Russians "as a systematic and deliberate pressure on Russia's western frontiers."

Similarly, the Russians "could well have interpreted" the American refusal of a loan to the Soviet Union, combined with cancellation of lend-lease, "as deliberate sabotage" of Russia's postwar reconstruction or as "blackmail." In both cases, of course, there would have been no basis for these suspicions; but "we have thought a great deal more in recent years," Schlesinger says, ". . . about the problems of communication in diplomacy," and we know how easy it is for one side to misinterpret what the other is saying.

This argument about difficulties of "communications" at no point engages the evidence uncovered by Alperovitz and others—evidence which seems to show that Soviet officials had good reason to interpret American actions exactly as they did: as attempts to dictate American terms.

In reply to the assertion that the refusal of a reconstruction loan was part of such an attempt, Schlesinger can only argue weakly that the Soviet request for a loan was "inexplicably mislaid" by Washington during the transfer of records from the Foreign Economic Administration to the State Department! "Of course," he adds, "this was impossible for the Russians to believe." It is impossible for some Americans to believe. As William Appleman Williams notes, "Schlesinger's explanation of the "inexplicable" loss of the Soviet request "does not speak to the point of how the leaders could forget the request even if they lost the document."

When pressed on the matter of "communications," Schlesinger retreats to a second line of arguments, namely that none of these misunderstandings "made much essential difference," because Stalin suffered from "paranoia" and was "possessed by convictions both of the infallibility of the Communist word and of the inevitability of a Communist world."

The trouble is that there is very little evidence which connects either Stalin's paranoia or Marxist-Leninist ideology or what Schlesinger calls "the sinister dynamics of a totalitarian society" with the actual course of Soviet diplomacy during the formative months of the cold war. The only piece of evidence that Schlesinger has been able to find is an article by the Communist theoretician Jacques Duclos in the April, 1945, issue of *Cahiers du communisme,* the journal of the French Communist party, which proves, he argues, that Stalin had already abandoned the wartime policy of collaboration with the West and had returned to the traditional Communist policy of world revolution.

Even this evidence, however, can be turned to the advantage of the revisionists. Alperovitz points out that Duclos did not attack electoral politics or even collaboration with bourgeois governments. What he denounced was precisely the American Communists' decision, in 1944, to withdraw from electoral politics. Thus the article, far from being a call to world revolution, "was one of many confirmations that European Communists had decided to abandon violent revolutionary struggle in favor of the more modest aim of electoral success." And while this decision did not guarantee world peace, neither did it guarantee 20 years of cold war.

Schlesinger first used the Duclos article as a trump card in a letter to *The New York Review of Books,* Oct. 20, 1966, which called forth Alperovitz's rejoinder. It is symptomatic of the general failure of orthodox historiography to engage the revisionist argument that Duclos' article crops up again in Schlesinger's more recent essay in *Foreign Affairs,* where it is once again cited as evidence of a "new Moscow line," without any reference to the intervening objections raised by Alperovitz.

Sooner or later, however, historians will have to come to grips with the revisionist interpretation of the cold war. They cannot ignore it indefinitely. When serious debate begins, many historians, hitherto disposed to accept without much question the conventional account of the cold war, will find themselves compelled to admit its many inadequacies. On the other hand, some of the ambiguities of the revisionist view, presently submerged in the revisionists' common quarrel with official explanations, will begin to force themselves to the surface. Is the revisionist history of the cold war essentially an attack on "the doctrine of historical inevitability," as Alperovitz contends? Or does it contain an implicit determinism of its own?

Two quite different conclusions can be drawn from the body of revisionist scholarship. One is that American policy-makers had it in their power to choose different policies from the ones they chose. That is, they could have adopted a more conciliatory attitude toward the Soviet Union, just as they now have the choice of adopting a more conciliatory attitude toward Communist China and toward nationalist revolutions elsewhere in the Third World.

The other is that they have no such choice, because the inner requirements of American capitalism *force* them to pursue a consistent policy of economic and political expansion. "For matters to stand otherwise," writes Carl Oglesby, "the Yankee free-enterpriser would . . . have to . . . take sides against himself. . . . He would have to change entirely his style of thought and action. In a word, he would have to become a revolutionary Socialist whose aim was the destruction of the present American hegemony."

Pushed to what some writers clearly regard as its logical conclusion, the revisionist critique of American foreign policy thus becomes the obverse of the cold-war liberals' defense of that policy, which assumes that nothing could have modified the character of Soviet policy short of the transformation of the Soviet Union into a liberal democracy—which is exactly the goal the containment policy sought to promote. According to a certain type of revisionism, American policy has all the rigidity the orthodox historians attribute to the U.S.S.R., and this inflexibility made the cold war inevitable.

Moreover, Communism really did threaten American interests, in this view. Oglesby argues that, in spite of its obvious excesses, the "theory of the International Communist Conspiracy is not the hysterical old maid that many leftists seem to think it is." If there is no conspiracy, there is a world revolution and it *"does* aim itself at America"—the America of expansive corporate capitalism.

Revisionism, carried to these conclusions, curiously restores cold-war anti-Communism to a kind of intellectual respectability, even while insisting on its immorality. After all, it concludes, the cold warriors were following the American national interest. The national interest may have been itself corrupt, but the policy-makers were more rational than their critics may have supposed.

In my view, this concedes far too much good sense to Truman, Dulles and the rest. Even Oglesby concedes that the war in Vietnam has now become irrational in its own terms. I submit that much of the cold war has been irrational in its own terms—as witness the failure, the enormously costly failure, of American efforts to dominate Eastern Europe at the end of World War II. This is not to deny the fact of American imperialism, only to suggest that imperialism itself, as J. A. Hobson and Joseph Schumpeter argued in another context long ago, is irrational—that even in its liberal form it may represent an archaic social phenomenon having little relation to the realities of the modern world.

At the present stage of historical scholarship, it is of course impossible to speak with certainty about such matters. That very lack of certainty serves to indicate the direction which future study of American foreign policy might profitably take.

The question to which historians must now address themselves is whether American capitalism really depends, for its continuing growth and survival, on the foreign policy its leaders have been following throughout most of the twentieth century. To what extent are its interests really threatened by Communist revolutions in the Third World? To what extent can it accommodate itself to those revolutions, reconciling itself to a greatly diminished role in the rest of the world, without undergoing a fundamental reformation—that is, without giving way (after a tremendous upheaval) to some form of Socialism? . . .

VI YALTA REVISITED

Diane Shaver Clemens
YALTA

Diane Shaver Clemens regards herself neither as an orthodox nor a revisionist historian of the Yalta Conference. With her attention focused directly on the conference, she gives the contents of the Yalta bargain a political scientist's scrutiny. Many of the thrusts and counterthrusts of negotiation depicted in her summary diagram will already have been encountered elsewhere in the readings. Those that are new may lead the reader to additional research, and her suggestion that perhaps the United States did not live up to all of its agreements after Yalta may stimulate the reader to further investigation. This recent work on the subject indicates that the Yalta controversy is not yet at an end.

"Today I remember the Crimean Conference with joy and grief. How many hopes, it seems, fully sincere, were expressed in those days, and how many disappointments did we derive from the international situation in the following years." These words, written by a Yalta participant on the twenty-fifth anniversary of the Conference, could have been uttered by any one of a number of men from any one of the three countries. They were written by Soviet Admiral Nicholai Kuznetsov. He concluded, sadly, "But even now, twenty-five years later, I am convinced that the Soviet Union is not to blame for this." This remark suggests the significance of Yalta as the watershed between wartime cooperation and the opening sorties of the postwar era—"the Cold War."

Kuznetsov's statement directs us to the underlying question: why did such a dramatic outward change in the relationships among the "Big Three (the United States, the Soviet Union, and Great Britain) occur? The West has blamed the Soviet Union, frequently citing as cause the Yalta agreements allegedly broken by the Soviet Union. Whittaker Chambers, with an even more stern appraisal, echoed the perception of the 1950s when he said: "The illusion of Yalta [was] that the Communists yearned for peace if only we'd be kind to them." The Soviet Union has denied this and has blamed the failure on the West. Regardless of these charges, the real test is whether Soviet policy, behavior, and cooperation during the war differed fundamentally or qualitatively from Western policy, behavior, and cooperation.

The diplomatic negotiations on the issues of the Yalta Conference provide one insight into answering this question. The amiability of the Allies and the workability of the wartime coalition reflect what Churchill and Roosevelt called in their correspondence "the three of us." Yet this cohesive structure was built upon fundamental and long-standing conflicts among all three "friends." The paradox of the Yalta Conference was that it convened at a time when the Allies were on the verge of military victory, but fundamentally had resolved little else through diplomatic agreement. At Yalta they made agreements that reflected their mutual interests and embodied traditional compromises. These decisions were later challenged and abandoned, and the world was propelled into the "Cold War." . . .

* * *

Yalta as a Negotiating Experience

Was Yalta the "dawn of the new day we had all been praying for and talking about for so many years," as Harry Hopkins stated as he left Yalta, or was it "the high point of Soviet diplomatic success and correspondingly the low point of American appeasement," as William Henry Chamberlin stated it?

These judgments lie at either end of a spectrum of sentiment obscuring that fateful meeting in February 1945. For too long the Conference has been viewed as a success if the Americans won on every point and the Russians lost on every point. Even from this perspective interpretations differ, because estimates of what the Americans or the Russians wanted differ.

Perhaps the only realistic way to consider Yalta is as a traditional diplomatic negotiating situation, removed from its emotionally charged context. Toward the end of the war several issues were being unilaterally resolved by the various sides. At Yalta the Three Powers thrashed out their perspectives on these issues.

There were five main issues that took up most of the time at Yalta, three of them problems related to a German settlement. It seems useful to recapitulate the process of reaching a decision on these issues in terms of what individual nations sought to accomplish by their negotiating positions. In this way some conclusion can be reached as to the reasonableness of the decisions and negotiating stances of the three nations at this tripartite meeting. . . . [Figure 1, p. 208] shows the initial proposal by the sponsoring nation in the upper left-hand corner; the opposing and subsequent positions over time can be followed in relation to this.

Reparations. The Soviet delegation presented a reparations plan (I-a) which Churchill opposed. Stalin was confronted from the onset with Churchill's pessimism and reluctance to accept a proposal for a specific payment in amount and kind by Germany because, argued the British Prime Minister, the Germans could not afford to pay. In contrast, Roosevelt's words were more lenient and without a definite commitment, aligned him with the Soviets who held a harsher view of Germany's responsibility. Readily agreeing to Churchill's suggestion to establish a Reparations Commission in Moscow (I-b) as an interim solution, Stalin then argued in favor of establishing instructions for the Commission.

Molotov proposed that the Soviet principles be accepted by the three nations as a guideline in deciding reparations (I-c). Without contest, Eden added a new principle, and the principles seemed mutually acceptable. The United States again brought the question into prominence by offering a concrete proposal (I-d) in a foreign ministers' meeting two days later, and this plan, close to the original Soviet proposal, became the basis of final agreement. But this strong stand was again rejected by Britain. Molotov settled on the spot for a written agreement of American support (I-e).

The following day, Britain attempted once again, this time by introducing a counterproposal (I-f), to alter the main features of the plan. When the heads of state met again in plenary session, Stalin immediately took umbrage at a remark made by Roosevelt which seemed to indicate a possible reversal of the American position and the adoption by the Americans of a British solution. Challenging both Washington and London to clarify their intentions, Stalin won further assurance from Roosevelt that he was completely in agreement with Soviet policy. Churchill continued to disassociate Britain from the agreement. Stalin then (I-g) sought minimal agreement from Britain, but when this also failed, he retreated to the Soviet-American agreement of a fixed sum for consideration by the Reparations Commission and the statement of principles.

The Dismemberment of Germany. Stalin altered the original agenda for February 5 (II-a) when he called for a discussion of Allied intentions to dismember Germany in light of the Morgenthau plan. Churchill reacted negatively to dismemberment, but Roosevelt positively. In the foreign ministers' meeting (II-b) Anthony Eden proposed that the word "dismemberment" be changed to "dissolution." Molotov vigorously disagreed and began to argue for an increased Allied commitment to dismember Germany. Stettinius stepped in (II-c), and the three nations were reconciled; they agreed to the inclusion of the word "dismemberment" in the protocol, the terms of surrender, and the immediate plan for postwar Germany.

The foreign ministers quibbled somewhat over the next question they had to resolve (II-d), namely, how the committee for dismemberment would work. Molotov envisioned that the committee should have the minimal function of studying procedure. Eden sought instructions that included France on the committee; and Stettinius suggested using the existing European Advisory Council. Unable to settle the question satisfactorily, the ministers agreed to let the Commission itself decide whether France was a member of it (II-e).

The Immediate Postwar Role of France. Through British initiative, the consideration of a zone for France was scheduled. Stalin, knowing from an earlier conversation with Roosevelt that America opposed elevating France to the role of a victor in the German settlement, played the antagonist. Tactically arguing the many (III-a) issues which this question provoked, Stalin assailed the proposal until Roosevelt announced (III-b) that American troops would leave Europe in two years. The immediate result of this announcement was that Churchill changed his argument from one that France should be an exception in the German settlement to the argument that France was necessary now to share in the protection of Europe. Stalin now moved to back Churchill. France could have a zone, he said, but not reparations.

In a foreign ministers' meeting, Molotov proposed that France be subordinate to the Control Council for Germany, but Eden insisted that France be an equal member of the Council (III-c). When Molotov

(III-d) called for approval of the Soviet proposal, Eden refused. Stettinius and then Molotov supported postponing the question until it could be considered by the European Advisory Council. Eden remained adamant that the decision be made immediately. The stalemate continued until February 10, when Roosevelt decided to switch to the support of Churchill, and Stalin went along (III-e).

Questions Relating to Poland. Churchill and Roosevelt (IV-a) broached the issue of Poland on the second day of the conference. They indicated acceptance of the old Curzon Line as the Soviet-Polish border, granted certain Soviet principles as operative, and stressed their predominant concern for guaranteeing a democratic Polish government. Recognizing the predominant Soviet interest in Poland, they asked for concessions. Stalin replied, outlining a strong case for Big Three agreement on existing Soviet policy for reasons of both democracy and security.

Roosevelt (IV-b) sent Stalin a letter just prior to the next plenary session, suggesting that Stalin's recommendation to bring the Poles to Yalta be implemented; the Poles could then form a government recognizable by the three Allies. Stalin briefly rebutted the proposal, then displaced the issue with one far closer to Roosevelt's heart—the American voting formula for the United Nations (refer to V-b). In a dramatic shift of emphasis, Russia accepted Roosevelt's formula. Molotov then went back to the Polish question, putting forth a proposal (IV-c) which incorporated Stalin's position of the previous day with some modifications that took into account the requests made by Roosevelt and Churchill. Roosevelt announced that he was pleased with the compromise, while Churchill remained aloof.

The following day both Roosevelt and Churchill presented proposals on Poland at the plenary session (IV-d). Stalin responded by asking what substantively the three did agree upon? (For example, was the West prepared to abandon the exiled Polish government?) Next, Stalin rejected Roosevelt's proposed Presidential Council on the basis that a Polish government (Lublin) already existed.

Summarizing the issues already agreed upon, Stalin gained assurance (IV-e) that the Polish-Soviet frontier was not in question. The question of elections showing popular support for a government remained a key issue, although all agreed that there would be free elections. Heated exchanges between Soviet and British diplomats indicated that no agreement, implicit or explicit, could be reached without acceptance of the Soviet proposal in some form. In the course of debate, Roosevelt's position began to shift again toward the agreement he had expressed the previous day (refer to IV-c); he clarified it by stating that, since elections would be held within a month, disagreement on the interim government was not of great consequence. Thus the alignment by the end of February 8 (IV-f) in a sense completed the shift of balance.

The next day President Roosevelt proposed a compromise (IV-g) which embodied the Soviet proposal and the established points of agreement up to that point. Molotov took the initiative by launching an attack on Britain on an *ersatz* issue, but Churchill nonetheless withstood the combined pressure. Roosevelt (IV-h), assuming the function of mediator, insisted that remaining differences in posture were only slight. Without diminishing the breadth of Soviet-American agreement, Molotov rejected wording in the proposal that required active implementation of observation of the elections. Simultaneously, Stalin accepted Roosevelt's terminology for the expanded Lublin government. Almost as a measure of friction during the crystallization of this alignment, Churchill broke out in anger over his suspicions of Roosevelt's United Nations trusteeship concept (refer to V-k).

The special foreign ministers' session scheduled for the evening of February 9 centered on the British proposal to modify the emerging Polish solution. After stating a clear stand taken in London by the War Cabinet, Eden asked for major changes. He submitted a revised formula of the American proposal. Molotov countered this by altering the unacceptable points and restructuring it until it substantively returned to the Soviet original and American compromise proposals (IV-i).

The final stage of agreement occurred on the next day, when the specific wording was agreed upon. Molotov incorporated into the Conference protocol the sum of agreements during different stages of the Conference. This was then the last agreement (IV-j).

Decisions Relating to the United Nations. Roosevelt raised the question of the United Nations, threatening trouble over the German peace unless the American voting formula for the United Nations were adopted (V-a). Stalin questioned the possible use of this formula against Russia, and Churchill insisted that Britain's imperial interests be protected.

Stalin (V-b) accepted the American voting formula (refer to scenario immediately above in chart to note timing, IV-b and c). The British also concurred. Stalin then requested United Nations membership for two or three Soviet Republics in addition. Churchill made a similar request by Britain (V-c). Roosevelt attempted to overlook this issue and moved on to the American list of nations to be invited to the San Francisco Conference and to the wording of the invitations. The three heads of state found they were unable to agree, so these issues were referred to the foreign ministers. Eden initiated the question of the two Soviet Republics (V-d); Stettinius followed Roosevelt's attempt to beg the question and move into invitations; and Molotov strongly stated his position, threatening discord on the question of invitations. Eden and Molotov (V-e) urged that the Republics be considered (Molotov favored immediate agreement on their treatment, but Eden wanted to delay agreement until the San Francisco Conference). Stettinius finally promised to take the question up with Roosevelt. After this meeting (V-f) and prior to the plenary session, Roosevelt agreed, stating that he did so because Britain backed the Soviet request.

Roosevelt (V-g) now could continue with his next item related to the formation of the United Nations, the list of nations to receive invitations to become original members. Stalin wanted the two Soviet Republics to be invited also and to become original members. Roosevelt (V-h) asked that his list be accepted. Parts of this session were confused, apparently because of the discrepancies in the criteria determining which nations would receive invitations. (Some had not signed the Declaration of the United Nations and yet would become original members, thus individually receiving invitations.) Stalin, with Churchill's backing, sought acceptance of the two Soviet Republics as signers of the Declaration, to make certain that they would be original members. Granting that the Soviet Republics fulfilled the criteria for membership as well or better than some already listed, and yet unwilling to jeopardize the United Nations project, Roosevelt professed embarrassment (V-i); and Stalin, in deference, withdrew his request. By the end of the meeting (V-j), Roosevelt had agreed

Figure 1
Patterns of the Yalta Negotiations

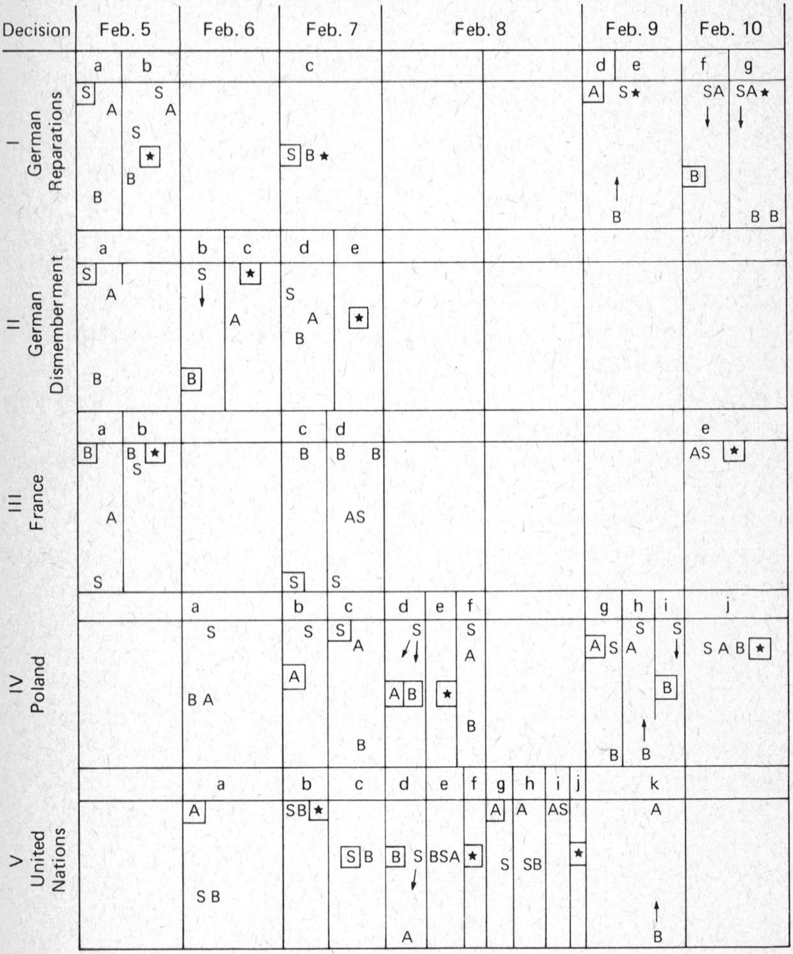

Key:
Placement from left to right signifies temporal sequence of statements. Placement from top to bottom signifies approximate distance between negotiating positions on a spectrum from unity (overlapping positions) . . . to diametrically opposed positions. The original position of the nation initiating the proposal is placed in the upper left-hand corner; opposition negotiating stances can be contrasted by scanning the chart.

A = USA   Ⓐ = USA Proposal   ⭐ = Tripartite decision

B = Great Britain   A = Intense USA verbal attack   ★ = Bilateral decision

S = Soviet Union

to membership at San Francisco of the Soviet Republics. Stalin continued to seek equal treatment of the Republics, and Churchill supported him.

A study of these decisions as they were made at Yalta indicates that several conclusions can be made about the Conference as a tripartite negotiating experience. Although the Great Powers differed in their initial viewpoints, a high incidence of consensus was reached at the Conference. The Allied coalition, which had been primarily military in nature, produced at last an impetus to nonmilitary agreement among all three parties—on the assumption that consensus was in the best interest of each of the parties. Most importantly, each nation had an issue of prime importance to it, and each gained support from its other two Allies. Britain's insistence on reviving France in the creation of a Western block was agreed to by Roosevelt and Stalin; America's voting formula for the United Nations, the subject on which the United States spent much of its diplomatic effort during the war, did not meet the opposition Washington feared; the Soviet Union, which was determined to prevent another hostile Polish government on its borders, gained support for the Lublin committee, although in a compromise form. But two Soviet desires, reparations and Poland's western frontier, remained unresolved, the former because of Churchill's instructions from the War Cabinet, and the latter because of an Anglo-American reluctance to make a frontier arrangement.

The Conference functioned reasonably on the basis of balanced diplomatic interaction. Agreement between two parties tended to assure agreement of the third, even if the third party was reluctant: Stalin used Roosevelt's support for dismemberment and reparations, and his agreement to an expansion of the Lublin committee as the basis for the government of Poland, in order to force British concurrence. (In the case of reparations, only a two-way agreement resulted on the details, but a three-way agreement was achieved on the establishment of a Reparations Commission.) British support for admission of two Soviet Republics to the United Nations led Roosevelt (by his own admission) to accept that proposal. Stalin's acquiescence to a zone for France in Germany promptly followed a shift by Roosevelt to the same position. When it seemed apparent that Britain would accept the American voting formula in the United Nations, Stalin also concurred.

A review of the contents of original proposals, compared with subsequent proposals and final agreements, indicates that the Soviet Union in particular tended to incorporate compromises and suggestions in order to achieve agreement. During the Conference the Soviet Union and the United States made six major proposals on prime topics and Britain made five. Of the five topics listed on the chart, the Soviet Union took the initiative on two issues, both on Germany, and eventually a third, on Poland (although the first proposal came from Roosevelt). America took the initiative on one issue, and Britain on one. Considering the favorable military position of the Soviet Union as well as the disappointments of her earlier diplomatic encounters with the West, the Soviet Union showed a co-operative and conciliatory stance, which at the time of the Conference was recognized by many participants.

Soviet "stubbornness" or "obstructionism" can be argued only if one accepts the hypothesis that the Soviet Union ought to have accepted as just and superior any proposal which differed from the Soviet position.

In retrospect, we see a diplomatic encounter in which all sides, not without misgivings and harsh words, struggled to achieve their aims, but an encounter in which they prized agreement by traditional negotiation as preferable to unilateral action which might undermine international stability. Herein lies the meaning of the Yalta agreements, which provided an alternative to a "Cold War."

During World War II the United States was treading a path of expanding global "responsibility" and simultaneously fighting four wars to that end. The first was the military war against Germany, and the second the military war against Japan in the Pacific. The third was a struggle with Great Britain, allegedly to "defeat colonialism" (in American terms) but actually to determine which power would control Europe and Asia economically and politically. The last was the long-standing ideological struggle against "bolshevist" Russia, which continued, though intermittently, during the war. That struggle increased in focus and intensity as the Soviet Union emerged from the war with Great Power status.

Although American policy reputedly rested on the high-minded principles of the Atlantic Charter, those principles were invoked mainly to ward off British or Soviet threats to American plans. During the war, cooperation, the cornerstone of wartime diplomacy, was sorely pressed. Roosevelt gave the Soviet Union several "opportunities" to demonstrate its cooperativeness. One critical "opportunity" came up in 1942, when the President invited Molotov to Washington to plan a second front for that year. Simultaneously Roosevelt encouraged the Soviet Union to drop the provision in the proposed Anglo-Soviet treaty which recognized the incorporation of the Baltic states into the Soviet Union. Molotov did so, and in return he received a written commitment for the invasion of France—which Roosevelt dropped when Churchill objected. At the same time the President seized the initiative on Stalin's request for a postwar guarantee of cooperation—Roosevelt began to plan the United Nations, a slightly updated League of Nations with its membership dominated by America's allies. (Russia, of course, had been expelled by the League after attacking Finland.)

By 1943, both Anthony Eden and Ivan Maisky were openly discussing the two policy alternatives which the Soviet Union would decide upon after the war: unilateral action, or cooperation with her Western Allies. Eden informed Washington that the Soviet Union preferred the latter course. Maisky emphatically affirmed this judgment. Washington hindered Great Britain from adjusting Anglo-Soviet policy and held out to the Soviet Union promises of postwar aid, cooperation, and amicable adjustments, while resolving nothing. The few tripartite negotiating experiences, such as the Italian surrender and the European Advisory Commission, raised serious questions about American intentions. On the other hand, the Soviet Union during the war remained basically cooperative. American officials complained of the frustrations of dealing with the Soviet central bureaucracy, but this did not constitute Soviet unwillingness to cooperate.

In the wake of Soviet military victories, Roosevelt at last decided it was time to resolve issues which he had postponed for three years. The Yalta Conference met with a sense of deliberation. It was to be a test of the ability of the three nations to resolve the issues dividing them. It was a moment when American ideology, normally submerged in moralistic phrases uncharacteristic of its actual behavior, was submitted to a traditional negotiating experience with binding results. Roosevelt and Churchill, when they met personally with Stalin, tended to treat the Soviet Union as the nation it was—an existing state with increasing influence in world affairs. The decisions at Yalta involved compromise by each nation, probably more by the Soviets than by the Western nations.

By abandoning the Conference agreements after Yalta, America created a self-fulfilling prophecy. Believing that the Soviets intended to take advantage of any opportunity at the expense of the United States, Washington tried to renegotiate the zonal agreements and held Western troops in Soviet occupation zones as a political pressure tactic. Further, the American government changed its interpretation of the Yalta decisions on Poland. After deserting the original American-Soviet viewpoint, the United States accused the Soviet Union of breaking the Yalta agreements. Finally, the Allies decided, contrary to Yalta, not to support reparations. In doing so they abandoned the Soviet Union. These decisions, and many others, left the Soviet Union with no alternative than to substitute unilateral action for a policy of cooperation which they had hoped for, but which had never emerged—except briefly, at Yalta.

The Yalta Conference has been more condemned than commended by Western commentators. Under most of these condemnations lies the implicit and unexpressed premise that the Soviet Union is in essence evil while the West embodies the virtues of the ages; and, further, a belief that the Soviet Union has and can have no interests which the West considers legitimate. American policy during the war and afterward has been studied in terms of what the United States failed to do to foil Soviet aims, or else in terms of what the United States could have done to alter a decision acceptable to the Soviet Union. The policies based on this ideological bent attributed false motives to the Soviet Union and created a situation in which the Soviet Union increasingly defended herself from Western hostility.

Roosevelt's departure from America's moralistic and anti-Soviet bias, combined with Churchill's usually consistent realism, served diplomacy for the week the leaders met at Yalta. But the postwar world bears little resemblance to what these men worked to achieve. Broken promises, bad faith, misperceptions, and self-righteousness have forced new and different policies upon the nations. We are living with the problems of a world that did not benefit from the experience at Yalta.

It is perhaps relevant to ask what the world would have been like if the spirit of Yalta had triumphed.

Suggestions for Further Reading

For the student who wishes to dig into primary source materials on the Yalta Conference, the best collection is the 1,000 page official U.S. State Department publication *Foreign Relations of the United States: The Conferences at Malta and Yalta, 1945* (Washington, 1955). One of the interesting things about these documents is how little they added to the memoir materials already available. The firsthand accounts by Winston Churchill, James Byrnes and Robert Sherwood could, therefore, profitably be read in their entirety. Two other useful accounts by participants are those by Admiral William D. Leahy, *I Was There* (New York, 1948) and Secretary of State Edward Stettinius, *Roosevelt and the Russians: The Yalta Conference* (New York, 1949).

Of the secondary descriptions of what went on at the conference, the one by Diane Clemens is probably most complete in that it provides the best treatment of the Russian bargaining perspective. Another careful account, mostly from the American viewpoint, is John L. Snell (editor) *The Meaning of Yalta* (Baton Rouge, 1956). Two major books that describe Yalta in the course of their more extensive (and divergent) discussions of wartime foreign policy are the ones by William H. McNeill, from which we have taken an excerpt, and Gabriel Kolko, *The Politics of War* (New York, 1969). Useful descriptions will also be found in Herbert Feis, *Churchill, Roosevelt, Stalin: The War They Waged and the Peace They Sought* (Princeton, 1957); and John R. Deane, *The Strange Alliance: The Story of Our Wartime Efforts at Cooperation with Russia* (New York, 1947).

Among the early favorable discussions of the conference are the following: Wickham Steed, "Fulfillment," *Contemporary Review* 167 (March 1945): 129–134; Henry Steele Commager, "Was Yalta a Calamity? A Debate," *New York Times Magazine*, August 3, 1952; Raymond Gram Swing, "What Really Happened at Yalta," *New York Times Magazine*, February 20, 1949; McGeorge Bundy, "The Test of Yalta," *Foreign Affairs* 27 (July 1949): 618–629; Rudolph A. Winnacker, "Yalta, Another Munich?" *Virginia Quarterly Review* 24 (October 1948): 521–537; Sumner Welles, *Seven Decisions That Shaped History* (New York, 1951), Chs. 5–7.

Among the unfavorable assessments of the conference are: Eugene Lyons, "Appeasement in Yalta," *American Mercury* 60 (April 1945): 461–468; Oswald Garrison Willard, "Poland, A Moral Issue," *Christian Century* 62 (March 14, 1945): 334–336; William C. Bullitt, "How We Won the War and Lost the Peace," *Life*, August 30, 1948, pp. 82–97, and September 6, 1948, pp. 86–103; G. F. Hudson, "The Lesson of Yalta," *Commentary* 17 (April 1954): 373–380. Three memoirs critical of the Polish settlement are: Jan Ciechanowski, *Defeat in Victory* (New York, 1947); Arthur Bliss Lane, *I Saw Poland Betrayed* (New York, 1948); Stanislaw Mikolajzyk, *The Rape of Poland* (New York, 1948). A scholarly presentation of the same viewpoint is Edward Rozek, *Allied Wartime Diplomacy* (New York, 1958). Sharp attacks on the Far Eastern agreements will be found in John T. Flynn, *While You Slept: Our Tragedy in Asia and Who Made It* (New York, 1951) and Freda Utley, *The China Story* (Chicago, 1951).

Chester Wilmot's analysis is more completely developed in the remainder of his book. A view similar to that of Wilmot is developed in Hanson Baldwin, *Great Mistakes of the War* (New York, 1949) and by the same writer in "Churchill Was Right," *Atlantic* 194 (July 1954): 23–32. Likewise, William Henry Chamberlin's criticism can be better understood in the light of his entire book and a later one, *Beyond Containment* (Chicago, 1953). The supporting intelligence estimates of Captain Ellis Zacharias will be found in his "The Inside Story of Yalta," *United Nations World* (January 1949) pp. 12–17.

The domestic give-and-take over Yalta, from 1945 to 1955, is indispensably detailed by Athan Theoharis. Two supplementary accounts of the domestic political climate are: Robert Griffiths, *The Politics of Fear: Joseph R. McCarthy and the Senate* (Lexington, Kentucky, 1970); and Earl Latham, *The Communist Conspiracy in Washington* (Cambridge, Mass., 1966). Further reading in the extensive MacArthur Hearings, from which the Harriman excerpt is taken, and in the Bohlen nomination hearings will provide additional material. Helpful in explicating Harriman's testimony and our Far Eastern diplomacy in general is Tang Tsou, *America's Failure in China 1941–1950* (Chicago, 1963). The context of the Bohlen testimony is described in James Rosenau, *The Nomination of "Chip" Bohlen,* Eagleton Institute Cases in Practical Politics (New York, 1960).

Two good treatments of cold war diplomacy, balanced between traditional and revisionist views, are: Walter LaFeber, *America, Russia and the Cold War, 1945–1971* (New York, 1972) and Martin F. Herz, *Beginnings of the Cold War* (Bloomington, 1966). The former covers the entire postwar period, the latter focuses on Yalta and its immediate aftermath.

More or less traditional accounts of the cold war owe much to the seminal work of George F. Kennan, *American Diplomacy 1900–1950* (Chicago, 1951). Some of these are: Norman A. Graebner, *Cold War Diplomacy, 1945–1960* (Princeton, 1962); Herbert Feis, *The Atomic Bomb and the End of World War II* (Princeton, 1966); William Neumann, *After Victory* (New York, 1967); Louis J. Halle, *The Cold War as History* (New York, 1967); and John L. Snell, *Illusion and Necessity: The Diplomacy of Global War, 1939–1945* (Boston, 1963).

The overall revisionist critique of American foreign policy can be examined in the remainder of Williams' book. His reply to Schlesinger will be found in William Appleman Williams, "The Cold War Revisionists," *Nation*, November 13, 1967, pp. 492–495. Other revisionist analyses of the cold war are: Gar Alperovitz, *Atomic Diplomacy: Hiroshima and Potsdam* (New York, 1965); Gar Alperovitz, *Cold War Essays* (New York, 1970); David Horowitz, *Free World Colossus* (New York, 1971); Carl Oglesby and Richard Shaull, *Containment and Change* (New York, 1968); D. F. Fleming, *The Cold War and Its Origins, 1917–1960,* 2 vols. (New York, 1961).

For an overview of Russian foreign policy, two starting points are: Adam Ulam, *Containment and Coexistence* (New York, 1967), and Philip Mosley, *The Kremlin in World Politics* (New York, 1960). American foreign policy is summarized in the annual volumes entitled *The United States in World Affairs* published by The Council on Foreign Relations in New York. A useful comparative study of U.S. and Russian views of foreign policy is Anatol Rapoport, *The Big Two: Soviet American Perceptions of Foreign Policy* (Indianapolis, 1971). See also Raymond Dennet and Joseph E. Johnson, eds., *Negotiating with the Russians* (Boston, 1951).

A helpful analysis of our stake in the United Nations is found in Lincoln Bloomfield, *The United Nations and U.S. Foreign Policy* (Boston, 1967). An introduction to various institutional and political factors in foreign policymaking is Andrew M. Scott and Raymond H. Dawson, *Readings in the Making of American Foreign Policy* (New York, 1965).